# DIPLOMATIC HANDBOOK

## Eighth Edition

D1339358

# DIPLOMATIC HANDBOOK

Eighth Edition

## Ralph G. Feltham

*Sometime Diplomat, Founder-Director
and Senior Tutor, Oxford University Foreign Service Programme*

MARTINUS NIJHOFF PUBLISHERS
LEIDEN/BOSTON

A C.I.P. Catalogue record for this book is available from the Library of Congress.

First published 1970
Second edition 1977
Third edition 1980
Fourth edition 1982
Fifth edition 1988
Sixth edition 1993
Seventh edition 1998

Previously published by Longman.

Printed on acid-free paper.

ISBN 90-04-14142-1
© 2004 *Koninklijke Brill NV, Leiden, The Netherlands*

Brill Academic Publishers incorporates the imprint Martinus Nijhoff Publishers.
http://www.brill.nl

All rights reserved. No part of this publication may be reproduced, stored in a retrieval system, or transmitted in any form or by any means, electronic, mechanical, photocopying, microfilming, recording or otherwise, without written permission from the Publisher.

Authorization to photocopy items for internal or personal use is granted by Brill Academic Publishers provided that the appropriate fees are paid directly to The Copyright Clearance Center, 222 Rosewood Drive, Suite 910, Danvers MA 01923, USA. Fees are subject to change.

Printed and bound in The Netherlands

# CONTENTS

# APPENDICES

# PREFACE

The aim of this book is to provide a concise but comprehensive source of relevant information for those who are embarking on an international and, particularly, a diplomatic career.

It has been revised with the assistance of diplomats from many countries and members of international organisations, to all of whom I am deeply indebted for their unfailing courtesy and assistance.

I would like to express my particular appreciation to Professor Stanley Martin CVO, Professor Maurice Mendelson Q.C., Marcel Boisard, Milan Jacobec, Annebeth Rosenboom, Henriette Feltham and Alison Nicol administrator of the Oxford University Foreign Service Programme; and above all to those diplomats whom I have had the privilege of teaching over the past forty years: they have provided inspiration, enthusiasm and good fellowship, and I am the richer for their company.

I would also like to take this opportunity to point out that the word 'diplomat' in the English language can have either a masculine or feminine connotation, and if at any point in the text it is followed by the masculine personal pronoun it is solely to avoid the tedium of 'he or she': it is not intended to have any other significance.

*Budleigh Salterton, Devon*                                                              *R.G.F.*

# ACKNOWLEDGEMENTS

We are indebted to the following for permission to reproduce copyright material: Butterworth + Co Ltd. for an extract from *An Introduction to International Law* by J.G. Starke; the author for items in the appendix from *Dictionary of Economic Terms* by A. Gilpin; the Controller of Her Majesty's Stationery Office for extracts from *Treaty Series Command Papers* and Martinus Nijhoff Publishers for an extract from *Conference Diplomacy* by J. Kaufmann.

# DIPLOMATIC RELATIONS

## INTRODUCTION

It is an exhilarating and at the same time disturbing experience to be living through a period of change unparalleled in recorded history: a transitional stage in the social, political and economic evolution of states and their relations with each other. There is no problem in recognising a revolution when the guns are going off in the streets and the politicians are hanging from the lamp posts, but there is a danger in failing to grasp the extent of the revolution that has overtaken us and of failing to adjust our attitudes, responses and policies accordingly. It could be said that we are witnessing not so much an earthquake of history – a sudden shock followed by tremors and then a return to normality – as an avalanche of history that develops its own momentum and moves inexorably on, sweeping away everything in its path. There are, in fact, three major revolutions of a structural nature that have broken out virtually – in historical perspective – simultaneously.

The revolution that has produced the most immediate and extensive impact has been a *political* one: the collapse of the Soviet Empire which has resulted in the end of a period of potential nuclear war on a global scale; the end of a period of military imperatives when diplomats, through no fault of their own, had little opportunity to act effectively; the break-up of Europe's last major conglomerate state and the end of the two-power world order.

The revolution that is gradually becoming self-evident to the popular mind is the *economic* one. The globalisation of the factors of production has resulted in the reduction of barriers to trade; the creation of a global capital market and the globalisation of entrepreneurship. The chip-based industrial revolution has reorientated and in many instances reduced employment opportunities; the belief in economic socialism and the corporate state has largely disappeared; and preferential trading blocs are being established with little thought for their eventual social consequences.

And finally, there is the *communications revolution* which has created a global society. It has helped to internationalise science and business and, through the medium of television and the Internet, has created a global sense of political awareness; and since the pen – in the long run – is mightier then the sword, it may well prove to be the most profound of the structural revolutions.

In addition there are several major factors contributing to the instability and uncertainty of the present transitional phase of which the most important are: the sudden economic liberation of the Chinese people – one-fifth of the world's population with a strong sense of national identity which provides the basis for a positive foreign policy; the process of unifying most of the states of Europe after centuries of struggle for hegemony, the rise of terrorism; the potentially adverse relationship between the world's resources and the world's population; the threats to the global environment; the ease and speed of the proliferation of weapons of mass destruction; the potentially destabilising effects of large-scale migrations; the problems of equating ethnic asperations with existing national frontiers and the apparent incompatibility of peoples with irreconcilable values.

Regrettably, the one major factor that has remained constant has been the failure of the members of the international community to act in accordance with the Charter the United Nations to which they are committed and legally bound. The primary purpose of the Charter remains the maintenance of international peace and security and the sanctioning of the use of armed force for this purpose in clearly specified circumstances; and if it fails on these counts it is inevitable that it will follow its predecessor the Covenant of the League of Nations into the dusty archives of history.

But the very failure of the international community to recognise the Charter as the basis for a peaceful world with sustainable development has made it increasingly self-evident that there is no alternative; and although it had come into force in 1945, it had never come into effect, Mutual hostility among the permanent members during the Cold War had inhibited the Security Council from taking action for the maintenance of international peace and the prevention of aggression; but that situation no longer applies, and not only the governments but the peoples of members states – motivated largely by the CNN-inspired global television coverage – now accept that they must resolve their differences by reason and diplomacy: not by the use of force. Following the end of the first World War, the Covenant of the League of Nations was an option: following the end of the second World War and the development of weapons of mass-destruction, the Charter of the United Nations is an imperative.

It will doubtless need to be revised one day in order to make it more acceptable, more transparent and more effective, and to tackle not only present responsibilities encompassed by the United Nations Universal Declaration of Human Rights but also fresh problems such as secession, the control of weapons of mass destruction and terrorism. Provision for its amendment exists in chapter XVIII of the Charter, and in the meantime it would not come amiss if all member-states were to sign a solemn declaration of re-dedication to the Charter and an unreserved commitment to uphold its principles and purposes.

# THE ESTABLISHMENT OF DIPLOMATIC RELATIONS AND OF PERMANENT DIPLOMATIC MISSIONS

## GENERAL PRINCIPLES AND PURPOSES

Diplomatic relations between states may be established by friendly contacts of any form between their governments; but permanent diplomatic relations are considered to exist only with the establishment of a diplomatic mission, or preferably with the exchange of diplomatic missions. These are established by mutual consent and on the basis of a mutual understanding of the functions that will be undertaken by the mission. These functions have become generally accepted over past centuries, and have been defined in the 1961 Vienna Convention on Diplomatic Relations as consisting, basically, of:

(a) representing the sending state in the receiving state;
(b) protecting in the receiving state the interests of the sending state and its nationals, within the limits permitted by international law;
(c) negotiating with the government of the receiving state;
(d) ascertaining, by all lawful means, conditions and developments in the receiving state, and reporting thereon to the government of the sending state;
(e) promoting friendly relations between the sending state and the receiving state, and developing their economic, cultural and scientific relations.

Apart from their diplomatic functions, members of the diplomatic staff of a mission may also act in a consular capacity.

## CLASSES OF HEADS OF MISSION

Heads of mission may be of one of three classes depending on the mutual agreement of the governments concerned:

1. Ambassadors, Apostolic Nuncios, and other heads of mission of equivalent rank (e.g. High Commissioners exchanged between Commonwealth countries) who are accredited to Heads of State.
2. Envoys, Ministers and Papal Internuncios who are accredited to Heads of State. This class is now virtually non-existent.
3. Chargés d'Affaires (*en titre*, *en pied*, or titular) who are accredited to Ministers for Foreign Affairs. This class is also rare.

No differentiation may be made between heads of mission on account of their class, except in matters of precedence and protocol, and in that the right of reception by a Head of State is normally reserved to those of ambassadorial rank.

## TITLES OF HEADS OF MISSION

It is usual for an Ambassador to be styled 'Ambassador Extraordinary and Plenipotentiary'. (An Ambassador Extraordinary and Plenipotentiary was at one time superior in status to a resident Ambassador.) Similarly the head of a legation is likely to be styled 'Envoy Extraordinary and Minister Plenipotentiary'.

## APPROVAL OF A HEAD OF MISSION BY THE HOST STATE

Before a head of mission is appointed to a post, the approval or *agrément* of the receiving state is sought confidentially. This approval will normally be given, but may be withheld if it is considered that the person concerned is not acceptable and in this event no reason has to be given. In practice, an official (but usually informal) hint of unacceptability would normally be enough for a nomination to be withdrawn.

## CREDENTIALS

A head of mission is provided with credentials to prove his authenticity to the Head of State to whom he is accredited. These are alternatively referred to as Letters of Credence and are somewhat ornate in style, e.g.

*For Ambassadors*

To [full name and title of head of state]

Excellency:
I have appointed X.Y.Z., a distinguished citizen of [name of sending state], to represent me before your Government as Ambassador Extraordinary and Plenipotentiary of [name of sending state].
He is well aware of the mutual interests of our two countries and shares my sincere desire to preserve and enhance the long friendship between us.
My faith in his high character and ability gives me entire confidence that he will carry out his duties in a manner fully acceptable to you.
Accordingly I entrust him to your confidence. I ask that you receive him favourably, and give full credence to what he shall say on the part of [name of sending state] as well as to the assurances which he bears of my best wishes for the prosperity of [name of receiving state].

Yours very truly

[Signature of Head of State]

By the head of state

[Signature of Minister for Foreign Affairs]

[Place] [Date]

In the Commonwealth the Sovereign is Head of State of several of the member states, and when heads of mission are exchanged between such states they are provided with a *letter of introduction* from Prime Minister to Prime Minister.

When a Head of State who is a sovereign dies or otherwise ceases to reign, the credentials of all heads of mission accredited to the sovereign become invalid; similarly the credentials issued by the sovereign become invalid; and in both instances require renewal. This requirement does not, however, apply in the event of the death of a President or the termination of his period of office. It is also no longer effective in some countries and is likely to disappear gradually from the diplomatic scene.

## DATE OF ASSUMPTION OF FUNCTIONS

A head of mission of ambassadorial rank is considered to have taken up his functions in the state to which he is accredited when he has presented his credentials to the Head of State. In a few states (notably the UK) he is considered to have taken up his functions when he has notified the appropriate ministry (usually the Ministry of Foreign Affairs) of his arrival and has presented them with a working copy (*copie d'usage*) of his credentials. The ceremonies for the formal acceptance of heads of mission are held strictly in the order that they arrived to take up their functions.

## NATIONALITY OF A HEAD OF MISSION

A head of mission will, save in most exceptional circumstances, have the nationality of the state he is representing; but this requirement does not necessarily apply to his spouse. In many diplomatic services officers may be given special permission to marry foreign nationals provided the circumstances and the particular nationality involved are such that they do not in any way jeopardise or interfere with the officer's career. In Arab countries it is the general rule that diplomats may not marry foreigners, though in certain instances the Head of State may authorise marriage to other Arabs.

## NATIONALITY OF MEMBERS OF THE DIPLOMATIC STAFF

The members of the diplomatic staff of a mission should in principle be nationals of the state they serve, but in exceptional cases they may be nationals of the state in which the mission is situated; in this event, the specific approval of the host state must be obtained, and it may be withdrawn at any time. Such diplomats will enjoy only limited privileges and immunities (see p. 44).

## ACCREDITATION TO MORE THAN ONE STATE

A head of mission may be accredited (and members of the diplomatic staff assigned) to more than one state, provided there is no objection on the part of any of the states concerned. In the event of such an arrangement, Chargés d'Affaires *ad interim* (or in certain circumstances members of the diplomatic staff of lesser standing) may be established in diplomatic missions in those capitals where the head of mission does not have his permanent seat.

## INTERNATIONAL ORGANISATIONS: ACCREDITATION OF HEADS OF MISSION

A head of mission (or any member of the diplomatic staff of his mission) may act as representative of his state to any international organisation, and in this instance the state to which he is accredited need not be informed, nor may it raise any objection.

## THE SEAT OF A DIPLOMATIC MISSION

A diplomatic mission is established in the capital of a state; additional offices forming part of the mission may only be established in other parts of the state if special permission is given by that state. In a few instances, e.g. The Netherlands, the diplomatic capital (The Hague) is different from the capital of the country (Amsterdam).

## THE SIZE OF A MISSION

The size of diplomatic missions may be agreed on a reciprocal basis; alternatively a state may require that the number of members of a mission should be kept within reasonable limits taking into consideration the circumstances and conditions in the host state and the needs of the mission. Within such limits, and provided that the principle of representation by its own nationals is adhered to, a state should be free to appoint whomsoever it wishes to any of its diplomatic missions. In the case of military, naval and air attachés it is within the discretion of the Ministry of Foreign Affairs to require their names to be submitted in advance, and for approval to be obtained before any appointment is made. A state may also refuse to accept officials of a particular category, provided that the restriction is applied on a non-discriminatory basis to all diplomatic missions in the state.

## ACCREDITATION BY MORE THAN ONE STATE

Two or more states may, in exceptional circumstances, accredit the same person as head of mission to another state, unless objection is raised by the receiving state.

## DECLARATION OF *'PERSONA NON GRATA'* OR *'NON-ACCEPTABLE'*

A state has the right to declare a head of a mission or member of his diplomatic staff to be unacceptable (*persona non grata*) and to inform his government accordingly. In this event the diplomat's functions are terminated and he is (unless a national or permanent resident of the state in which he is serving) recalled. If his government takes no such step, the host state may refuse to recognise him as being a member of the mission. The declaration of *persona non grata* may be made either before or after the diplomat's arrival, and no reasons for it have to be given.

Similarly, members of the administrative and technical staff may be declared *non-acceptable*.

There are two principal grounds on which a diplomat may be declared *persona non grata*: those which spring from personal weakness, and result in criminal or anti-social behaviour; and deliberate acts hostile to the security or other interests of the state, carried out under the cloak of diplomatic immunity. A further possible pretext for a diplomat being so declared is as a retaliation against a state that has declared one of its own diplomats to be *persona non grata*; but although such practice is contrary to the spirit of international relations, it is regrettably not infrequent.

## OBLIGATIONS ACCEPTED BY A HOST STATE

By agreeing to the establishment of a permanent diplomatic mission a state implicitly accepts certain obligations: it must provide such facilities and immunity as will enable the mission to function satisfactorily, and it must grant to those who work in the mission the personal privileges and immunities necessary for them to carry out their functions without fear or hindrance. These obligations are set out in the Chapter dealing with 'Diplomatic privileges and immunities'.


# THE CONDUCT OF DIPLOMATIC RELATIONS IN THE ABSENCE OF A FULL DIPLOMATIC MISSION OR WHEN DIPLOMATIC RELATIONS HAVE BEEN SEVERED

No state maintains a diplomatic mission in every capital in the world; most have to be selective, and balance their national interest against the cost involved. The problem of not having full diplomatic representation in a particular state can be resolved in any of four ways:
(a) by requesting a government which is represented by a permanent mission in the state concerned to act on its behalf, which it may do with the approval of that state. In these circumstances the head of the permanent mission would normally limit his activities to transmitting messages between the two governments concerned and dealing with consular matters; and if any conflict arose between the interests of his own government and those of the foreign government on whose behalf he was acting, the interests of his own government would prevail;
(b) by accrediting one of its heads of mission resident in another state as a non-resident or 'visiting' head of mission in the state concerned;
(c) by establishing a diplomatic mission headed by a duly accredited non-resident head of mission, but with a Chargé d'Affaires *ad interim* in charge. In practice, owing to the difficulty encountered by several states in finding adequate senior diplomatic staff for the posts they wish to fill, it is not uncommon for a host state to agree to such a mission being headed by a diplomat of lesser standing;
(d) by accrediting a very senior official (e.g. the Permanent Secretary of the Foreign Ministry) as a non-resident or 'visiting' head of mission in a number of states while maintaining his residence in his own capital.

In certain instances diplomatic missions may be withdrawn as a result of mutual agreement between the states concerned, for example on the grounds that changed circumstances have resulted in the missions being unnecessary or uneconomic. Missions may also be withdrawn as a deliberate act of foreign policy, and in the days of straightforward gunboat diplomacy the withdrawal of a mission with the consequent breaking off of diplomatic relations was a logical prelude to war; in practice, the threat of such action by a big power was usually sufficient to convince the smaller power that it was time that it reviewed its foreign policy. Today this manoeuvre is occasionally used, not so much as a threat but as a protest; but as such its effect is limited, and usually disproportionate to the inconvenience that it causes to all concerned.

Even when a mission is withdrawn and diplomatic relations formally broken off, contacts are rarely terminated: the states of the world are to an increasing extent interdependent, and diplomatic relations frequently carry on in varying degrees as before, but (provided the host state has no objection) through the intermediary or 'good offices' of a state that is represented by a permanent mission in that country. In some cases only the head of the mission leaves, usually 'for consultation', and returns within a short space of time. In more serious circumstances the head of mission and the majority of the staff depart, leaving behind a token 'Interests Section' as part of the mission of a protecting power which looks after the interests of their country. They retain their personal diplomatic privileges and immunities, communicate with their government under privilege in the name of the 'protecting' power, and continue to function normally except that they may not fly their national flag or display their national emblem on their official premises. If they display a flag or emblem it will be that of the 'protecting' power.

# THE MINISTRY OF FOREIGN AFFAIRS

## ORGANISATION AND FUNCTIONS

The governments of all states include among their members one who is responsible for relations with other states and with international organisations. The extent of his personal responsibility varies from country to country, as does his title: Minister for Foreign Affairs, Secretary of State (USA), Secretary of State for Foreign and Commonwealth Affairs (UK), etc. The Minister's executive function is to implement the foreign policy of his government, and to manage its international relations. This he does with the help of deputy or assistant Ministers (politicians like himself) and the permanent staff of his Ministry and the heads of his own missions abroad, and through the intermediary of the heads of foreign missions accredited to his state.

The composition of Ministries varies considerably from country to country, but on the basis of the functions that they perform might be divided into the following sections, and grouped according to convenience:

*Political Affairs* – usually subdivided into regional departments, e.g. Latin America, Australasia.

*The United Nations* – including the provision of directives or 'briefs'.

*Other international and regional organisations* – including interdepartmental coordination and the provision of non-technical briefs.

*Treaties* – this section works in close relations with the legal department.

*Legal* – a separate department in the larger states; it normally deals with all international instruments and all questions of international law. Smaller countries may appoint part-time professional or academic advisers or obtain advice from a general Ministry of Justice. The legal department may advise both in matters of home and foreign affairs. In certain states a Department of International Law exists as a separate entity from the Legal Department, the latter concerning itself with legal assistance, frontier problems, nationality law, national property abroad, etc.

*Protocol* – responsibility for all personal dealings with heads of foreign missions on such matters as privileges, immunities and formalities; also for the organisation of conferences, reception of visitors, etc.

*Trade and economic relations*

*Cultural relations*

*Disarmament*

*Press, Media and Information*

*Scientific*

*Personnel*

*Commodities*

*Consular relations*
*Administration, communications and security*
*Archives and library*

When a country maintains close international relations on a wide variety of matters of national concern its Ministry of Foreign Affairs would be overloaded and even technically out of its depth if it were to try to maintain a close control over the negotiations concerned. An example of this situation is the relationship between the countries of Western Europe, where matters of defence, social welfare, health, economic relations, etc., are of close mutual concern, and policies are constantly under discussion and negotiation between the departmental experts rather than through the traditional channels of the Ministry of Foreign Affairs. But although a Ministry of Foreign Affairs may in many instances relinquish immediate responsibility to other departments, it has an essential coordinating function and must always remain responsible for background information, political advice, personal relationships and follow-up; and it must always be in a position to step in and take action, or at least make recommendations, if it considers that a particular department, in pursuing its particular interest, is in danger of losing sight of the national interest as a whole.

## RELATIONS WITH ITS OWN MISSIONS

The prime responsibility of a head of mission is to carry out the instructions of his Ministry and to report back to it the information that he is asked to provide. He is, however, expected to use his initiative in recommending the policy that he thinks his government should adopt, and also in reporting back information that he personally considers significant, whether he has been asked to do so or not. The relationship between Ministry and heads of mission is thus very much a matter of give and take, and the extent to which the Ministry or the mission dominates in the shaping of policy varies from country to country and in accordance with the national requirements and resources. Modern technology now helps Ministry and mission to keep in almost instantaneous contact, thus fusing their contributions to the formulation of policy.

If policy decisions are reached essentially within the Ministry and the task of the head of mission is mainly that of implementing them, emphasis in terms of numbers of staff (and often ability) is likely to be placed on the Ministry, leaving fewer to serve abroad; but if policy-making is to be influenced strongly by the advice of the heads of mission, then the staff of the Ministry need be relatively few, and the overseas posts may be strongly manned. Staff distribution policy will also determine the length of time that diplomats serve abroad compared with the time that they spend at home, and there is a marked contrast not only between the policies of different countries but also between types of officers: for example, a commercial or press attaché for whom wide local contacts are essential might be of greatest value if his stay in a country were five years or longer, while for an embassy secretary the standard period might be three or four.

The arguments in favour of a diplomat remaining in a post for a lengthy period are:
(a) he – or of course she – (and his/her family) need time to settle down domestically before he can really concentrate on his work;
(b) he will have an adequate opportunity of getting to know and understand the country in which he is serving – its language, history, politics and national temperament;
(c) he will have time to make personal contacts and friendships;
(d) there will be a saving for the government of expense on travel and costs of transfer.

The main disadvantage is that he may become emotionally involved in the problems of the country in which he is living and serving, and so be unable to act and advise his own government in a detached and realistic manner. Also he is liable to find himself out of touch with sentiment and events in his home country.

The head of the personnel department has one of the most important tasks in the Ministry, deciding whom to send where and for how long. A diplomat is subject to a wide variety of pressures in different posts abroad, and some can cope with particular circumstances better than others: a posting that suits his temperament and personality is in many ways as important as one that suits his ability.

## RELATIONS WITH FOREIGN MISSIONS

The Ministry of Foreign Affairs (or its equivalent) is the channel through which all representations should be made to a government by another state, its diplomatic representative or an international organisation. If the enquiry is of an essentially technical or routine nature the Ministry may authorise the appropriate technical department to carry on further correspondence direct with the mission or organisation concerned; but the initial approach and all matters of substance are traditionally addressed to the Ministry.

In practice, with the great increase in the scope and extent of international cooperation since the establishment of the United Nations and regional economic and political groupings, there has been a tendency for home government departments to assume even greater responsibility for international negotiations within their particular field.

When a Minister for Foreign Affairs assumes office he usually writes to all the diplomatic representatives of foreign states and informs them accordingly, and (depending on the size of the capital) may subsequently make arrangements for them to meet him individually or collectively. When he relinquishes the post he also advises them accordingly and gives them the name of his successor. In addition, the Minister informs the diplomatic representatives of his own country abroad of such moves.

The head of a diplomatic mission (unless he is a Chargé d'Affaires *en titre*) is the representative of one Head of State to another; and although it is no longer practical for him to claim the right of access to the Head of State, or, in many countries, to the head of government, he has by custom and courtesy the right of access to a Minister of the Foreign Ministry at any time in order to discuss matters of major concern between the two countries. Dealings of a routine matter, however, are normally carried out between the head of mission or a member of the diplomatic staff of the mission and the appropriate official in the Ministry of Foreign Affairs.

When a Minister for Foreign Affairs wishes to convey a message to another government he has two possible means of communication: through his country's own diplomatic representative in the foreign country concerned; or through that country's representative to the Minister's own government. (Since any government is the instrument of the Head of State, a head of mission may correctly be said to be the representative of one government to another.) Generally speaking a government makes formal approaches through its own representative abroad, but formal protests are often made to the foreign representative who is perhaps more immediately available; effectiveness being the obvious key to the choice of method. Sometimes both are used at the same time. By summoning a head of mission and speaking directly person-to-person. a Minister for Foreign Affairs can doubtless stress the extent of his displeasure when asking for a clarification, particularly if the time chosen for the summons is known to coincide with the diplomat's breakfast or golf.

## RELATIONS WITH THE DIPLOMATIC CORPS

Matters concerning the Diplomatic Corps in its entirety and the government of the state to which its members are accredited or assigned are dealt with by the senior head of mission (who is known as the Doyen) and the appropriate minister or chief of the Department of Protocol. The term 'Doyen' of the Corps Diplomatique might reasonably be transposed to 'Dean of the Diplomatic Body'; but common usage among English speakers is 'Dean of the Diplomatic Corps'.

In determining the appointment of the Dean or Doyen, the seniority of a head of mission is based on the length of time that he has continuously held his appointment at that post. In certain countries (especially in Latin America) the Apostolic Nuncio is always Dean; and the practice is not uncommon, especially in Latin America, for special provision to be made for Armed Services attachés by the appointment of protocol officers in the Ministry of Defence.

# THE DIPLOMATIC MISSION

## GENERAL OBSERVATIONS AND DEFINITIONS

A diplomatic mission consists of a diplomatic representative duly nominated by one state and accepted by another, together with his staff and established in the diplomatic capital of the state. As far as the receiving state is concerned there is only one person who may represent another state, and he is head (or acting head) of that mission who, as such, is entirely responsible for its activities; his staff, strictly speaking, have no direct representative function and merely assist their head.

The terminology of diplomacy is often obscure and misleading, and the 1961 Vienna Convention on Diplomatic Relations usefully defined the staff of a diplomatic mission (with the French expression in brackets) as follows:

(a) The 'head of the mission' *(chef de mission)* is the person charged by the sending state with the duty of acting in that capacity;

(b) the 'members of the mission' *(membres de la mission)* are the head of the mission and the members of the staff of the mission;

(c) the 'members of the staff of the mission' *(membres du personnel de la mission)* are the members of the diplomatic staff, of the administrative and technical staff and of the service staff of the mission;

(d) the 'members of the diplomatic staff' *(membres du personnel diplomatique)* are the members of the staff of the mission having diplomatic rank;

(e) a 'diplomatic agent' *(agent diplomatique)* is the head of the mission or a member of the diplomatic staff of the mission;

(f) a 'member of the administrative and technical staff' *(membre du personnel administratif et technique)* is a member of the staff of the mission employed in the administrative or technical service of the mission;

(g) a 'member of the service staff' *(membre du personnel de service)* is a member of the staff of the mission in the domestic service of the mission;

(h) a 'private servant' *(domestique privé)* is a person who is in the domestic service of a member of the mission and who is not an employee of the sending state.

The term 'diplomatic agent', which formerly referred only to the head of a mission, now includes the members of the diplomatic staff of the mission; and 'the members of the diplomatic staff' are not only members of a diplomatic service, but also attachés, advisers and members of other ministries, provided that they hold diplomatic rank.

The term 'diplomatic rank' is not defined, but is used in this context to describe the range of appointments in a diplomatic mission which by tradition entitle the holders to full diplomatic privileges and immunities; and although the term 'diplomatic agent' is the correct word to describe the head of mission and members of the diplomatic staff of a mission, the commonly accepted (though less precise) terminology is 'diplomat'.

The functions of a mission are reflected in its structure, and the following pattern remains valid even if, as may happen in some instances, they are all performed by a single person.

## THE HEAD OF MISSION

The head of mission is responsible for all matters connected with his mission. He may, and does, delegate various functions to his staff, but he alone is responsible both to his own government and to the government to which he is accredited for the conduct of the mission.

Irrespective of the size of his staff there are certain basic priorities to which a head of mission normally devotes his personal attention:

(a) the formulation of diplomatic policy;
(b) transmitting to the host government the views of his own government on important matters of common interest and common policy, and acting as the channel of communication between the two in such matters;
(c) reporting to his Ministry on events of political or economic significance, whether they are of direct significance (e.g. the national budget or ministerial changes) or of indirect significance (e.g. changes and trends in social or economic conditions), and commenting on the views of third parties in the country (e.g. articles from the local press, opinions of other diplomats);
(d) being aware of the people of influence and the sources of national power in the state in which he is serving;
(e) conducting himself in his official and personal behaviour in such a way as to bring credit to his country;
(f) cultivating as wide and as varied a circle of friends as is possible in order to be able to fulfil (a), (c), (d) and (e) above.

The formulation of the diplomatic policy of a mission is a major responsibility of the head of mission, and in this he is assisted by his principal advisers – the heads of the various sections of his mission. The diplomatic policy of a mission can best be defined as the positive attitude adopted towards all matters relating to intercourse between the head of mission's own state and the one to which he is accredited. It is the product of political judgment, political sense and political wisdom, and is based on an intimate knowledge and understanding of the people and governments of the two states concerned. It may take the form of the head of mission recommending policies to his own government or seeking clarification of their instructions and suggesting a different line of approach; or alternatively suggesting to the government to which he is accredited that a communication that they have instructed him to refer to his government should be reconsidered. It is reflected in the advice given to visiting politicians or businessmen on how to approach people or problems, and is the function that differentiates a diplomatic mission from a post office.

## ADMINISTRATION AND COORDINATION

In most diplomatic services a single officer (the Deputy Head of Mission) is responsible for the coordination of the political and economic activities of the mission and the oversight of the administration of the mission. He or she ensures that the various sections of the mission are properly coordinated; that the staff is properly organised and contented; and that communications and the premises of the mission are secure and adequately maintained. The welfare of his staff is a matter of particular concern, for the younger members and those who do not enjoy the privileges of being members of the diplomatic staff may find themselves subject to loneliness and its related ills.

One of the administration's more important duties is to compile and keep up to date files containing all the items of local information that an incoming head of mission or member of the staff might want to know.

Such files would normally include:

(a) The organisation of the Ministry of Foreign Affairs of the host state and any other departments or institutions with which the mission deals; which section deals with which matters; how to obtain an interview, whom to approach (and whom to avoid);

(b) a short account of recent local history;

(c) a 'Post Report' containing matters of domestic interest to members of the staff; medical, dental, travel and sporting facilities; climate; housing; domestic help; schools; churches, etc. (this would normally be sent to the Personnel Department at home for the briefing of future members of the mission);

(d) a list of personalities which would include distinguished or up-and-coming persons of influence in the political, media, military, administrative, industrial, commercial, academic and social sphere.

With such information at his disposal an incoming head of mission can quickly grasp the local situation and find his way around. In particular he can know straight away who is significant in relation to his country's interests; social blunders can be avoided, and entertaining *(q.v.)* greatly facilitated.

## COMMERCIAL AND ECONOMICS SECTION

Economic and commercial work play an increasingly important part in the functions of a mission.

Economic work focuses on analysing the economic and financial policy of the host government, assessing its effects on other domestic and external policies, predicting future trends and reporting (and as necessary negotiating) on economic issues affecting the bilateral relationship. While this involves the collection and analysis of relevant statistics, it also requires a wide range of contacts in the relevant Ministries and in the banking and financial sector. With the aid of modern technology, statistics can quickly be available to a diplomat's own government: but it is the diplomat's job, following events and picking up information on the spot, to understand the facts behind the figures and thus determine their relevance and significance.

The commercial element is concerned with two separate functions: trade and investment promotion, and trade policy. Trade promotion is self-explanatory and involves a high degree of personal communication skills, dealing with both one's own exporters and potential importers. Diplomats must be prepared to assist visiting businessmen to find their way around, to reply to specific queries and generally provide background information that will enable them to assess the local market and contact the right people. It also involves up-to-date knowledge of markets, how they are structured and who operates them; a close watch on the calling for tenders as well as a keen eye for promotional opportunities.

Trade policy relates to an understanding of the host government's legislation and attitude to commercial relations, and is of increasing significance in view of the trend towards the creation of regional preferential trading areas as governments search for a solution to the problems raised by unemployment and the globalisation of the factors of production. While concentrating on their own country's interests, which is their prime concern, diplomats will also deal with enquiries in the opposite sense from local businessmen, and these they will do their best to satisfy in the interests of good bilateral relations.

Negotiations on the sale of weapons are in many cases conducted through Defence Attachés rather than the Commercial Section. Where important contracts with the host government are concerned – for weapons or other manufactures – the head of mission may play a key role in exerting diplomatic pressure in appropriate quarters.

For many countries a major foreign policy objective is the encouragement of inward investment, and this depends not only on the state of the infrastructure such as transport and communication facilities, security, access to a local market, a skilled labour supply and efficient service industries, but also to business-friendly legislation and a judicial system that operates fairly and without undue delay. Especial areas of concern for potential investors are property rights, bankruptcy laws, financial services and contractual legislation

## SECRETARIAL AND ARCHIVES SECTION

Members of the secretarial and archives staff who deal with confidential matters are normally of the same nationality as the mission, though non-political sections (e.g. cultural or commercial) may employ local residents provided that they maintain a separate secretarial and archival section. The maintenance of an efficient and well-indexed system of records is a time-consuming occupation, but one of fundamental importance.

## SECURITY

The task of the security staff is to ensure that the premises of the mission and the residences of the members of the mission are secure and not entered unlawfully; that persons entering the building on business are not able to obtain confidential information; and that access to computers, files and documents is restricted to those so entitled. The security staff are preferably of the same nationality as the mission.

## TECHNICAL AND COMMUNICATIONS SECTION

Communications with a diplomat's own Ministry of Foreign Affairs is normally effected by e-mail, but the technical staff are required to encode and decode, encypher and decypher, and operate and, when necessary, repair wireless transmitters and receivers (in those missions that have been granted permission by the host government to use this means of communication), fax machines, encoding and decoding equipment, and computers. Their work is of a confidential nature and they are invariably of the same nationality as the mission.

## LOCAL STAFF

Local staff are employed for non-confidential duties as part of the administrative and secretarial staff. They can be of immense value on account of their continuity of service and their knowledge of local customs, politics and personalities. They are commonly employed in the commercial, consular and information sections and as translators.

## ACCOUNTS

Accounts are unavoidable, and, if neglected, can cause more trouble than all the rest of the functions of the mission put together; a competent book-keeper (usually local staff under close scrutiny) is employed where circumstances permit. A good accounting system has the advantage of enabling local bills to be settled promptly; failure to do so often resulting in ill-will that can undo much of the good relations established by the mission.

# CONSULAR SECTION

A consular office in a capital city normally comes directly under the control of the head of the diplomatic mission, and often occupies part of the premises of the mission; it is, however, in some respects a separate entity governed by its own regulations. Its functions and organisation are dealt with in a subsequent chapter.

# PRESS, MEDIA AND INFORMATION SECTION

The member of the staff in charge of the Press, Media and Information section has to know what makes news in a particular country and who, locally, makes it, so that he may provide information concerning his country to the maximum effect. Apart from maintaining good relations with the producers of instant publicity – the press, radio and television – a press officer often finds it advantageous to maintain a web-site (especially for consular information), and circulate a news-sheet to persons who are known to be interested in and sympathetic to his country. He will usually need the services of a translator (local staff), for an article will only be acceptable if it is written in the language and idiom of the country in which it has to be used. He/she will also ensure that if the Embassy is asked to appear on television and comment on a matter that has arisen relevant to his country he will be able to provide a suitably trained and briefed member of the staff – preferably the Head of Mission – for this purpose: to refuse is likely to prove counter-productive.

# SERVICE AND SPECIALIST ATTACHÉS

Until quite recently there was a clear distinction between a career diplomat, who concerned himself with political or commercial relations, and an attaché, whose interests were limited to a particular field. The former was a member of the diplomatic service and in practice a link between his own Ministry of Foreign Affairs and that of the state to which he was accredited or assigned; the latter was a member of a different government department, and while coming under the auspices and control of the head of mission was primarily serving the interests of his own department. With the growing number of specialist personnel now needed in large diplomatic missions, however, the distinction between the two categories has lessened, and specialists in, for example, legal or labour matters may be either attachés or secretaries on the diplomatic staff. Whatever their function, it is essential that their work should be closely coordinated with that of the mission as a whole.

## ARMED SERVICES ATTACHÉS

Armed Services attachés are normally regular members of the Armed Forces who are attached to a diplomatic mission for a limited period of time. One of the major functions of a Military, Naval or Air attaché is to report on developments in his particular field of interest to his particular branch of the services either directly or, in important matters, through his head of mission. He can, in certain instances, help with the purchase or sale of war materials, and in most countries will be invited to visit military establishments and to take part in military exercises.

## CULTURAL AND EDUCATIONAL ATTACHÉS

Cultural agreements were at one time the last resort of governments which could find nothing else to agree upon. Today the work of the cultural attaché can be of great value in fostering understanding and goodwill between states by arranging exchange visits of professional or occupational groups, or visits of world-class artists, by the award of scholarships, and by facilitating the study of his national language. It is sometimes the practice to appoint as attaché a person eminent in the field of a particular cultural activity; but in such instances it is also the practice to appoint a good administrator as his assistant. In some instances separate cultural and educational attachés are appointed.

## OTHER ATTACHÉS

The range of possible attachés is limited only by the interest of the states appointing them and the willingness of the states receiving them. Their titles are indicative of their function, and include: Labour, Agriculture, Fisheries, Scientific, Industrial, Civil Aviation, Public Relations, Recruitment, Tourism, Legal, Immigration, Shipping and Timber. Chaplains are an important member of certain missions, who may be members of the diplomatic staff and enjoy diplomatic status.

# ABSENCE OR INDISPOSITION OF A HEAD OF MISSION

If a head of mission is absent or otherwise unable to perform his functions (e.g. through serious illness), or if the post of head of mission is vacant, a member of the diplomatic staff of the mission (usually the next senior) will fill the post as Chargé d'Affaires *ad interim*. In these circumstances the head of mission or his Ministry informs the appropriate authorities of the host state of the change, and advises them when the head of mission resumes his functions. If no member of the diplomatic staff is available to take charge during the absence of a head of mission, a member of the administrative or technical staff may, with the approval of the host state, be appointed by his government to take charge of the current administrative business of the mission. If a Chargé d'Affaires *ad interim* is unable to continue his functions, he may not appoint a Chargé in his place: this can only be done by his Ministry of Foreign Affairs.

# APPOINTMENTS, ARRIVALS AND DEPARTURES

### NOTIFICATION OF APPOINTMENTS

Although it is only the appointment of heads of mission and frequently that of Military, Naval or Air Attachés that require the formal approval of the host state in advance, all other appointments of diplomatic staff must be notified to the Ministry of Foreign Affairs at the earliest opportunity.

## NOTIFICATION OF ARRIVALS AND DEPARTURES

The head of a mission should, where possible, advise the Protocol Department of the Ministry of Foreign Affairs well in advance of the date, place and time of the intended arrival or final departure of any member of the staff of the mission or of their families. In addition, in some countries it is the practice to provide the Consular Department of the Ministry with details of the engagement or discharge of any residents or nationals of the country in which the mission is situated.

## PROCEDURE ON ARRIVAL

On arrival at his post to take up his duties, a head of mission will be met by the Chief of Protocol (or his representative). This will not, however, be the case in the event of his arrival coinciding with a national or religious holiday or (in an increasing number of countries) over a weekend or very early or very late in the day. He immediately informs the Minister for Foreign Affairs (as well, of course, as informing his own Minister) that he has arrived, and requests an appointment so that he may call on him and, according to the practice in a number of countries, present him with a copy of his credentials.

In the UK, for example, an Ambassador would do this by handing to the Chief of Protocol, when he calls on him or her very soon after arrival, a letter, addressed to the Secretary of State for Foreign and Commonwealth Affairs, on the following lines.

Sir/Madam,
I have the honour to inform you of my arrival in London on [date] in order to take up my duties as Ambassador of ................. to the Court of St. James's.
I should appreciate it if arrangements could be made for me to call on the appropriate Ministers and senior officials of the Foreign and Commonwealth Office and, in due course, for me to have an Audience with Her Majesty the Queen for the presentation of my credentials the Working Copies of which I shall deliver [or] which have already been sent to your department.
With the assurance of my highest consideration,
I have the honour to be, Sir/Madam,

Your obedient Servant,
[Usual signature of Ambassador]

The Rt Hon. .................,
Secretary of State for Foreign and Commonwealth Affairs,
Foreign and Commonwealth Office,
London

According to UK practice the receipt of the working copy of the Ambassador's credentials (and of his predecessor's letter of recall where appropriate), together with the letter announcing his arrival, constitute the formal assumption of his duties.

His next call will be a ceremonial one on the Head of State (to present the original of his credentials), arrangements for which will usually be made through the head of the Department of Protocol. If it is the practice to deliver a formal speech at this audience, he should ensure that the Minister for Foreign Affairs has a copy of it in advance. If the head of mission holds the rank of Chargé d'Affaires *en titre* he will be accredited to the Minister for Foreign Affairs and will deliver to him his letter of appointment.

The procedure adopted by a state for the reception of a particular class of head of mission (i.e. Ambassador, Minister or Chargé d'Affaires) must be uniform in all cases.

Once a head of mission has officially assumed his functions he advises the Dean (Doyen) of the Diplomatic Corps and other heads of mission accordingly, and proceeds to call on them in accordance with the diplomatic protocol.

In a city of considerable diplomatic activity such as, for example, London, where the number of diplomatic missions has trebled in the past thirty years, the traditional practice for newly arrived heads of mission has been adapted to present-day circumstances. After paying courtesy calls on Ministers and senior officials of the Foreign and Commonwealth Office (usually within a week or ten days of arrival), heads of mission call on the Doyen of the Diplomatic Corps, a selected number of their fellow heads of mission (chosen, in order of seniority, according to the political interests and geographical position of the newcomer's country), and on prominent figures in British life of their own choosing. Because a new head of mission has entered *fully* on his functions by presenting to the FCO, shortly after his arrival, the working copies of his credentials, his call on the Queen to present the credentials themselves is in the nature of a symbolic last act of the arrival procedure rather than (as in many other countries) an essential first act. Because of the Queen's absence from London, it can sometimes be a month or so before a new head of mission presents his credentials, but meanwhile he can, quite properly, circulate a note to other missions announcing his arrival and assumption of functions.

If a head of mission is replacing a colleague (as opposed to opening up a mission) he ensures that the appropriate procedure has been carried out with regard to his predecessor's *letter of recall*.

## PROCEDURE ON DEPARTURE

Shortly before a head of mission relinquishes his or her post (except in the event of his recall having been requested by the host state) he sends a note announcing his recall to the Minister for Foreign Affairs and asks for an audience with the Head of State. If it is still the customs in the country concerned an outgoing head of mission's letter of recall (a formal document signed by the Head of State) will be combined with his successor's letter of credence.

A departing head of mission writes to the Dean of the Diplomatic Corps and to other heads of mission and informs them that he is leaving, e.g.

Your Excellency (or Monsieur le Chargé d'Affaires),
I have the honour to inform Your Excellency (you) that I shall be leaving
.................. [place] on .................. [date], on the termination of my mission.
Until the arrival of my successor, the direction of this Embassy will be assumed
by Mr .................. Counsellor [e.g.] of this Embassy, as Chargé d'Affairs *ad
interim*.
I should like to take this opportunity to express to Your Excellency (you) my sincere gratitude for your cooperation which has contributed to the good relations, both official and personal, which so happily exist between our two countries and our two missions.
Please accept, Your Excellency (Monsieur le Chargé d'Affaires), the assurance of my highest (high) esteem.

Ambassador's name

His Excellency .................., etc.
or Mr .................., Chargé d'Affaires, etc.)

The head of mission's diplomatic functions come to an end either when he leaves the country or on an earlier date if this is specified in his note announcing his recall. (If he does not leave on the date specified it is customary for him, together with his family, to be allowed full privileges and immunities for a reasonable period until his departure.) He is normally seen off at his point of departure by a representative of the Department of Protocol.

# THE DIPLOMAT

The diplomat needs to acquire all the normal attributes of his compatriots who are successful businessmen, administrators or civil servants, but he is a specialist in that he needs an added dimension: he must understand other countries, other cultures and other societies, and know what makes them tick. He must like people, and be genuinely interested in them.

He needs specialist knowledge, professional skills and personal qualities, which may be summarised as follows:

*Specialist knowledge*
A knowledge and understanding of his own country: its geography, history and culture, its political, social, economic and demographic structure and institutions, its human and economic resources – agriculture, industry, finance – in short the determinants of its foreign policy priorities.

A similar knowledge and understanding, as far as is possible, of other states and regional organisations, priority being given to his neighbours, the regional organisations of which his county is a member, and the super-states, actual and potential.

A knowledge of the mechanism and procedures of international intercourse. This involves a knowledge of the worldwide network of diplomatic missions and consular posts, their functions, their practice and structure; the worldwide network of trading and financial establishments and how they operate; the United Nations and other inter-governmental institutions, global and regional, for international political, social and economic cooperation; also the code of public international law which establishes rules of behaviour between states and the laws regulating international institutions. Not least, he should have an understanding of the social and political consequences of the current 'Media Revolution'.

*Professional skills*
The intellectual discipline of foreign policy analysis and reporting
Skill in negotiating and in day-to-day diplomacy
Skill in representation
Skill in the management of a mission
Skill in communication and public diplomacy including television presentation skills
Cross-cultural skills
Foreign languages

*Personal qualities*
Political awareness
Personal warmth and acceptability
Intellectual curiosity and the drive to go on learning
Intellectual versatility
Leadership
Common sense

The compendium of knowledge and the table of virtues required for the perfect diplomat are rarely found in one man or woman: which is perhaps just as well for those ordinary mortals who would have the trying task of working with them.

# PROTOCOL AND PROCEDURE

## ORDERS OF PRECEDENCE

A diplomat is concerned with four orders of precedence:

## 1. PRECEDENCE BETWEEN HEADS OF DIPLOMATIC MISSIONS

The precedence of a head of mission is based on the class into which he falls:
Ambassador, High Commissioner or Apostolic Nuncio;
Envoy Extraordinary and Minister Plenipotentiary or Inter-nuncio (a rank rarely used);
Chargé d'Affaires *en titre* (titular or *en pied*).

Within each class, seniority is based on the date on which the head of mission assumed his duties as such. This is either the date on which he presented his credentials to the Head of State, or alternatively the date on which he notified his arrival to the Ministry of Foreign Affairs and sent or handed to the Minister or Ministry a copy of his credentials, depending on the practice of the country. In most countries the date is that of the presentation to the Head of State, but in some, including the UK, it is the date of handing over the copy of credentials.

If two heads of mission present their credentials (or copies of their credentials) on the same day precedence may be determined either by the place in the alphabet of the first letter of the state (in French) of the representatives concerned; or, more commonly, by the relative times of day they officially commenced their functions. Whichever practice of determining precedence is adopted by a state, it must be applied consistently, and not altered without prior notification.

In certain states the diplomatic representative of the Holy See takes precedence over all other heads of mission of the same category.

At gatherings at which all heads of mission are present a Chargé d'Affaires *en titre* will follow heads of mission of ambassadorial or ministerial rank, and Chargés d'Affaires *ad interim* will come third, each Chargé taking precedence within his class according to the date of his assumption of duty. When other members of the diplomatic staff of a mission (including spouses) are present they take their place with the head of mission or Chargé in accordance with his precedence.

Precedence is not affected by a head of mission's credentials becoming temporarily invalid owing to the death of the Head of State who signed or accepted them.

## 2.  INDIVIDUAL PRECEDENCE WITHIN A MISSION

The individual precedence of members of the 'political' staff below head of mission is:
Minister Plenipotentiary
Minister-Counsellor
Counsellor
First Secretary
Second Secretary
Third Secretary

The place of service and specialist attachés is determined by individual missions. They usually come before a First Secretary but rarely above the diplomat next senior to the head of mission. The precise order of precedence is normally found in the diplomatic list which every state receiving diplomatic representatives produces, though in certain states the list is arranged in functional sections. It is the responsibility of the head of mission to notify the Ministry of Foreign Affairs of the precedence of the members of his mission.

## 3.  INDIVIDUAL PRECEDENCE *INTER SE* OF DIPLOMATS AT FORMAL OR DIPLOMATIC FUNCTIONS

Individual precedence at formal or diplomatic functions is based on rank, and is as follows:
Apostolic Nuncio (in those countries where he is Doyen *ex officio*)
Ambassador, High Commissioner, Apostolic Nuncio
Envoy Extraordinary and Minister Plenipotentiary
Chargé d'Affaires *(en titre)*
Chargé d'Affaires *(ad interim)*, usually a senior member of the diplomatic staff
Minister Plenipotentiary
Minister-Counsellor
Counsellor
First Secretary
Second Secretary
Third Secretary

Service and specialist attachés are usually placed immediately after Counsellors, but practice varies.

## 4. PRECEDENCE OF HEADS OF MISSION WITHIN THE NATIONAL ORDER OF PRECEDENCE

Heads of mission are placed according to custom, but usually after members of the cabinet and the presidents of the legislative assemblies. In the United Kingdom heads of mission of ambassadorial or equal rank are placed after the seven very high dignitaries who rank immediately after the Sovereign and close members of the Royal Family in the national order of precedence.

# THE DIPLOMATIC LIST

The Diplomatic List is a record of the names and designation of (a) the heads of diplomatic missions accredited to a state at a particular date, together with the names and diplomatic rank of the members of the diplomatic staff of their mission, and (b) other institutions and individuals received in a diplomatic capacity (e.g. United Nations senior staff).

Also shown is the address of the mission and sometimes the residences of the diplomats; whether or not they are married; whether or not their spouses have accompanied them; and in some countries the names of unmarried daughters over the age of eighteen.

If the post of head of mission is temporarily vacant the designation of the holder is shown with the word 'vacant'. If the head of mission is non-resident, his place of residence is indicated after his name and the address of his mission and sometimes residence are given.

It is customary to add a list of heads of mission in order of their precedence (naming the Doyen), together with a list of the national days of the states represented in the host state.

The Diplomatic List is regularly revised and reprinted (the interval depending on the size of the state and the rate of diplomatic turnover); states are listed alphabetically (usually in the language of the issuing state); and the responsibility for the correctness of the information it contains rests jointly with the host government (in practice with the Department of Protocol) and the heads of diplomatic missions: both have a vested interest in the accuracy of the List, if only because it is used for reference by both parties, and because it is *prima facie* evidence of the right to diplomatic status.

The List does not normally have any security rating, and in some countries it is on sale to the public. It is issued to all foreign missions, and to ministers and officials of the host government who may need to refer to it, e.g. customs and immigration officials, police and mayors, as well as to the heads of the issuing government's missions abroad.

In certain instances a combined Diplomatic and Consular List is issued containing, in addition, details of career and honorary consular officers; otherwise a separate Consular List is sometimes issued, depending on need.

# CORRESPONDENCE AND COMMUNICATION BETWEEN DIPLOMATIC MISSIONS AND THE HOST GOVERNMENT

All formal communications between a diplomatic mission and the foreign government in whose capital it is situated are made (a) by or on behalf of the head of mission, and (b) to the Ministry of Foreign Affairs (or its equivalent), except where special permission has been given for dealing with another department, or in the case of specialist attachés who are by custom permitted to deal direct with the relevant department on technical (but not policy) matters. In practice, the complexity of modern diplomacy has reduced the strict formalities in many countries.

## PERSONAL INTERVIEWS

The Ministers in the Foreign Ministry are customarily accessible to heads of mission, and appointments are usually made by telephone. Such top-level approaches are normally limited to matters of special importance; those of lesser importance are best dealt with by the head of mission or a member of the diplomatic staff of the mission arranging (once again by telephone) to see an appropriate member of the ministry staff. Ministers and ministry officials are normally very busy people, and tend to be sympathetic to visiting diplomats who, after the initial courtesies, are brief and to the point, and take their leave when there is no further business to conduct.

## WRITTEN CORRESPONDENCE

*(a) The Official Note in the third person*
The customary method of correspondence between a diplomatic mission and a Ministry of Foreign Affairs is the Official Note. The note is typed in a recognised international language on official paper headed with the national crest and address, and begins as follows:

> The ................ Embassy presents its compliments to the Ministry of Foreign Affairs and has the honour to inform them that ... [or] to bring to their attention the following matter ...

The substance of the note then follows, and the document terminates with a formula on the following lines:

> The Embassy takes [or avails itself of] this opportunity of assuring the Ministry of its highest consideration.
> Date [Sender's initials and Embassy stamp]

In some countries (e.g. the United States of America) this final courtesy is omitted. The Official Note is also the standard form of communication between Diplomatic Missions.

*(b)  The note verbale*
The *note verbale* is written in the third person and its general form is that of the official note.

*(c)  The Official Letter in the first person*
A less formal approach to a Minister for Foreign Affairs (by a head of mission) or to an official in the Ministry (by a member of the diplomatic staff of a mission) is the letter in the first person. This is written on correspondence paper with the address and date at the top, and would be on the following lines:

*Head of mission to Minister for Foreign Affairs*
An official letter from a head of mission to a Minister of Foreign Affairs usually begins 'Your Excellency' or sometimes just 'Sir' or 'Excellency', followed by:

I have the honour …

*and ends with the sentence*:

I avail myself of the opportunity to assure Your Excellency of my highest consideration

*or*

Accept, Excellency, the renewed assurances of my highest consideration.

[Name of sender]

Alternatively, and depending on the Ambassador's relationship with the Minister, a letter might begin 'My dear Minister', and end with the words 'Yours sincerely'. This less formal approach is used in the UK since no British Minister or official there is properly addressed as 'Excellency'.

If the letter is addressed in the form 'Your Excellency', it ought strictly to continue in the same way, e.g. 'My government has studied Your Excellency's proposal …' However, such phraseology can become tedious, and the judicious and occasional use of the second person (you, your) is permissible, and avoids pomposity.

*Official to official*
As a general rule correspondence between officials begins, 'My dear (name of addressee)', and ends 'Yours sincerely (name of sender)'.

*(d) Methods of providing records of verbal discussions*
Heads of mission are frequently instructed by their governments to 'make representations' to the Ministry of the country to which they are accredited or to ask for clarification of an issue. This necessitates a personal visit during which the diplomat

'states his case', and in order that there can be no room for doubt as to the purpose of his visit, he leaves behind a summary of his remarks. This may take the form of:

> An *aide-mémoire* which explains a government's action or point of view, or puts forward a proposition. It is headed 'Aide-Mémoire' and bears the date at the end, but has no signature, address or Embassy stamp.

or

> A *bout de papier* which is typed on paper without heading, signature or date, the theory being that its provenance could be denied if necessary. It is thus less 'official' than the *aide-mémoire*.

Diplomats may wish to put forward a tentative suggestion at a conference, or may be instructed by their government to make representations on a matter of great delicacy, about which their own Ministry does not yet wish to take a stand. The diplomat may then choose to discuss the issue and leave a *non-paper* in which the matter is clarified in a non-committal way.

*(e) Rejection of a note or letter*
If a Ministry of Foreign Affairs considers that a communication from another government is offensive in any way it may 'refuse to accept' it, even though it has already taken delivery of it and studied it. In these circumstances the Ministry – or invariably the Minister in such a serious situation – would summon the appropriate head of mission and hand back to him the document concerned informing him at the same time that it was unacceptable to his government.

# DEMONSTRATIONS

A diplomatic mission may find itself approached by a group of people asking for an interview with the Ambassador, or a member of his staff. An embassy thus approached has various options, the last being most commonly adopted:
- to keep the door shut,
- to accept the petition without comment,
- to invite the spokesman/men of the group in and explain the home government's position.

If the demonstration appears to be getting out of hand the Chief of Protocol (or, better still, the Police Diplomatic Protection Unit, if such exists) should be advised without delay: 'The receiving State is under a special duty to … prevent any disturbance of the peace of the mission or impairment of its dignity' (1961 Vienna Convention on Diplomatic Relations, Article 22, paragraph 2).

# FLAGS

Heads of mission are entitled to fly their national flag on their residence and the premises of their mission at all times, and it is the practice to do so to mark (a) their own national occasions, and (b) those of the state in which they are situated. They are also entitled to fly their national flag on their official car, although many choose to do so only on formal occasions or in dangerous situations.

On occasions when national mourning is officially prescribed, whether in the sending state or in the host state, flags are flown at half mast. They are normally flown in this manner only on the day of the funeral; but in the event of the death of a Sovereign it is customary for them to be flown from the day of death until (and including) the day of the funeral except on the date of the proclamation of the accession of the new Sovereign. The flag is first raised to the top of the mast, and after a brief pause lowered to half-mast. Before being lowered at the end of the day it is raised briefly to the mast-head.

Traditionally flags are raised first thing in the morning and lowered at sunset.

Consular officers who include a port within their consular area are normally permitted – subject to any existing convention, and dependent on local custom – to fly their national flag on a boat (at the bow) when on official duty. It is also common practice for heads of consular posts to fly their national flag on their official car when making official visits to the local authorities or when they are invited to take part in ceremonies or festivities in their official capacity; but the precise conditions are often regulated by a consular convention. The flying of the national flag on a consular post may be prohibited if the premises are situated in the same city as the diplomatic mission.

On the occasion of the visit of a distinguished foreign guest, the national flag of the visitor's state and that of the host state are often flown at the same place, e.g. on either side of a saluting base or platform. In this instance the flag pole on the right hand of a person sitting on the platform would be the 'guest' one: and as such would fly the visitor's flag.

When a number of flags of different countries are flown from individual flagstaffs the place of honour should be assigned to the national flag, the others being arranged alternately to right and left of this central point (looking outwards from the site) in the alphabetical order of the countries represented.

When a flag is flown on a car, the seat behind the flag is highest in the order of precedence.

# DRESS

The rules regarding dress for diplomats vary considerably between countries, and depend largely on tradition, custom and climate; the increasing trend being towards informality. There are, however, certain standard forms of dress which it is useful to be aware of (in addition to the diplomatic uniform or national dress that diplomats of certain states wear); these are normally indicated when invitation cards are sent. Dress for ladies can only be defined as 'appropriate'. Unlike that of the dull and standardised male it enlivens otherwise formal occasions, and makes a personal visual statement. For males the options are:

## MORNING COAT

Occasionally worn for daytime ceremonies, especially in the open, e.g. farewells to, or arrivals of, distinguished visitors.

Black tail coat; black waistcoat and black high silk hat for solemn occasions, alternatively grey waistcoat and grey top hat for festivities; white shirt, black striped 'pepper and salt' trousers; turndown (i.e. plain) collar; sombre tie, black shoes. Medal ribbons are not worn, but full-size medals are worn on the left breast if the occasion demands, e.g. military or remembrance.

## TAIL COAT ('WHITE TIE' OR 'FULL EVENING DRESS')

Usually restricted to formal evening functions such as dinners, balls or receptions; occasionally for more formal indoor ceremonies during the day (e.g. the presentation of credentials in the UK because it is the highest form of civilian national dress).

Long black tail coat; white waistcoat; stiff white shirt; wing collar; white bow tie; black trousers with two black silk stripes; black silk hat; black patent leather shoes; miniatures of decorations and orders (the ribbon of any neck decoration going under the white tie, and the sash of an order going across the white waistcoat).

## DINNER JACKET ('BLACK TIE' OR 'SMOKING')

For informal evening functions.

Black jacket with silk-faced lapels; black trousers with one silk stripe; white shirt (usually soft with soft collar); black bow tie; black shoes. Miniatures of decorations and medals are worn when indicated on the invitation card.

The greater the degree of informality of the evening (and the climate), the greater is the liberty with regard to dress. In some situations cummerbunds (black, or sometimes coloured, silk sashes) are worn with dinner jackets; also coloured bow ties. White tuxedos are customarily worn when the climate so demands.

## NATIONAL DRESS

Formal national dress is suitable for all diplomatic functions, and is always a welcome relief from the tedium of diplomatic representation.

# STATE CEREMONIES

It usually falls to the Chief of the Department of Protocol to plan and execute arrangements for state ceremonies and these (assuming the once-and-for-all nature of independence celebrations) are most commonly: inaugurations, visits, anniversaries of national significance and funerals.

On all the above occasions (funerals being a possible exception) detailed plans are produced several weeks, even months, in advance and the Ministry might well consult the Dean of the Diplomatic Corps if the Corps as a whole would be involved.

The cooperation of various organisations is essential for most functions, and it is usual to create an *ad hoc* planning and coordinating committee which might include representatives of the police (for parking and the regulation of traffic); the army (for a band and guard of honour); the press relations office and civic authorities; and, if foreign visitors are expected in any number, representatives of the customs, immigration and airports.

On the occasion of the visit of a foreign Head of State or member of the government or other person of distinction, the head of mission of the state concerned is invited to all the official functions and entertainments which the visitor attends; and in return the visitor offers hospitality at his head of mission's residence or an appropriate place for the corresponding dignitary in the host country (e.g. Head of State to Head of State, Foreign Minister to Foreign Minister, Head of Church to Head of Church).

A formal diplomatic visit begins when the visitor arrives in the diplomatic capital of the state (which normally must be his first objective) and it is there that the official reception takes place. The visitor's national anthem will be played, the guard of honour inspected, and compliments paid to the host's flag. If, however, the port, airport, or frontier post by which the visitor enters the state is some distance from the capital, the visitor is met by members of the local authority and an official representative who accompanies him to the capital. A procession with motor-cycle or horse escort is then arranged with the visitors riding in a carriage or motor car (depending on the distance involved). The general rule for the seating of state visitors in carriages and cars in a procession is that they are placed in the vehicles in descending order of precedence with the senior person in each vehicle seated behind the flag.

It is a recognised practice that the host of a state visit should be invited to make a return to visit to the other's capital within a reasonable time.

# OFFICIAL MOURNING

The observance of official mourning may be declared (a) by a head of mission's own government, in which event it applies to him and to the members of the staff of the mission; or (b) by the host government, in which case it applies to the Diplomatic Corps as a whole.

In the former instance, which might be occasioned by the death of the Head of State, the head of government or a member of the royal family or by a national catastrophe, a head of mission would receive instructions from his Ministry concerning the period of official mourning, the flying of the flag at half mast, etc. During this time he and members of the staff of his mission would wear black ties or their equivalent (ladies being appropriately dressed); and he would as far as possible refrain from giving or attending social engagements. Previously arranged official commitments might justifiably be cancelled, but state functions would have to be attended. Private functions, if given, would be unostentatious and relatively solemn. A 'condolences' book would be available at the Embassy or sometimes at the head of mission's residence to receive the signatures of persons wishing to express their sympathy, together with a tray for cards. In certain instances a photograph of the deceased is displayed surrounded by black ribbon; and black-edge stationery used for correspondence for a limited period of time.

In the event of official mourning being declared in the host country, the Diplomatic Corps acts as a body and receives its guidance through the Doyen who would be in close touch with the Chief of the Department of Protocol. Its members would be required to fly their flags at half mast for a given period, and to cancel all but the most informal gatherings. They would be expected to attend official ceremonies and generally to behave in conformity with the solemnity of the times. Heads of Mission would individually send formal letters of sympathy to the Minister for Foreign Affairs, and their cards marked 'p.c.' *(pour condoléances)* at the Ministry where a suitable receptacle would be provided, together with a condolences book.

If a distinguished national of a diplomatic colleague's state dies, heads of mission would express their condolences in a similar fashion, but there would be no general mourning. They would similarly express their condolences – by letter or by card, and by attendance at the funeral – on the death of a diplomatic colleague.

A note to the other diplomatic missions might take the following form:

> The Embassy of .................. presents its compliments to the Diplomatic Missions accredited to the Court of St James's and in deep sorrow has the duty to inform them that .................. died on ..................
>
> A Book of Condolence will be opened at the Embassy .................. (address) .................. from Thursday 9 to Friday 10 September .................. between the hours of 10.00 a.m. and 2.00 p.m.
>
> The Embassy of .................. avails itself of this opportunity to renew to the Diplomatic Missions accredited to the Court of St James's the assurance of its highest consideration.

# DIPLOMATIC PRIVILEGES AND IMMUNITIES

The privileged position of diplomats in society is traditional, but it is not for this reason that it continues to be respected; it is because representatives of a state can only carry out their diplomatic functions satisfactorily if they are utterly free from pressures, whether legal, physical or moral, that the state in which they are serving may be able to impose on them. In the majority of peaceful law-abiding countries the privileges and immunities to which they are entitled may appear pointless and excessive, and thus may cause resentment on the part of the host population; but in exceptional times and in exceptional countries it is only the recognition of mutually applicable privileges and immunities that enables diplomatic relations to be maintained.

Privileges and immunities are applicable both to the diplomatic mission and its functions, and to the individual.

The privileges and immunities accorded to diplomatic missions and their functions are also applicable to the United Nations and its functions under the 1946 Convention on the Privileges and Immunities of the United Nations, though the application of the Convention varies in different states.

The following is a summary of the principles contained in the 1961 Vienna Convention on Diplomatic Relations which has been accepted by an overwhelming majority of the members of the United Nations as representing an internationally agreed codification of modern diplomatic law.

## PRIVILEGES AND IMMUNITIES IN RESPECT OF THE MISSION AND ITS FUNCTIONS

### INVIOLABILITY AND IMMUNITY OF PREMISES AND PROPERTY

The premises of a mission and the private residence of the head of a mission are inviolable, as are those of members of the diplomatic and administrative and technical staff of the mission provided that they are not nationals or permanent residents of the host state. They may not be entered by agents of the host state without the permission of the head of mission concerned; the host state is obliged to ensure that all appropriate steps are taken to protect such premises against intrusion or damage, and to prevent any disturbance of the peace of the mission or impairment of its dignity. The premises, together with their contents and the means of transport belonging to the mission, are immune from search, requisition, legal attachment or execution. Motor vehicles belonging to members of the diplomatic and administrative and technical staff enjoy the same immunity, but special provisions apply to traffic offences in different countries. Generally speaking diplomats are treated as nationals in respect of such offences, save that they are not prosecuted, but the offence is reported to the head of mission.

## INVIOLABILITY OF RECORDS, DOCUMENTS, CORRESPONDENCE AND ARCHIVES

The records, documents, correspondence and archives of a mission are inviolable at any time and wherever they may be.

## FREEDOM AND INVIOLABILITY OF COMMUNICATIONS

A diplomatic mission is entitled to communicate freely for all official purposes and to have access to every facility for this in the state in which it is situated. It may use any appropriate means including couriers and messages in code or cypher to communicate with its own government and with any of its government's missions and consulates wherever they may be situated. A wireless transmitter, however, may be installed and used only with the consent of the host government.

## THE DIPLOMATIC BAG, POUCH OR VALISE

This is a sealed bag or container clearly marked as such, containing only official documents and articles for official use. A diplomatic bag usually falls into one of two categories depending on the importance of its contents: accompanied or unaccompanied. The diplomatic bag is inviolable: it may not be opened or detained, and every facility must be given for its swift despatch. It may be carried by a *diplomatic courier* who is entitled to the protection of the state which he is visiting or in which he is serving in the performance of his functions. He enjoys personal inviolability, and is not liable to any form of arrest or detention. A diplomatic courier is usually a full-time employee of a Ministry of Foreign Affairs, and on every journey must be provided by his Ministry or head of mission with a document indicating his status and the number of packages constituting the diplomatic bag. Where there is no regular diplomatic courier a state or mission may designate an individual – often an official of appropriate nationality who is making the journey for other reasons – as a diplomatic courier for a specific journey. Provided that he is furnished with the appropriate documents by his Ministry or head of mission he will be granted the same immunities and personal inviolability as a regular courier until such time as he has delivered the diplomatic bag in his charge. In normal circumstances a diplomatic bag may be entrusted to the captain of an aircraft, provided he enters or leaves the country through an authorised place of entry. A member of the mission concerned is entitled to hand the bag directly and freely to the captain, and similarly to receive it from him. The captain concerned must be provided with a document stating the number of packages constituting the bag; but he himself is not considered as being a diplomatic courier.

When communications between a state and its diplomatic mission have to pass through a third state, that state must furnish the same inviolability as is accorded by the receiving state. Diplomatic bags properly identified are inviolable while in transit through third states, as are diplomatic couriers. Couriers must, however, obtain any appropriate visas.

## EXEMPTION FROM TAXATION

A diplomatic mission is exempt from all national, regional and municipal dues and taxes in respect of the mission premises, whether owned or leased, except for those charges which represent payment for specific services rendered (e.g. water, electricity, refuse collection). This exemption does not extend to persons entering into contracts with a head of mission or his government – for which reason such contracts usually stipulate that it is the head of the mission or his government who are responsible for any rates or taxes on the premises.

A diplomatic mission is also exempt from dues and taxes in respect of any fees and charges that it levies as part of the normal functions of a mission.

## RIGHT TO IMPORT, AND EXEMPTION FROM CUSTOMS DUTIES

A diplomatic mission is entitled to import (subject to existing laws) articles for the official use of the mission, and is exempt from customs and other similar duties in respect of such articles. It is not exempt from charges for related services, e.g. storage or cartage. Goods imported duty free may not be sold or otherwise disposed of in the host state except in accordance with the conditions laid down by the state.

# PERSONAL PRIVILEGES AND IMMUNITIES

## GENERAL PROVISIONS

*Full diplomatic privileges and immunities* are applicable to (a) diplomats, and (b) members of their families forming part of their household provided they are not nationals or permanent residents of the state in which the diplomat is serving.

The interpretation of the term 'family' varies between states. The spouse and minor children of the diplomat are always included. Normally a diplomat who is a bachelor or widower or not accompanied by his wife would be entitled to count his mother or sister as part of the family if they are living with him; sons and daughters for whom the diplomat is legally responsible are included, as are widowed mothers.

*Limited diplomatic privileges and immunities* are afforded to three categories of members of the staff of a mission: those who are nationals or permanent residents of the state in which they are serving; members of the administrative and technical staff; and private servants of members of the mission.

As a counterpart to the enjoyment of immunity a diplomat may not practice for profit any professional or commercial activity in the state in which he is serving.

It is customary (but not universally accepted) practice for members of diplomatic missions to be issued with diplomatic identity cards by the host state. These carry the photograph and signature of the holder, together with whatever instructions the host state may see fit to add for the benefit of its officials with regard to the privileges, facilities and immunities which should be accorded to the bearer.

The immunity granted to a diplomat and members of his family by the host state does not exempt them from the jurisdiction of their own state.

## DURATION OF PRIVILEGES AND IMMUNITIES

Personal privileges and immunities apply from the moment the member of a mission enters the host country to take up his post or, if already in the country, from the moment his appointment is notified to the appropriate Ministry. Privileges and immunities come to an end when he leaves the country on the conclusion of his functions, or (if he does not leave immediately) after a reasonable interval of time (e.g. 4-6 weeks in the UK); but immunity from jurisdiction in respect of acts carried out in the course of his official duty has no limit in time. Immunity from jurisdiction in respect of any act carried out in a private capacity, however, does not continue after the conclusion of the diplomat's functions. In the event of the death of a member of a mission, the members of his family continue to enjoy the privileges and immunities to which they were entitled for a reasonable period of time sufficient to enable them to leave the country.

# FULL PRIVILEGES AND IMMUNITIES

## PERSONAL INVIOLABILITY AND PROTECTION

All diplomats enjoy personal inviolability, and members of their family forming part of their household similarly enjoy inviolability provided that they are not nationals or permanent residents of the host state. A state which accepts the establishment of a foreign diplomatic mission is bound to ensure complete protection to all members of that mission and to their families against physical violence whatever its source, and from attacks on their dignity and freedom.

## IMMUNITY FROM CRIMINAL JURISDICTION

A diplomat and members of his family forming part of his household (provided that they are not nationals or permanent residents of the host state) are immune from the criminal jurisdiction of the host state.

## IMMUNITY FROM CIVIL AND ADMINISTRATIVE JURISDICTION

A diplomat and members of his family forming part of his household (provided they are not nationals or permanent residents of the host state) are immune from civil and administrative jurisdiction in the host state except in the case of:

(a) a real action (i.e. an action to claim ownership or possession) relating to private immovable property situated in the host state, unless he holds it on behalf of the state he serves for the purposes of the mission;

(b) an action relating to succession in which he is involved as executor, administrator, heir or legatee as a private person and not on behalf of the state he serves;

(c) an action relating to any professional or commercial activity exercised by him in the host state outside his official function. This limitation applies in practice to his spouse and family.

## WAIVER OF DIPLOMATIC IMMUNITY

The immunity from jurisdiction of an individual entitled to such protection may be waived only by his government. A waiver of immunity from civil or administrative proceedings does no more than allow the person concerned to stand trial; a second and specific waiver is required before the judgement can be put into effect.

## COUNTERCLAIMS

If legal proceedings are started by a person enjoying diplomatic immunity he is not entitled to claim immunity from jurisdiction in respect of any counterclaim directly connected with the principal claim.

## INVIOLABILITY OF CORRESPONDENCE

The papers and correspondence of a diplomat and of members of his family forming part of his household (provided that they are not nationals or permanent residents of the host state) are inviolable.

## INVIOLABILITY OF PROPERTY

The property of a diplomat and of members of his family forming part of his household (provided that they are not nationals or permanent residents of the host state) is inviolable.

## EXEMPTION FROM LIABILITY FOR PUBLIC SERVICE

A diplomat and members of his family forming part of his household (provided that they are not nationals or permanent residents of the host state) are exempt from all personal and public services and from military obligations such as requisitioning, billeting or military contributions and from jury service.

## EXEMPTION FROM LIABILITY TO SERVE AS A WITNESS

A diplomat and members of his family forming part of his household (provided that they are not nationals or permanent residents of the host state) are not obliged to give evidence as witnesses (but in many cases do so in order to assist justice).

## EXEMPTION FROM NATIONAL AND LOCAL TAXATION

A diplomat and members of his family forming part of his household (provided that they are not nationals or permanent residents of the host state) are exempt from all dues and taxes, personal or real, national, regional or municipal, except for:

(a) Indirect taxes of a kind normally incorporated in the price of goods or services, e.g. value-added tax (though in some instances a refund of such taxes and excise duties is made on a reciprocal basis or to promote sales of goods manufactured in the receiving state).

(b) Dues and taxes on private immovable property situated in the territory of the host state, unless it is held on behalf of the sending state for the purposes of the mission.

(c) Estate, succession or inheritance duties levied by the host state, subject to the provisions referred to in Article 39 of the Vienna Convention. Generally speaking, such duties are not levied on an individual's movable property provided that its presence in the receiving state could reasonably be related to his official functions, and provided that he or she was not a permanent resident or national of the state concerned.

(d) Dues and taxes on private income originating in the host state, and capital taxes levied on commercial undertakings in that state.

(e) Charges levied for specific services rendered. (In UK practice this covers one-quarter approximately of local authority rates or taxes relating to services such as roads, street lighting and refuse collection from which a diplomat is deemed to derive direct benefit.)

(f) Registration, court or record fees, mortgage dues and stamp duty in respect of immovable property (except for immovable property required as part of the premises of the mission in which case fees and dues are payable only in respect of specific services rendered).

## EXEMPTION FROM CUSTOMS DUTIES

A diplomat and members of his family forming part of his household (provided that they are not nationals or permanent residents of the host state) are entitled (in accordance with local regulations, which must not defeat diplomatic privilege) to import articles for their personal use, including articles required for the upkeep of their establishment, and are exempt from customs and other similar duties in respect of such articles. They are, however, liable to related charges for services, e.g. storage and cartage; and must comply with the regulations of the host state in respect of any articles imported duty-free that they subsequently sell or otherwise dispose of.

## EXEMPTION FROM SOCIAL SECURITY PROVISIONS

A diplomat and members of his family forming part of his household (provided that they are not nationals or permanent residents of the host state) are exempt from the social security provisions of the host state. Private servants in the sole employ of a diplomat are also exempt, provided that they are not nationals or permanent residents of the host state and that they are covered by the social security provisions of their own state; and a diplomat is obliged to comply with the social security provisions in force in respect of any person he employs who is not so exempt. In some states he may be permitted to participate in their social security scheme if he so wishes; and in others his position may be covered by an existing agreement between the host state and his own state.

## EXEMPTION FROM INSPECTION OF PERSONAL LUGGAGE

A diplomat and members of his family forming part of his household (provided that they are not nationals or permanent residents of the host state) are exempt from the inspection of personal luggage, unless there are serious grounds for believing that it contains articles that do not come within the scope of the privileges permitted, or illegal imports or exports. In this event the inspection is conducted only in the presence of the diplomat or of his authorised representative.

## FREEDOM OF TRAVEL

All members of the staff of a diplomatic mission are entitled to travel freely and without restriction in the state in which they are serving, except in those areas to which access is limited on grounds of national security. This principle is not always adhered to, and certain states limit the freedom of certain diplomats to special travel zones; and in such cases a policy of reciprocity is usually adopted.

## TRAVEL THROUGH A THIRD STATE

Provided that they have any necessary visas, diplomats and members of their family, whether travelling with them or separately, are entitled to inviolability and all other immunities necessary to ensure a safe journey when passing through a third state on their way to or from a post. To ensure this they should be provided by their Ministry with a letter (preferably in the language of the third state or states) giving the purpose of their journey; or with a diplomatic visa issued by a diplomatic or consular representative of that state. It is not normal for their luggage to be inspected, and the authorities should have very good reasons before doing so.

## RECIPROCAL OBLIGATIONS OF DIPLOMATS

The granting of privileges and immunities by a state implies the acceptance of a high standard of responsibility and integrity on the part of the recipient. He may not interfere in the internal affairs of that state nor allow official premises to be put to any purpose other than their proper and recognised function; and he should not take advantage of his immunity from the jurisdiction of the courts to disregard its laws in such matters as motor-car accidents, speeding and parking.

## DIPLOMATIC PASSPORTS

Diplomatic passports are issued by most states to those of their nationals who are entitled to diplomatic immunity and in the case of some states, to persons of high standing or connection. The UK practice is to issue diplomatic passports on a strictly controlled basis and only to diplomats for the duration of their posting in a British diplomatic mission overseas. They are usually taken not as evidence of entitlement to immunity (this being a function *prima facie* of the Diplomatic List), but as evidence of appointment only; they nevertheless often serve a useful purpose. Identity cards may be issued by the receiving state for the same purpose.

## REPRESENTATIVES TO INTERNATIONAL ORGANISATIONS

In certain cases resident (and sometimes non-resident) representatives of states to international organisations are entitled to the same privileges and immunities as diplomats. Representatives to the United Nations and its Specialised Agencies normally receive a wide range of privileges and immunities under the 1946 Convention on the Privileges and Immunities of the United Nations, and the similar Convention regarding the Specialised Agencies. The few most senior officers on the staffs of these organisations are entitled to the full range of diplomatic privileges and immunities (unless they are nationals or permanent residents of the receiving state); the other staff members of the organisations enjoy more limited privileges and immunities. In the case of other organisations, such matters are normally included in the Agreement establishing the organisation or in an Agreement concluded between the host state and the international organisation before the latter is set up. Special provisions apply in Switzerland and the USA where such organisations are numerous.

## MEMBERS OF VISITING DIPLOMATIC MISSIONS

It is customary for states to grant privileges and immunities to visiting representatives of foreign states who, although not accredited as diplomats to any state, are exercising quasi-diplomatic or representative functions. Within this category come Heads of State or their representatives whether on a state occasion or on an informal visit, members of arbitration tribunals and government delegates to conferences or congresses. The New York Convention on Special Missions has now been drawn up to regulate the privileges and immunities given to such temporary special missions sent with the agreement of the receiving state.

# LIMITED PRIVILEGES AND IMMUNITIES

## NON-DIPLOMATIC STAFF OF A MISSION WHO ARE NOT NATIONALS OR PERMANENT RESIDENTS OF THE STATE IN WHICH THEY ARE SERVING

*Members of the administrative and technical staff* of a mission and members of their families forming part of their household (provided that they are not nationals or permanent residents of the state in which they are serving) are entitled to the full immunities given to a diplomat except that immunity from civil and administrative jurisdiction does not extend to acts performed outside the course of their duty; and to full diplomatic privileges except that they are not exempt from the inspection of their luggage, and exemption from customs duties is limited to articles imported at the time of their arrival in the state to take up their appointment there; nor are they entitled to privileges and immunities while travelling through third states to take up an appointment, though such states are obliged not to hinder their passage.

*Members of the domestic ('service') staff* of a mission who are not nationals or permanent residents of the state in which they are serving are entitled to immunity in respect of acts performed in the course of their duties, exemption from dues and taxes on the emoluments they receive in respect of their employment, and exemption from social security provisions in respect of their employment with a diplomatic mission provided that they are covered by the social security provisions of their own country.

*Private servants of members of the diplomatic staff* of a mission who are not nationals or permanent residents of the state in which they are serving are exempt from dues and taxes on the emoluments they receive in respect of their employment, but are not otherwise entitled to any privileges or immunities other than those that the host state may choose to grant; it is, however, bound to exercise its jurisdiction over them in such a manner as not to interfere unduly with the performance of the functions of the relevant mission.

## DIPLOMATS AND OTHER MEMBERS OF THE STAFF OF A MISSION WHO ARE NATIONALS OR PERMANENT RESIDENTS OF THE HOST STATE

Diplomats who are nationals or permanent residents of the state in which they are serving are entitled only to immunity from jurisdiction and personal inviolability in respect of official acts performed in the exercise of their functions, though other privileges and immunities may be granted in particular states. Other (non-diplomatic) members of the staff of a mission and private servants who are nationals or permanent residents of the state in which they are serving enjoy only those privileges and immunities that the host state considers appropriate. Any limitations placed on persons in these categories, however, must be such as not to interfere unduly with the performance of the functions of their mission.

# CONSULAR OFFICERS AND CONSULAR POSTS

## THE ESTABLISHMENT OF CONSULAR POSTS

The establishment of diplomatic relations between states implies agreement in principle to the establishment of consular relations unless the contrary is specifically stated; but the severance of diplomatic relations does not automatically signify the severance of consular relations.

The establishment of a consular post requires the prior approval of the host state, which may ask to be provided with details of the location and status of the post (i.e. Consulate-General, Consulate, Vice-Consulate or Honorary Consulate) and its area of consular jurisdiction. Its prior approval must also be obtained for any subsequent changes in these particulars, and also for the establishment of any subsidiary consular offices elsewhere in the consular area.

## CONSULAR FUNCTIONS

Consular functions are described in general terms in the 1963 Vienna Convention on Consular Relations as follows:
(a) protecting in the receiving state the interests of the sending state and of its nationals, both individuals and bodies corporate, within the limits permitted by international law;
(b) furthering the development of commercial, economic, cultural and scientific relations between the sending state and the receiving state and otherwise promoting friendly relations between them in accordance with the provisions of the Convention;
(c) ascertaining, by all lawful means, conditions and developments in the commercial, economic, cultural and scientific life of the receiving state, reporting thereon to the Government of the sending state and giving information to persons interested;
(d) issuing passports and travel documents to nationals of the sending state, and visas or appropriate documents to persons wishing to travel to the sending state;
(e) helping and assisting nationals, both individuals and bodies corporate, of the sending state;

(f) acting as notary and civil registrar and in capacities of a similar kind, and performing certain functions of an administrative nature, provided that there is nothing contrary thereto in the laws and regulations of the receiving state;

(g) safeguarding the interests of nationals, both individuals and bodies corporate, of the sending state in cases of succession *mortis causa* in the territory of the receiving state, in accordance with the laws and regulations of the receiving state;

(h) safeguarding, within the limits imposed by the laws and regulations of the receiving state, the interests of minors and other persons lacking full capacity who are nationals of the sending state, particularly where any guardianship or trusteeship is required with respect to such persons;

(i) subject to the practices and procedures in force in the receiving state, representing or arranging appropriate representation for nationals of the sending state before the tribunals and other authorities of the receiving state, for the purpose of obtaining, in accordance with the laws and regulations of the receiving state, provisional measures for the preservation of the rights and interests of these nationals, where, because of absence or any other reason, such nationals are unable at the proper time to assume the defence of their rights and interests;

(j) transmitting judicial and extra-judicial documents or executing letters rogatory or commissions to take evidence for the courts of the sending state in accordance with international agreements in force or, in the absence of such agreements, in any other manner compatible with the laws and regulations of the receiving state;

(k) exercising rights of supervision and inspection provided for in the laws and regulations of the sending state in respect of vessels having the nationality of the sending state, and of aircraft registered in that state, and in respect of their crews;

(l) extending assistance to vessels and aircraft mentioned in (k) above and to their crews, taking statements regarding the voyage of a vessel, examining and stamping the ship's papers, and without prejudice to the powers of the authorities of the receiving state, conducting investigations into any incidents which occurred during the voyage, and settling disputes of any kind between the master, the officers and the seamen in so far as this may be authorised by the laws and regulations of the sending state;

(m) performing any other functions entrusted to a consular post by the sending state which are not prohibited by the laws and regulations of the receiving state or to which no objection is taken by the receiving state or which are referred to in the international agreements in force between the sending state and the receiving state.

These functions may, with the consent of all governments concerned, be exercised by a consular officer on behalf of a third state.

It will be noted that in a substantial number of cases the right to act is not absolute, but dependent on the law of the receiving state. Also, despite the quasi-legal nature of many of his functions, a consul is not a substitute for a lawyer or other specialist.

More detailed provisions are included in many bilateral conventions, and a comprehensive outline of consular functions may be found in the Council of Europe, *European Convention on Consular Functions*

A consular officer whose government has no diplomatic representative in the state in which he is serving and is not represented diplomatically by a third state may, with the authority of his host state, and without affecting his consular status, be authorised to perform certain diplomatic acts, including the representation of his state at intergovernmental organisations.

## CONSULAR OFFICERS, CONSULAR EMPLOYEES AND MEMBERS OF THE SERVICE STAFF

*Consular officers* are persons designated as such and responsible for the exercise of consular functions. They hold the rank of Consul-General, Consul or Vice-Consul and are divided into two categories:

(a) *career consular officers* who are full-time servants of their government and are appointed by their Head of State or Foreign Minister;
(b) *honorary consular officers* who are non-career officials for whom consular functions are usually a part-time occupation.

Career officers may not normally carry on for personal profit any professional or commercial activity in the host state, and should in principle have the nationality of the country they serve; the appointment of a national of the host state may only be made with that government's permission which may be withdrawn at any time. An honorary consular officer, on the other hand, though often a national of the country whose interest he serves, need not necessarily be so.

*Consular employees* are members of the consular staff who are not responsible for the exercise of consular functions, but who are employed in an administrative or technical capacity.

*Members of the service staff* are those employed as chauffeurs, cleaners, domestics, etc. Persons falling within these categories are usually local residents.

*Consular agents and pro-consuls* are appointed by certain states but there is no standard definition of the terms. Generally they refer to consular employees with limited responsibilities ranking below vice-consul, but their precise status and functions vary considerably in different states.

# THE APPOINTMENT OF CONSULAR OFFICERS

It is traditional practice for the head of a consular post to be provided by his government with a written authority in respect of each appointment showing his full name, consular rank, consular district and post. This document (a *Commission*) is sent through diplomatic channels to the host government who, if they have no objection, issue a corresponding document (an *Exequatur*) authorising the appointment. In the rare event of its declining to issue an Exequatur, a government need give no reasons for its action. A similar procedure is normally adopted in respect of officers appointed to the consular staff; but, alternatively, a simple notification of relevant details in advance may be acceptable, and the granting of formal Exequaturs, though customary, is not obligatory.

The UK practice follows the Vienna Convention on Consular Relations, Article 12(1), whereby 'the Head of a Consular post is admitted to the exercise of his functions by an authorisation from the receiving State termed an exequatur whatever the form of this authorisation'. All officers performing consular functions are recognised by simple letter from the Protocol Department, and a Head of State exequatur is issued only to the career head of a consular post.

On arrival at his post, the head of a consular post informs the Dean of the Consular Corps accordingly, and makes calls on the local authorities and on the other heads of consular posts.

As soon as a head of a consular post is admitted to his functions, and even though the formalities of his appointment may not have been completed, the host government notifies the official authorities in the consular district concerned and ensures that all necessary facilities are provided for him to carry out his functions. Customs and immigration authorities are also advised of the arrival and departure of a consular officer and members of his family so that appropriate arrangements can be made.

In the absence of the head of a consular post (whether through illness, or the post falling temporarily vacant) the position may be held provisionally by a diplomat or consular officer or, if the host state has no objection, by some other person. In any event the name of the acting head of post must be furnished to the host government, advance notification usually being required.

A consular officer may at any time and without explanation be declared *persona non grata*. In this event he is recalled by his government; failing which his letter of appointment or Exequatur is cancelled and he ceases to be considered a consular officer.

# SEVERANCE OF CONSULAR RELATIONS

In the event of consular relations being broken off, the consular premises, property and archives must be respected and protected by the host state; and the business of the consulate, together with the property and archives, may be entrusted by the appointing state to a third state acceptable to the host state.

# PRIVILEGES, FACILITIES AND IMMUNITIES

The Vienna Convention on Consular Relations was drawn up in 1963 with the aim of providing the basis for a uniform practice in respect of consular privileges and immunities; but many states with wide consular interests have preferred to conclude bilateral agreements to suit their particular requirements, and these usually accord a more liberal scale of privileges, though not usually of immunities. Some states such as the United Kingdom are parties both to the Vienna Convention and to prior and subsequent bilateral conventions. In case of any conflict they apply the more generous treatment in matters of privileges and immunities, on being assured of reciprocity. Nevertheless the advantages of a standard practice are self-evident, and the following are the main provisions of the Vienna Convention.

# CAREER CONSULAR OFFICERS AND POSTS HEADED BY THEM

## RELATING TO THE CONSULAR POST

The facilities granted by the host state to a consular post are those necessary to ensure the effective fulfilment of its functions: the premises used exclusively for consular purposes are (with specific exceptions such as an emergency requiring prompt action on the premises) inviolable and may not be entered except with the permission of the head of the consular post or the head of the diplomatic mission of the country concerned; the host state is obliged, where necessary, to help in finding suitable premises for the consular post (and accommodation for staff) and to ensure that all appropriate steps are taken to protect the premises from damage or insult; the consular archives and official correspondence are inviolable; there is freedom of movement for members of the post (save in generally restricted zones) and freedom and inviolability of communication by bag and other recognised means, although wireless transmitters may be used only with the permission of the host government; furthermore the host government may ask for a bag to be opened if it has serious reason to believe that its contents are unauthorised (if, however, the sending state refuses to do this the bag shall be returned to its place of origin); and the head of post has the right to fly his national flag and display his national coat of arms on his premises and residence, and fly his flag on his car, boat or aircraft when on official business.

The consular premises, including the residence of the head of the post but not those of other members of the staff, are not directly liable to taxation (though this exemption does not apply to the vendor or lessor of the premises if he is liable under the law), but charges for services, e.g. refuse collection, must be met.

In addition, consular fees and charges may be levied for services rendered, e.g. the granting of visas, certification of documents; these are exempt from all dues and taxes in the host state.

## RELATING TO CONSULAR DUTIES

*Right of access to nationals who are detained*
In view of a consular officer's particular responsibility within his consular district towards nationals of his own state (and those of any other state or states whose interests he represents) he must be free to visit and communicate with them; and such individuals, conversely, have the right to communicate with and have free access to their consular officer. Moreover, if the authorities detain a foreign national they must inform him that he is free to communicate with his consular officer, who must be given the appropriate facilities to visit the national if the latter so wishes. If a consular officer makes enquiries as to whether an individual for whom he is responsible has been detained, he must be given an immediate reply and be permitted, where he considers it necessary and with the concurrence of the person concerned, to arrange for appropriate legal representation.

*Right of access to information in cases of death, guardianship or trusteeship, wrecks and air accidents*
The appropriate authorities have the duty to notify a consular officer without delay of any incident of which they are aware occurring within his district and affecting individuals for whom he is responsible, such as a death, a case where the appointment of guardians or trustees is needed, or a wreck or accident occurring to a ship or aircraft registered in his state.

*Right of access to appropriate authorities*
In the exercise of his official functions a consular officer is entitled to communicate with the competent local authorities in his consular area; and in exceptional cases with the central authorities if custom and circumstances permit.

## PERSONAL PRIVILEGES AND IMMUNITIES

*General*
The privileges to which a career consular officer is entitled under the 1963 Vienna Convention on Consular Relations are similar to those of members of the diplomatic staff of a mission. The extent of his immunity from jurisdiction and personal inviolability, however, is considerably less except where specific agreements provide otherwise. Privileges and immunities apply from the moment he enters the host state to take up his appointment or, if already in the country, from the moment he takes up his duties. They terminate when he leaves the country or (if he does not leave immediately) a reasonable time after he relinquishes his appointment.

*Personal protection*
The host state is obliged to treat a consular officer with due respect and must take all appropriate steps to prevent any attack on his person, freedom or dignity.

*Personal inviolability and immunity from jurisdiction*
A consular officer or consular employee is not liable to the jurisdiction (judicial or administrative) of the host state in respect of acts performed in the exercise of his consular functions. It is expressly made clear that his immunity does not apply to civil actions by third parties, (i) for damage arising within the state from an accident caused by a vehicle, vessel or aircraft or (ii) arising out of any contract that he concluded if he did not contract expressly or impliedly as an agent of the state which he was serving at the time. His government may, if it sees fit, waive his immunity.

He must, however, appear before the competent authorities if criminal proceedings are brought against him, and he is liable to imprisonment if convicted by the competent judicial authorities. In the event of his being accused of a grave crime (but only in such an event) he may be detained pending trial.

It is, nevertheless, some consolation for him to know that proceedings will be carried out with the minimum delay, with due respect to him by reason of his official position, and, if the charge is not serious, with the minimum interference to his consular functions; and that the head of his consular post must be informed of his predicament unless he himself holds that position, in which case his government will be informed immediately through diplomatic channels.

*Proceedings initiated by a consular officer or consular employee*
If a consular officer or consular employee initiates proceedings, he loses any immunity from jurisdiction in respect of any counterclaim directly connected with the main claim to which he would otherwise have been entitled.

*Liability to give evidence*
No member of a consular post is obliged (unless his government waives the immunity) to give evidence on official matters or to produce official correspondence and documents concerning matters connected with the exercise of his functions; nor is he bound to give evidence as an expert witness with regard to the law of his state. In other matters he may be called on to attend as a witness at judicial or administrative proceedings and would normally do so. If a consular officer (as opposed to a consular employee or member of the service staff) should decline to do so, however, no penalty or coercive measure may be applied to him.

*Residence permits, work permits, and registration as aliens*
Career consular officers, consular employees (provided that they are permanent employees of the state they serve and are not engaged in any gainful occupation in the state in which they are serving) and members of their families forming part of their household are exempt from local regulations concerning residence permits, the registration of aliens and the employment of aliens.

*Social security*
Career consular officers and other members of the consular post (i.e. consular employees and members of the service staff) together with members of their families

forming part of their household are exempt from social security requirements in force in the host state in respect of their official duties. They may, however, be permitted to participate voluntarily; and if they have any individuals in their private employ, they are responsible for complying with the social security requirements in respect of such persons.

*Taxation*
Career consular officers and consular employees and members of their families forming part of their household, provided that they do not carry on any private gainful occupation in the host state, are exempt from all national and local taxes, except:
(a)  indirect taxes of a kind normally incorporated in the price of goods or services;
(b)  dues or taxes on private immovable property in the territory of the host state (this provision does not apply to the premises of a career consular post or to the residence of the head of such post);
(c)  estate, succession or inheritance duties and duties on transfers levied by the host state (this provision does not normally apply to movable property of a deceased person which is sent out of the country);
(d)  dues and taxes on private income (including capital gains) originating in the host state, and capital taxes on investments in commercial or financial undertakings in the host state;
(e)  charges levied for specific services rendered;
(f)  registration, court or record fees, mortgage dues and stamp duties (this provision does not apply to the premises of a career consular post or to the residence of the head of such post).

Members of the service staff are exempt from dues and taxes on the wages that they receive for their services.

*Customs duties and inspection*
Exemption from all customs duties, taxes and related charges (other than those for storage, cartage, etc.) and unrestricted right of entry (except for articles generally restricted by law) are granted in respect of:
(a)  articles for the official use of the *consular post*;
(b)  articles for the personal and domestic use of a *consular officer* and members of his family (forming part of his household) in reasonable quantities;
(c)  articles for the personal and domestic use of a *consular employee* and members of his family (forming part of his household) imported at the time of his first arrival to take up his duties.

*Insurance against third-party risks*
All members of a consular post must comply with national and local legislation concerning third party insurance in respect of any vehicle, vessel or aircraft.

# HONORARY CONSULAR OFFICERS AND POSTS HEADED BY THEM

## RELATING TO THE CONSULAR POST

A certain number of the facilities and immunities granted to career posts (with the same provisos as to their use exclusively for consular functions) are granted to consular posts headed by honorary consuls:

(a) full facilities for the performance of the functions of a consular post;

(b) the right to display the national flag and emblem at the consular post and consular residence and on a vehicle when on official business;

(c) assistance in the acquisition of premises and accommodation;

(d) freedom of movement and travel of all members of the consular post (save in generally restricted areas);

(e) freedom and inviolability of communication (including the right of communication through third states); but the exchange of consular bags between two consular posts headed by honorary consular officers in different states is not permitted without the consent of the two host states concerned;

(f) the right to levy consular fees and charges, and their exemption from taxation in the host state;

(g) more limited protection by the host state of the consular premises against intrusion, damage, disturbance and impairment of its dignity;

(h) exemption from all forms of taxation of the consular premises of which the sending state is owner or lessee except for those representing the payment for specific services rendered: but this exemption does not extend to the individual who leases or sells the premises to the sending state if he is liable to pay under the law;

(i) inviolability of consular archives and documents at all times and wherever they may be, provided that they are kept separate from other papers and documents and, in particular, from the private correspondence of the head of a consular post and of any person working with him, and from the materials, books or documents relating to their profession or trade;

(j) exemption from customs and other similar duties on coats-of-arms, flags, signboards, seals and stamps, books, official printed matter, office furniture, office equipment and similar articles supplied by or at the instance of the sending state to the consular post provided that they are for official use.

## RELATING TO CONSULAR DUTIES

(a) the right of access to nationals for whom the post is responsible;

(b) the right of access to information in cases of deaths, the need for guardianships or trusteeships, wrecks and air accidents;

(c) the right of access to the appropriate authorities in the host state.

## FACILITIES, PERSONAL PRIVILEGES AND IMMUNITIES

An honorary consular officer enjoys a certain number of the facilities, privileges and immunities enjoyed by a career consular officer in connection with the performance of his functions, though, as with career officers, they may be waived by the government he serves; and if he himself initiates legal proceedings he loses the immunity (see below) in respect of a counterclaim directly connected with a principal claim.

They start the moment the officer enters the territory of the state to take up his post, or if he is already in the territory, the moment that he takes up his duties, and come to an end when he leaves the territory or (if he does not do so immediately) a reasonable period thereafter.

These facilities, privileges and immunities are as follows:

(a) The obligation of the host state to notify his consular or diplomatic representative in the event of his being arrested, detained or prosecuted.

(b) Immunity from jurisdiction in respect of acts performed in the exercise of his consular functions except for civil actions (i) in respect of third-party claims arising from an accident caused by a vehicle, vessel or aircraft, or (ii) arising out of a contract not expressly or implicitly carried out as an agent of the state which he, as an honorary consular officer, serves. The immunity is of indefinite duration, i.e. it does not necessarily cease on the termination of the officer's period of duty.

(c) Freedom from the obligation to give evidence or to produce official correspondence or documents on matters connected with the exercise of his consular functions; and the right to decline to give evidence as an expert witness with regard to the law of the state he serves.

The following additional provisions also apply to an honorary consular officer:

(d) If criminal proceedings are instituted against him he must appear before the competent authorities. He is, however, treated with the respect due to his official position; proceedings are instituted with the minimum of delay; and unless under detention, his ability to carry on his consular functions is hampered as little as possible.

(e) He is exempt from all obligations in the host state in regard to the registration of aliens and residence permits provided that he does not engage there in any professional or commercial activity for personal profit.

(f) He is exempt from all dues and taxes on the remuneration and emoluments that he receives from the government of the state he serves in respect of the exercise of his consular functions.

(g) He is exempt from all personal and public services and military contributions in the state in which he is serving.

(h) He is entitled to receive from the host state such protection as is needed on account of his official position; and in return must undertake to respect the laws of that state and not to interfere in its internal affairs.

(i) Privileges and immunities granted to an honorary consular officer do not apply to members of his family, nor to the family of a consular employee in a post headed by an honorary consul.

# THE UNITED NATIONS

*We, the peoples of the United Nations, determined to save succeeding generations from the scourge of war, which twice in our lifetime has brought untold sorrow to mankind ...*

(Opening words of the Charter of the United Nations)

The United Nations is first and foremost the custodian of the U.N. Charter, which is a multilateral treaty dating from the end of World War II and the advent of the nuclear age. Together with the Statute of the International Court of Justice it is the legal basis for the peaceful conduct of relations between states. The Charter was formulated primarily to maintain international peace and security (Art. 1) and to ensure that the scourge of war did not bring untold sorrow to mankind for a third – and seemingly last – time; and it accordingly commits member-states to the peaceful settlement of international disputes (Art. 2.3) and 'to refrain in their international relations from the threat or use of force against the territorial integrity or political independence of any state' (Art. 2.4). It recognises 'the inherent right of individual or collective self-defence' in the event of an armed attack on a member-state, until such time as the Security Council shall have taken measures necessary to maintain international peace and security (Art. 51); and authorises the Security Council to take action on the basis of 'an affirmative vote of nine members including the concurring votes of the per-manent members* (Art. 27.3) in two specific cases:

(i) the pacific settlement of disputes and the maintenance of international peace and security (Ch VI) with the proviso that 'nothing contained in the present Charter shall authorise the U.N. to intervene in matters which are essentially within the domestic function of any state' (Art. 24.2, and Purposes and Principles 2.7). The Charter provides that the Security Council shall investigate and mediate and endeavour to obtain a peaceful settlement of the dispute; and that Regional arrangements should be encouraged for the maintenance of international peace and security. Moreover, no enforcement action may be taken under regional arrangements or by regional agencies without the authorisation of the Security Council... (Art. 53.1)

---

*   So long as the Soviet Union was a permanent member of the Security Council it was able, by its absence from meetings, to nullify the precondition for action that required the 'concurring votes' of the permanent members. This predicament was overcome by agreeing that action could be taken if no nega-tive vote were cast. Now, with the advent of Russia as a permanent member, this derogation from the Charter lacks validity: and *pacta sunt servanda.*

(ii) where there is any threat to the peace, breach of the peace or act of aggression (Ch VII); in which event the Security Council *'may take such action by land, sea or air forces as may be necessary to maintain or restore international peace and security':* the proviso precluding intervention in matters which are within the domestic function of any state *not* being applicable in these circumstances. Moreover, in the event of a conflict between the obligations of members of the United Nations under the present Charter and their obligations under any other international agreement, Article 103 stipulates that 'their obligations under the present charter shall prevail'.

The United Nations is, in practice, a Standing Diplomatic Conference: it is a world-wide association of states which, on signing the Charter of the United Nations, sub-scribe to its purposes and agree to act in accordance with its principles; these are:

## PURPOSES

I   To maintain international peace and security, and to that end: to take effective col-lective measures for the prevention and removal of threats to the peace, and for the suppression of acts of aggression or other breaches of the peace, and to bring about by peaceful means, and in conformity with the principles of justice and international law, adjustment or settlement of international disputes or situations which might lead to a breach of the peace;

II   To develop friendly relations among nations based on respect for the principle of equal rights and self-determination of peoples, and to take other appropriate measures to strengthen universal peace;

III  To achieve international cooperation in solving international problems of an eco-nomic, social, cultural, or humanitarian character, and in promoting and encour-aging respect for human rights and for fundamental freedoms for all without dis-tinction as to race, sex, language, or religion; and

IV   To be a centre for harmonising the actions of nations in the attainment of these common ends.

## PRINCIPLES

I   The United Nations is based on the principle of the sovereign equality of all its members.

II   All members, in order to ensure to all of them the rights and benefits resulting from membership, shall fulfil in good faith the obligations assumed by them in accordance with the Charter.

III  All members shall settle their international disputes by peaceful means in such a manner that international peace and security, and justice, are not endangered.

IV   All members shall refrain in their international relations from the threat or use of force against the territorial integrity or political independence of any state, or in any other manner inconsistent with the Purposes of the United Nations.

V   All members shall give the United Nations every assistance in any action it takes in accordance with the Charter, and shall refrain from giving assistance to any state against which the United Nations is taking a preventive or enforcement action.

VI  The United Nations shall ensure that states which are not members of the Organisation act in accordance with these Principles so far as may be necessary for the maintenance of international peace and security.

VII Nothing contained in the Charter shall authorise the United Nations to intervene in matters which are essentially within the domestic jurisdiction of any state or shall require the members to submit such matters to settlement under the Charter; but this principle shall not prejudice the application of enforcement measures under chapter VII.

## THE UNITED NATIONS CHARTER

The Charter is divided into 111 articles grouped in nineteen chapters:

| | | |
|---|---|---|
| I | Purposes and Principles | (articles 1 and 2) |
| II | Membership | (articles 3-6) |
| III | Organs | (articles 7 and 8) |
| IV | The General Assembly | |
| | Composition | (article 9) |
| | Functions and powers | (articles 10-17) |
| | Voting | (articles 18 and 19) |
| | Procedure | (articles 20-22) |
| V | The Security Council | |
| | Composition | (article 23) |
| | Functions and powers | (articles 24-26) |
| | Voting | (article 27) |
| | Procedure | (articles 28-32) |
| VI | Pacific settlement of disputes | (articles 33-38) |
| VII | Action with respect to threats to the peace, breaches of the peace, and acts of aggression | (articles 39-51) |
| VIII | Regional arrangements | (articles 52-54) |
| IX | International economic and social cooperation | (articles 55-60) |
| X | The Economic and Social Council | |
| | Composition | (article 61) |
| | Functions and powers | (articles 62-66) |
| | Voting | (article 67) |
| | Procedure | (articles 68-72) |
| XI | Declaration regarding non-self-governing territories | (articles 73 and 74) |
| XII | International Trusteeship system | (articles 75-85) |
| XIII | The Trusteeship Council | |
| | Composition | (article 86) |

Membership of the United Nations consists of the 'original members' (those states which signed the Washington Declaration in 1942 or took part in the United Nations Conference on International Organisation in San Francisco in 1945, and signed and ratified the Charter in accordance with the prescribed procedure); and those states subsequently accepted as members in accordance with the provisions of the Charter.

Membership is further open to all other 'peace-loving' states which accept the obligations contained in the Charter and, in the judgement of the United Nations, are able and willing to carry them out. The admission of new members is dependent on the approval of the General Assembly on the recommendation of the Security Council.

A member which has persistently violated the principles of the Charter may be expelled from the United Nations by the General Assembly on the recommendation of the Security Council; or may have its rights and privileges of membership suspended by the General Assembly on the recommendation of the Security Council if it has been the object of preventive or enforcement action taken by the Security Council. These rights and privileges, however, may be restored by the Security Council.

Each state is entitled to one vote in the General Assembly and in its dependent committees and councils.

Provision is made in chapter XVIII for amendments to the Charter, and these come into force when they have been (a) adopted by a vote of two-thirds of the members of the General Assembly, and (b) ratified in accordance with their respective constitutional processes by two-thirds of the members of the United Nations including all the permanent members of the Security Council.

The official languages of the United Nations are Arabic, Chinese, English, French, Russian and Spanish.

The United Nations, in terms of its Charter, is based on six principal organs: the General Assembly, the Security Council, the Economic and Social Council, the Trusteeship Council, the International Court of Justice, and the Secretariat. Generally speaking the Assembly and Security Council are the political and legislative bodies, ECOSOC and the Trustee-ship Council are specialist bodies dependent on the General Assembly, and the International Court of Justice is an independent body.

Whilst recognising that the maintenance of international peace and security is the prime contributor to social and economic development, the U.N. also focuses on human needs through the Commission on Sustainable Development – a functional commission of ECOSOC – and the activities of the U.N. Environmental Programme. Moreover at the Millennium Summit in 2000 the U.N. adopted the Millennium Goals aimed at eradicating extreme poverty and hunger; achieving universal primary education; promoting gender equality and empowering women; reducing child mortality, improving material health; combating HIV/AIDS, malaria and other diseases, and ensuring environmental sustainability through a set of measurable targets to be achieved by the year 2015.

## THE GENERAL ASSEMBLY

The General Assembly consists of all members of the United Nations. In terms of the Charter, the United Nations may not intervene in matters which are essentially within the jurisdiction of a state, except in respect of the application of enforcement measures in accordance with chapter VII (threats to the peace, breaches of the peace and acts of aggression). Subject to this proviso, the functions of the Assembly are:

*To consider and discuss* (i) any matter within the scope of the Charter or relating to the powers and functions of any of the organs provided for in the Charter, (ii) general principles of cooperation in the maintenance of international peace and security, including principles governing disarmament and the regulation of armaments, and (iii) any question relating to the maintenance of international peace and security.

*To call the attention* of the Security Council to situations which are likely to endanger international peace and security.

*To make recommendations* to the Security Council or to member states (or both) or to a non-member state involved in questions relating to the maintenance of international peace and security in respect of (ii) and (iii) above; for the purpose of promoting international cooperation in the political field and encouraging the progressive development of international law and its codification; and for promoting international cooperation in the economic, social, cultural, educational and health fields, and assisting in the realisation of human rights and fundamental freedoms for all without distinction as to race, sex, language or religion.

*To make recommendations* – subject to the proviso that if the Security Council is already exercising its prescribed function in respect of such matters, recommendations will only be made if asked for relating to:
(a) any matter within the scope of the Charter or relating to the powers and functions of any of the organs provided for in the Charter;
(b) the peaceful adjustment of any situation, regardless of origin, which it deems likely to impair the general welfare or friendly relations among nations, including situations resulting from a violation of the provisions of the Charter setting forth the Purposes and Principles of the United Nations.

*To receive and consider annual and special reports* from the Security Council (including an account of the measures that it has decided upon or taken to maintain international peace and security), and from the other organs of the United Nations.

*To perform such functions* with respect to the international trusteeship system as are assigned to it under chapters XII and XIII, including the approval of the trusteeship agreements for areas not designated as strategic.

*To consider and approve* the United Nations budget and any financial and budgetary arrangements with the Specialised Agencies and to examine the administrative budgets of such Specialised Agencies with a view to making recommendations to the Agencies concerned.

In the event of a non-member state being involved in a question relating to the maintenance of international peace and security, the Assembly may make recommendations to the state concerned; and any question on which action is necessary in such circumstances shall be referred to the Security Council by the Assembly either before or after discussion.

The regular sessions of the Assembly as a rule begin in New York on the third Tuesday in September each year and continue until mid-December, but special sessions may be called by the Secretary-General at the request of the Security Council or of a majority of the members of the United Nations. At the start of each regular session, the Assembly elects a new President, twenty-one Vice-Presidents and the Chairmen of the Assembly's seven Main Committees. To ensure equitable geographical representation, the Presidency of the Assembly rotates each year among groups of States who select their own candidate.

The work of the General Assembly is coordinated and to a considerable extent organised by two procedural committees: the *General Committee*, which is made up of the President and Vice-Presidents of the General Assembly and the heads of the seven *Main Committees* and the *Credentials Committee*.

The *Main Committees*, which consider in advance matters placed on the agenda of the General Assembly and (when so requested) make recommendations for consideration by the Assembly in plenary session, are:

First Committee: Disarmament and related international security matters
Special Political Committee
Second Committee: Economic and Financial
Third Committee: Social, Humanitarian and Cultural
Fourth Committee: Special Committee for Political Issues and de-colonisation.
Fifth Committee: Administrative and Budgetary
Sixth Committee: Legal

The Special Political Committee was created primarily to relieve the First Committee; and there are two *Standing Committees*: the Committee on Contributions, and the Advisory Committee on Administrative and Budgetary Questions. Subsidiary and *ad hoc* committees are set up from time to time to deal with specific problems.

Voting in the Assembly is by simple majority of the members present and voting, except in the following circumstances, when the necessary majority is the affirmative vote of two-thirds of the members present and voting:

- recommendations with respect to the maintenance of international peace and security,
- the election of non-permanent members of the Security Council,
- the election of members of the Economic and Social Council,
- the election of members of the Trusteeship Council,
- the admission of new members to the United Nations,
- the suspension of the rights and privileges of members,
- the expulsion of members,
- matters relating to the operation of the trusteeship system,
- budgetary questions,
- any other matters considered by the Assembly (by a simple majority of the members present and voting) to be sufficiently important to require a two-thirds majority.

A member in arrears in the payment of its financial contributions to the United Nations is not entitled to vote if its arrears equal or exceed the amount of its contributions due for the preceding two full years, unless the General Assembly is satisfied that failure to pay is due to circumstances beyond the member's control.

Much of the work of the United Nations is conducted on the basis of regional groups: e.g. African States, Asian States, Latin American States and Western European and Other States. For election purposes the USA falls within Western European and Other States.

## THE SECURITY COUNCIL

The Security Council consists of fifteen members: China, France, Russia, the United Kingdom and the USA, who constitute the five permanent members; and ten non-permanent members elected by the General Assembly for a term of two years (provided that no member is elected for two consecutive periods). In order that it may function continuously, a representative of each of its members must be present at all times at the United Nations Headquarters. It has primary responsibility for the maintenance of international peace and security, and for this purpose acts on behalf of the members of the United Nations and in accordance with its Purposes and Principles. The members of the United Nations, for their part, agree to accept and carry out the decisions of the Security Council in accordance with the Charter.

The powers of the Security Council are specified in chapters VI and VII of the Charter. In terms of chapter VI the Council may investigate any dispute or situation which is referred to it by a state or which it considers may lead to international friction; and if it determines that its continuation is likely to endanger *the maintenance of international peace and security* it will try to resolve it by peaceful settlement.

If, however, it determines the existence of any *threat to the peace, breach of the peace or act of aggression*, the Security Council is empowered in terms of chapter VII to decide what measures shall be taken to maintain or restore international peace and security; these may take the form of non-violent measures or, if they fail, the use of force by land, sea or air. The provision of armed forces by member states is governed by article 43 of the Charter, and is subject to special agreements requiring ratification between such states and the Security Council.

The Security Council is required to submit annual and, where necessary, special reports to the General Assembly for its consideration, including plans for the establishment of whatever subsidiary organs it may consider necessary for the performance of its functions (e.g. the United Nations Truce Supervision Organisation in Palestine).

The General Assembly or any member state (or a non-member state under certain conditions) may bring to the attention of the Security Council any dispute or situation likely to endanger international peace and security.

Any state, whether it is a member of the United Nations or not, which is a party to a dispute under consideration by the Security Council and is not itself a member of the Council, has the right to participate (but not vote) in the deliberations. Similar provisions apply to any member state which, not being a party to a dispute nor a member of the Security Council, is nevertheless considered by the Council to be affected by the dispute.

In terms of articles 27 and 109(1) of the Charter (as amended), decisions of the Security Council require the affirmative votes of nine members *including the concurring votes of the permanent members*; except (a) on procedural matters and (b) for deciding to hold and for fixing a date and place for a Conference to review the Charter, when the affirmative votes of *any* nine members suffice. Amendments to the Charter require to be ratified by all the permanent members of the Council.

In decisions under chapter VI (pacific settlement of disputes) and article 52, paragraph 3 (the pacific settlement of local disputes through regional arrangements) any member of the Security Council who is a party to a dispute is required to abstain from voting.

## THE ECONOMIC AND SOCIAL COUNCIL

ECOSOC consists of fifty-four members elected for a three-years term of office by the General Assembly, and operates under the Assembly in conjunction with the Specialised Agencies and other governmental and non-governmental international organisations. Its major functions are: to serve as the central forum for discussing international economic and social issues, and for formulating policy recommendations addressed to Member States and the United Nations system; to make or initiate studies and reports and make recommendations on international economic, social, cultural, educational, health and related matters; to promote respect for, and observance of, human rights and fundamental freedoms; to assist in preparing and organizing major international conferences in the economic, social and related fields and promote a coordinated follow-up to these conferences, and to coordinate the activities of the specialized agencies, through consultations with and recommendations to them, and through recommendations to the General Assembly.

Through its discussion of international economic and social issues and its policy recommendations, ECOSOC plays a key role in fostering international cooperation for development and in setting the priorities for action.

The Council generally holds several short sessions throughout the year to deal with the organization of its work, as well as one four-week substantive session in July, alternating between New York and Geneva, and decisions in the Council are reached on a simple majority of those members present and voting.

ECOSOC functions on the basis of *standing committees*, *standing expert bodies*, various *functional commissions* and five *regional commissions*; as well as various *ad hoc* expert bodies.

The *standing committees* are on Non-Governmental Organisations; Programme Coordination; Natural Resources; and Development Planning.

The *functional commissions* are:
Commission on Statistics
Commission on Human Rights (including the Sub-Commission on the Prevention of Discrimination and Protection of Minorities)
Commission for Social Development
Commission on the Status of Women
Commission on Narcotic Drugs
Commission on Population and Development
Commission on Crime Prevention and Criminal Justice
Commission on Science and Technology for Development
Commission on Sustainable Development

The *regional commissions*, which act on behalf of the United Nations in all social and economic matters are:
Economic Commission for Europe (Geneva)
Economic and Social Commission for Asia and the Pacific (Bangkok)
Economic Commission for Latin America and the Caribbean (Santiago, Chile)
Economic Commission for Africa (Addis Ababa)
Economic and Social Commission for Western Asia (Baghdad)

The *standing committees and expert bodies* are the Committee for Programme and Coordination, the Commission on Human Settlements, the Committee on Non-Governmental Organizations, the Committee on Negotiations with Intergovernmental Agencies and the Committee on Energy and Natural Resources. The expert bodies deal with subjects such as development planning, natural resources, and economic, social and cultural rights.

The Council cooperates with, and to a certain extent coordinates, the work of United Nations programmes (such as UNDP, UNEP, UNICEF and UNFPA) and the specialized agencies (such as FAO, WHO, ILO and UNESCO), all of which report to the Council and make recommendations for its substantive sessions.

## NON-GOVERNMENTAL ORGANISATIONS

In terms of the Charter, ECOSOC maintains close co-operation with non-governmental organisations (N.G.Os.) and provides them with an opportunity to express their views in their fields of special competence. Over 1,600 N.G.Os. have consultative status with ECOSOC, and these may send observers to meetings of the Council and its subsidiary bodies and may submit statements in writing relevant to their work. NGOs are seen increasingly as parties to be consulted on policy matters and programmes, and as valuable links with civil society. In their particular fields the Red Cross (ICRC) which has been relieving suffering with total integrity for 150 years, and the International Organisation for Migration founded 50 years ago to tackle the problems associated with the migration of peoples in Europe are outstanding, but the similar humanitarian organisations are equally beyond praise.

# THE TRUSTEESHIP COUNCIL

The Trusteeship system was established under the authority of the United Nations for the administration and supervision of certain territories falling within the categories defined in article 77 of the Charter and placed under trusteeship by means of individual agreements with the states directly concerned (including mandatory powers where such already existed). The agreements require the approval of the General Assembly, and the principles of trusteeship are defined in article 76. Eleven territories have been placed under United Nations' Trusteeship, and have now achieved independence. Although its work is completed, the possibility remains for other territories to come within the scope of the Council at some time in the future, and it is relevant to note that Trust territories are directly controlled by the administering states in terms of their particular Trusteeship Agreement; that the Trusteeship Council consists of the administering state and the permanent members of the Security Council; and that it meets annually in New York, receives reports from the administering state, accepts petitions and makes periodic visits of inspection.

# THE INTERNATIONAL COURT OF JUSTICE

The International Court of Justice is situated in The Hague and is the principal judicial organ of the United Nations. It functions in accordance with the provisions of its Statute to which all members of the United Nations automatically subscribe. The Court is composed of fifteen suitably qualified judges elected by secret ballot by the

General Assembly and by the Security Council (independently) for a term of nine years. They retire in groups of five every three years (their re-election is permitted); and no two judges may be nationals of the same state.

Access to the Court is open to states which subscribe to its Statute, and to non-subscribing states under certain conditions. The functions of the Court are twofold: to give judgement on all contentious cases referred to it by states by mutual consent, and on all matters specially provided for in the United Nations Charter, in treaties or in conventions; and to give advisory opinions on legal questions referred to it by any branch of the United Nations or its Agencies. The Court will normally reach its conclusions in accordance with international treaties and conventions currently in force, international custom and general principles of law. It will also take into consideration judicial comments and decisions, and may reach a decision, if both parties agree, *ex aequo et bono*, i.e. on general principles of fairness and natural justice.

A state may at any time lodge a declaration to the effect that it recognises as compulsory, in relation to any other state accepting the same obligation, the jurisdiction of the Court in certain specific instances. These are listed in article 36(2) of the Statute (the co-called 'Optional Clause'), namely:

(a) the interpretation of a treaty;
(b) any question of international law;
(c) the existence of any fact which, if established, would constitute a breach of an international obligation;
(d) the nature or extent of the reparation to be made for the breach of an international obligation.

The declaration may be made unconditionally; on condition of reciprocity on the part of several or certain states; or for a certain time. In practice the forty-seven states that have lodged declarations in terms of article 36 have tended to add other provisos.

The official languages of the Court are English and French, but the Court is bound to allow a party to use whatever language it chooses. The procedure consists of two parts: written and oral, and the hearings in Court are public unless the Court decides otherwise or the parties concerned so desire. All questions are decided by a majority vote of the judges present, and in the event of an equality of votes the President or the judge who acts in his place has a casting (i.e. deciding) vote. A judgement is final and without appeal, though the court may subsequently recognise the discovery of fresh evidence of a decisive nature, and permit an application for a revision of judgement to proceed. Since its inception, the Court has delivered 73 judgements on subjects such as land frontiers, marine boundaries, nationality, diplomatic relations and hostage-taking; and more than 30 Advisory Opinions. A further nine contentious cases are awaiting judgement.

The ICJ should not be confused with the International Criminal Tribunal for the former Yugoslavia in The Hague which was established by the Security Council in 1993 as part of the Bosnian peace process which led up to the Dayton Accord. The purpose of the Tribunal is the prosecution of persons responsible for serious violations of international humanitarian law committed in the territory of the former

Yugoslavia since 1991. It consists of 16 Judges elected by the General Assembly of the U.N. for a period of 4 years. The maximum penalty that they can impose is life imprisonment.

## THE SECRETARY-GENERAL AND THE SECRETARIAT

In terms of the United Nations Charter the Secretary-General is the chief administrative officer of the Organisation. He acts as such at all meetings of the General Assembly, the Security Council and the Trusteeship Council, and carries out whatever functions these bodies assign to him. He submits an annual report to the General Assembly on the work of the Organisation, and may bring to the attention of the Security Council any matter which in his opinion may threaten the maintenance of international peace and security. He is appointed by the General Assembly on the recommendation of the Security Council for a period of five years, and he is responsible for the appointment of the staff of the Organisation in accordance with the regulations drawn up by the General Assembly. Selection of staff is primarily on the basis of merit, but representation on a balanced geographical basis is also a relevant factor. The Secretary-General and his staff are bound to act as international civil servants and may not seek or receive instructions from any government, or from any authority outside the Organisation; and member states similarly undertake not to try to influence them in any way.

## UN PEACE-KEEPING OPERATIONS

The UN Charter is based on the principle of the sovereignty of the state, and makes provision for the maintenance of peace and security between states: it does not, however, make specific provision for peace-keeping operations within states. Nevertheless such operations are to an increasing extent authorised by the Secretary-General and the Security Council with a specific mandate. The state concerned must give its consent, and provisions relating especially to impartiality and the use of force on the part of the peace-keeping forces are specified. The basic conditions are that peace-keeping forces will in no way seek to influence the outcome of a dispute or be perceived as doing so; and that they will use force only if directly attacked or, to a lesser extent, if their property is under direct threat. The UN Secretary-General defines peace-keeping in 'An Agenda for Peace' as 'a technique that expands the possibilities for both the prevention of conflict and the making of peace'. He then defines four additional forms of related activities:

1. *Preventative diplomacy* is action to prevent disputes from arising between parties, to prevent disputes from escalating into conflicts and to limit the spread of the latter when they occur.
2. *Peace-making* is action to bring hostile parties to agreement by peaceful means. Means for peace-making would be negotiation, inquiries, methods of reconcilia-

tion, arbitrations or methods of judgement, and the help of the territorial organisations and agreements. Parties concerned normally involve the United Nations military and/or police personnel and frequently civilians as well.

3. *Peace-building* is action to identify and support structures which will tend to strengthen and solidify peace in order to avoid a relapse into conflict.
4. *Peace enforcement* is action to enable the United Nations to deploy troops quickly to enforce a cease-fire by taking coercive action against either party or both, if they violate it. This kind of operation would be authorised by the Security Council.

Since 1948 the UN has authorised over 55 military observer and peace-keeping operations, including – as examples of their diversity – the UN Mission for the Referendum in Western Sahara, the UN Mission of Observers in Tajikistan (UNMOT), UN Assistance Mission to Rwanda (UNAMIR) and the UN Peace-keeping force in Cyprus.

The Department of Peace-keeping operations comes under the direction of the Secretary-General.

# INTERGOVERNMENTAL AGENCIES RELATED TO THE UNITED NATIONS (INCLUDING SPECIALISED AGENCIES)

The intergovernmental agencies related to the United Nations by special agreements are separate, autonomous organisations which work with the United Nations and each other through the coordinating machinery of the Economic and Social Council. Sixteen of the agencies are known as specialised agencies, a term used in the United Nations Charter. They report annually to the Economic and Social Council. The International Atomic Energy Agency (IAEA), established in 1957 under the aegis of the United Nations, reports annually to the General Assembly and, as appropriate, to the Security Council and the Economic and Social Council.

## FOOD AND AGRICULTURE ORGANIZATION

The FAO has extensive functions covering all aspects of food production and related activities. It collects, reviews, and makes available information and statistics on world agriculture, forestry and fisheries; it includes within its scope production, trade, consumption, nutrition, marketing, land tenure, and the protection of natural resources. It arranges for the provision of technical experts, assists in the negotiation of commodity and other related agreements, and encourages sustainable agriculture and rural development. The primary aim is to meet the needs of both present and future generations by promoting development that does not degrade the environment, is technically appropriate, economically viable and socially acceptable. Policy is determined by a Conference of representatives of all member countries which meets every two years and on which each member state is represented; responsibility in the period between its sessions rests with a Council of forty-nine elected by the Conference.

The Director-General and Secretariat are in Rome, and there are regional offices in Accra, Bangkok, Santiago and Cairo, and liaison offices in Geneva, Washington and New York.

## INTERNATIONAL ATOMIC ENERGY AGENCY

The IAEA encourages and coordinates research into the peaceful uses of atomic energy. It advises members on such subjects as the development of nuclear power, the uses of radioactive material in the fields of medicine, agriculture, etc., the disposal of radioactive waste, and water desalination; it provides experts where necessary, and offers research fellowships and training facilities.

In addition to its purely technical role the IAEA has increased responsibility under the 1968 Treaty of the Non-proliferation of Nuclear Weapons for ensuring adequate safeguards and preventing the diversion of nuclear energy from peaceful uses to nuclear weapons in those non-nuclear states which are signatories of the treaty.

It is also responsible for implementing the International Nuclear Information System (INIS) which collects and disseminates information relating to nuclear matters. There are 130 members and a Board of Governors of 34, 13 of whom are appointed by the Council, and 22 elected by the General Conference. The headquarters of the Agency is at the UN City in Vienna, and it is controlled by an annual Conference of member states.

## INTERNATIONAL CIVIL AVIATION ORGANIZATION

Established in 1944 in Chicago on the basis of the Convention on International Civil Aviation (ratified in 1947), ICAO was formed to assure the safe, orderly and economic development of world civil air transportation. ICAO has developed a worldwide system of standards, practices and rules common to all nations. The Organisation serves the world today as a medium through which over 185 nations cooperate to ensure safety for the air-travelling public and for agreement in the technical, economic and legal fields of civil aviation.

The legislative body of ICAO is the Assembly which is composed of representatives of all member states and meets at least once in three years to review in detail the work of the Organisation performed during the last triennium and to decide on future policies.

The Council, which is the executive body of ICAO, comprises thirty-three members elected by the Assembly; they must be representative of the major civil aviation interests and facilities, as well as providing representation on a worldwide basis. The Council is responsible to the Assembly and meets in virtually continuous session. One of the major duties of the Council is to adopt international standards and recommended practices and to incorporate these as Annexes to the Convention on International Civil Aviation. It directs the work of the Organisation, establishes and supervises subsidiary technical committees, can act as arbiter between member states on matters concerning the interpretation and application of the Chicago Convention, provides technical assistance to developing nations, elects the President, appoints the Secretary-General, administers the finances of the Organisation and considers any matter relating to the Convention which any contracting state refers to it.

The Council is assisted by the Air Navigation Commission (in technical matters), the Air Transport Committee (in economic matters), the Committee on Joint Support of Air Navigation Services, the Finance Committee and the Legal Committee.

The headquarters of ICAO are in Montreal and there are regional offices in Bangkok, Cairo, Dakar, Lima, Mexico City, Nairobi, Nenilly-sur-Seine and Paris.

## INTERNATIONAL FUND FOR AGRICULTURAL DEVELOPMENT

The agreement establishing the International Fund for Agricultural Development (IFAD) was adopted on 13 June 1976 at a United Nations conference. It was opened for signature on 20 December 1976, following the attainment of initial pledges of US$1 billion, and entered into force on 30 November 1977. The main purpose of IFAD is to mobilise additional resources to help developing countries improve their food production and nutrition, fisheries, processing and storage – and concentrates on rural areas. Its primary goal is to help efforts to end chronic hunger and malnutrition. It lends money for projects which will have a significant impact on improving food production in developing countries, particularly for the benefit of the poorest sections of the rural populations. It seeks to bring small farmers and the landless into the development process: thus, the fund is concerned not only with production objectives but with the impact each project may have on employment, nutrition and income distribution. Loan operations of IFAD fall into two groups: projects initiated by the Fund and projects 'co-financed' with other financial and development institutions, such as the World Bank and IDA and the various development banks (African, Asian, Inter-American, Islamic). IFAD loans represent only a part of total project costs; the governments concerned contribute a share.

The Fund's operations are directed by the Governing Council, on which all member states are represented, each of the three categories of members (developed countries, oil-exporting developing countries and other developing countries) having the same number of votes. Thus, the donor countries hold two-thirds of the total number of votes and the developing countries, at the same time, hold two-thirds of the votes. Current operations are overseen by the Executive Board, composed of eighteen Executive Directors, 8 from the first category, 4 from the second and 6 from the third and eighteen alternates, and chaired by the President of the Fund. The headquarters of the fund are in Rome.

## INTERNATIONAL LABOUR ORGANIZATION

The ILO was founded in 1919 and seeks to raise the standards and dignity of human labour throughout the world. In particular it encourages freedom of association and the rights of workers' organisations. It formulates conventions, makes recommendations, receives reports on labour conditions and related matters, and undertakes research and enquiries. Policy is determined by a Conference of all members which meets annually, member states being represented by two government delegates, one employers' delegate and one employees' delegate, and decisions being on the basis of a two-thirds majority. The executive of the organisation is the fifty-six-member Governing Body which meets quarterly and is responsible for determining programmes, convening conferences, preparing the budget and appointing the Director-General. It is part-nominated and part-elected by the Conference, and consists of twenty-eight government members, fourteen employers' members and fourteen employees' members. In order to play a more positive role in major international councils on social and economic development a policy of decentralisation of activities and resources was introduced under the ILO's Active Partnership Policy.

The ILO has its headquarters and secretariat (the International Labour Office) in Geneva, regional offices in Abidjan, Addis Ababa, Bangkok, Beirut, Istanbul and Lima, and an International Centre for Advanced Technical and Vocational Training in Turin.

## INTERNATIONAL MARITIME ORGANIZATION

The organisation changed its name from Inter-governmental Maritime Consultative Organisation (IMCO) to International Maritime Organisation (IMO) in May 1982. It is responsible for international cooperation in all technical matters relating to shipping. It was established on the basis of the Maritime Convention which resulted from the United Nations Maritime Conference held in Geneva 1948, and seeks to improve maritime safety and prevent maritime pollution from ships, disseminates information, convenes conferences, and promotes and administers international maritime conventions. It has an Assembly of all member states meeting every second year and a Council of 40 members. There are five main Committees: on maritime safety, legal matters, marine environment protection, the facilitation of maritime trade and technical cooperation. The headquarters and Secretariat are in London.

## INTERNATIONAL TELECOMMUNICATION UNION

The ITU is the body responsible for international cooperation, research and the dissemination of knowledge in all branches of telecommunications, and for the administration of its Convention. Policy decisions are made by a Plenipotentiary Conference of all member states meeting every five years; executive control lies with the Administrative Council elected by the Assembly and meeting annually, and their three permanent organs: the International Frequency Registration Board, the International Radio Consultative Committee and the International Telegraph and Telephone Consultative Committee. A wide-ranging set of reforms is under consideration, emphasising the increasing function of the ITU as a global co-ordinator and expert advisor in a period of rapid developments in communications, and its increasing partnership role with the private sector. The General Secretariat is in Geneva.

## THE INTERNATIONAL MONETARY FUND

The International Monetary Fund is an intergovernmental organisation based on a treaty drafted at Bretton-Woods, New Hampshire, in 1944 (amended in 1969 and in 1978), and membership of the Fund is a prerequisite of membership of the World Bank. Current membership is 184 countries.

The essential purpose of the Fund is to promote international monetary cooperation and thereby foster expanded international trade. It is a permanent forum where countries can work to coordinate their economic and financial policies, and is concerned not only with the problems of individual countries but also with the working of the international monetary system. As the world monetary system has changed, so too has the Fund, but the underlying purposes of the organisation and of membership in it remain the same. It has both regulatory and financing functions.

Members agree to abide by a code of economic behaviour and to cooperate with the Fund and with each other in order to ensure orderly exchange arrangements, to promote exchange stability and to avoid restrictions that would harm national and international prosperity. The Fund is required to exercise surveillance over their exchange rate policies and it maintains a large pool of currencies from which to help finance the temporary imbalances of its members, and this financial assistance – provided for short-term to medium-term periods and usually subject to conditions – allows member countries to correct their payment imbalances without having to resort to the trade and payment restrictions that they have pledged themselves to avoid. The policy adjustments that countries make in connection with the use of Fund resources support their creditworthiness and thereby facilitate their access to financial markets. In 1969, the Fund created SDRs (special drawing rights) as a reserve asset. One SDR equals approximately US$1.25.

The work of the Fund is carried out by a Board of Governors, an Executive Board, a Managing Director, and staff. Each member country is represented by a Governor and an Alternate Governor on the Board of Governors, which is the Fund's senior decision-making body. The Board of Governors meets annually, but may be asked by the Executive Board to vote on important matters by mail or e-mail between meetings. A member country's voting power is related to its subscription to the Fund's financial resources, and is broadly reflective of its relative size in the world economy (i.e. trade, gross national product and monetary reserves). The daily business of the Fund is conducted at its headquarters in Washington, DC, by an Executive Board consisting of twenty-four Executive Directors, chaired by the Managing Director. Each of the five members having the largest quotas, and thus the highest voting power – the United States, the United Kingdom, Germany, France and Japan – appoints an Executive Director. In addition, there are three Executive Directors representing single country constituencies: China, Russia and Saudi Arabia. Sixteen Executive Directors are elected by members or groups of member countries.

The Board of Governors is advised on policy issues by two ministerial-level committees whose membership reflects that of the Executive Board: the International Monetary and Financial Committee of the Board of Governors on the International

Monetary System, and the Joint Ministerial Committee of the World Bank and the Fund on the Transfer of Real Resources to Developing Countries (the Development Committee). The Interim and Developing Committees normally meet twice a year – in the spring at Fund headquarters in Washington, and in the autumn at the site of the Annual Meetings of the Fund and Bank.

The Fund also maintains small permanent offices in Paris, in Geneva, and at the United Nations in New York.

### Consultations

The Fund conducts consultations with each member country – in principle, annually – to appraise the member's economic and financial situation and policies. The consultation procedure begins with meetings in the member country between Fund staff and representatives of the member government. On the basis of these discussions, the staff prepares a report on economic conditions and policies for the Executive Board. The Board then discusses and comments on the report. The Board's views, as summarised by the Managing Director, are then transmitted to the member government by the Fund.

### Quotas and resources

The Fund's resources stem largely from its members' subscriptions, and these are based on a quota system which broadly reflects a member's weight in the world economy: these have been raised by 45 per cent to SDR 210 billion. Quotas also determine the voting power of members, their contributions to the Fund's resources, their access to these resources, and their share in allocations of SDRs.

While subscriptions constitute its basic resources, the Fund supplements them by borrowing. Under the General Arrangements to Borrow (GAB), which became effective in October 1962, ten industrial member countries together with non-member Switzerland (constituting the eleven-nation 'Group of Ten') extended credit lines to the Fund. The GAB has been renewed periodically, and in 1984 Saudi Arabia associated itself with the other eleven participants.

Additionally, the IMF agreed in 1997 to establish a scheme entitled *New Arrangements to Borrow* (NAB) as a facility of first recourse whereby twenty-four countries agree to make loans to the Fund totalling SDR34 billion wherever additional resources are needed to forestall or cope with an impairment of the international monetary system, or to deal with an exceptional situation that poses a threat to the stability of the system.

### Financial facilities

Members have access to the financial resources of the Fund under a variety of permanent and temporary facilities to help meet balance of payments needs. The mechanics of the transaction are as follows. The member uses its own currency to 'purchase' from the Fund an equivalent amount of the currencies of other members (or SDRs), and these in turn can be used to finance the member's balance of payments deficit or to supply its need for reserves. Within a specific period – or earlier if the member's balance of payments and reserve position improves – the member must repay the Fund by repurchasing with SDRs or the currencies of other members specified by the Fund the amount of its own currency that it used in order to make the drawing, except to the extent that the Fund sells the member's currency. Credit from the Fund is available in four tranches, each tranche being the equivalent of 25 per cent of the quota.

If the country suffers serious payments imbalances related to structural problems in production, trade, or prices, the adjustment process is likely to require both a longer period of time and greater resources than normally permitted under the credit tranche facility. In such situations, the member may make use of the *Extended Fund Facility*, under which up to 140 per cent of its quota may be purchased beyond the first credit tranche. Depending on whether the credit tranche or the extended Fund facility is used, resources are provided through lines of credit called *stand-by* or extended arrangements, and normally take place over a period of one year, although the period may be extended up to three years. Drawings are repayable within three to five years under the credit tranche facility and four to ten years under the extended Fund facility.

When a member receives financial assistance under the Fund's credit facilities, it must adopt a programme of specific measures to overcome its payments imbalance and thus provide assurance that it can repay the funds received. This aspect of Fund policies is known as *conditionality*. The Fund staff help member countries design adjustment programmes having due regard to their domestic, social and political objectives, economic priorities, and general circumstances. Drawings under both the credit tranche policy and the extended Fund facility are subject to a one-time service charge of 0.5 per cent, plus a charge at an annual rate on outstanding drawings.

The Fund also makes resources available under two special purpose facilities: the compensatory and the buffer stock financing facilities. *Compensatory financing* is available to members facing payments difficulties resulting from temporary shortfalls in their export earnings that are due largely to conditions beyond their control, such as falling commodity prices or natural disasters, including bad weather. In 1981, this facility was broadened to provide assistance to members facing payments difficulties owing to an excess in the cost of cereal imports. *Buffer stock financing*, available up to 45 per cent of quota, is available to members having payments difficulties to finance their contributions to international buffer stocks that are maintained to stabilise world markets for commodities.

### Structural adjustment facilities

The structural adjustment facility provides loans to low-income member countries that are facing protracted balance of payments problems and that agree to undertake medium-term structural adjustment programmes. They fall within the category of concessionary Assistance and include the Poverty Reduction and Growth Facility and the Heavily Indebted Poor Countries Initiative which is applicable in exceptional circumstances.

## SDRs (special drawing rights)

The SDR is an international reserve asset created by the Fund to supplement existing reserve assets. It is the unit of account of the Fund, and is also used as such by a number of international and regional organisations and in capital markets as a denominator and a unit of contract, such as in SDR-denominated deposits with commercial banks. It is the members' declared intention, expressed in the Fund's Articles, that the SDR shall eventually become the principal reserve asset in the international monetary system. The method of valuation of the SDR is determined by the Fund, and since January 1981, the 'basket' has consisted of the currencies of the five members with the highest value of exports of goods and services.

## Technical assistance

Member countries of the Fund may make use of its technical assistance for helping to improve the management of their economies. Experts sent to member countries by the Fund advise on fiscal, monetary, and balance of payments policies, central and general banking, statistics, accounting, exchange and trade systems, and operational aspects of Fund policies.

## THE WORLD BANK

The World Bank's goal is to reduce poverty and improve living standards by promoting sustainable growth and investment in people. The bank provides loans, technical assistance, and policy guidance to help its developing-country members achieve this objective. Moreover, mindful of the challenges ahead, the Bank is working with developing countries to pilot a more inclusive and more integrated approach to its development mission – the *Comprehensive Development Framework (CDF)*. As the Bank has moved beyond simply financing projects – and even beyond supporting only discrete policy reforms, such as trade liberalization – to addressing broader issues such as human and social development, governance, and institutions, the need for an integrating framework of this kind became apparent. The CDF approach calls for a development plan 'owned' by the country itself, focused on a long-term vision of the results to be achieved, and supported by strong partnerships among governments, donors, civil society, the private sector and other development actors. In launching the CDF, the Bank has focused attention on what it sees as the essential building blocks for effective development:

- *Structural:* good governance and clean government, an effective legal and judicial system, a well-organized and supervised financial system, and social safety net and social programs.
- *Physical:* water and sewerage, energy, roads, transport and telecommunications, and environmental and cultural issues.
- *Specific strategies:* for rural, urban, and private sector development.

The CDF is essentially a process. It is a new way of doing business, a tool to achieve greater development effectiveness in a world challenged by poverty.

The following form part of the World Bank group:

*The International Bank for Reconstruction and Development (IBRD)* – founded in 1944 – is the single largest provider of development loans to middle-income developing countries and a major catalyst of similar financing from other sources. While the World Bank has traditionally financed a wide variety of capital infrastructure such as roads and railways, telecommunications, and ports and power facilities, its development strategy also places an emphasis on investments that can directly affect the well-being of the masses of poor people of developing countries by making them more productive and by integrating them as active partners in the development process. It also works on a basis of partnership with non-governmental organisations, UN agencies, the business community, regional organisations, and its 184 member counties.

The Bank's concept of 'development' is based on targeting 'human needs' rather than relying on the 'trickle down' theory, and special emphasis is placed on sustainability, environmental protection, the increased participation of women in economic decision-making, family planning, greater transparency and open forms of government and recognition of the benefits of entrepreneurship, competitive private sector activity and a 'market friendly' approach to development. It also provides assistance for the process of economic transition undertaken in Russia, the Baltics, and the countries of East and Central Europe.

The Bank's capital is subscribed by its member countries, and it finances its lending operations primarily from its own borrowing in the world capital markets. A substantial contribution to the IBRD's resources also comes from its retained earnings and the flow of repayments on its loans. These generally have a grace period of five years and are repayable over twenty years or less. They are directed towards developing countries at more advanced stages of economic and social growth. The interest rate that the IBRD charges on its loans is calculated in accordance with a guideline related to its cost of borrowing. The IBRD's Charter spells out certain basic rules that govern its operations. It must lend only for productive purposes, and must stimulate economic growth in the developing countries where it lends. It must pay due regard to the prospects of repayment, and each loan is made to a government or must be guaranteed by the government concerned. The use of loans cannot be restricted to purchases in any particular member country, and the IBRD's decision to lend must be based on economic considerations.

*The International Development Association (IDA)*, founded in 1960, assists the poorest countries by providing interest-free credits. The terms of IDA credits, which are made to governments only, are ten-year grace periods, up to fifty-year maturities, and no interest. In all some sixty countries are eligible for such loans. IDA is primarily funded by government contributions.

*The International Finance Corporation (IFC)*, established in 1956, assists the economic development of less-developed countries by promoting growth in the private sector of their economies through loan and equity financing as well as advisory services, and helping to mobilise domestic and foreign capital for this purpose. Membership in the IBRD is a prerequisite for membership of the IFC. Legally and financially, the IFC and the IBRD are separate entities. The IFC has its own operating and legal staff, but draws upon the Bank for administrative and other services.

*The Multilateral Investment Guarantee Agency (MIGA)* – offers investors insurance against non-commercial risk and helps governments in developing countries to attract foreign investment.

*The International Center for the Settlement of Investment Disputes (ICSID)* – encourages the flow of foreign investment to developing countries through arbitration and conciliation facilities.

## UNITED NATIONS EDUCATIONAL SCIENTIFIC AND CULTURAL ORGANISATION

The aims of UNESCO are concentrated on practical projects for raising educational standards throughout the world, the exchange of knowledge, and the encouragement of international cooperation in the fields of education, science and culture. It seeks to provide better living conditions through scientific research and cooperation and to improve the scope and quality of mass communication throughout the world. It has its headquarters and Secretariat in Paris, and is controlled by a General Conference of all member states meeting every two years and an Executive Board of fifty-one meeting at least three times a year. National commissions extend the sphere of UNESCO activities to include the majority of member countries, and there are branch offices in New York and Havana; regional education offices in Santiago, Bangkok, Dakar and Beirut; and regional science offices in Nairobi, Montevideo, Cairo, Delhi and Jakarta.

## UNITED NATIONS DEVELOPMENT PROGRAMME

UNDP became a specialised agency of the UN on January 1 1986. It is an amalgam of the United Nations Special Fund and the Expanded Technical Assistance Programme providing technical advice and aid to developing countries, its funds being obtained from donations by member states. In partnership with governments it undertakes high priority, pre-investment projects; makes available experts and consultants as well as specialised equipment and contract services, and offers fellowship awards for training abroad. Assistance is given in support of projects to increase agricultural and industrial productivity, to conduct feasibility studies and to establish or expand applied research institutes and facilities for training and education, as well as to strengthen the administrative and institutional framework for development, and work in a variety of other essential fields.

The UNDP is controlled by a Governing Council composed of forty-eight members elected by ECOSOC and maintains Resident Representatives in 130 recipient countries. Its headquarters are in New York.

## UNIVERSAL POSTAL UNION

The UPU is responsible for the maintenance and development of postal services throughout the world. It has its headquarters in Berne and is controlled by the Universal Postal Congress composed of all member states meeting every five years and a permanent Executive Council of forty-one elected on a geographical basis by the Congress which meets annually.

## WORLD HEALTH ORGANIZATION

The aim of the WHO is the improvement of world standards of health – principally physical, but also mental and social. In view of the extent and diversity of the problems it has to face it has established regional offices in Alexandria, Brazzaville, Copenhagen, Delhi, Manila and Washington, and committees of experts in a wide number of fields. It has its headquarters and Secretariat in Geneva and is controlled by the World Health Assembly consisting of all member states meeting annually and an Executive Board of thirty-one elected by the Assembly.

## WORLD INTELLECTUAL PROPERTY ORGANIZATION

WIPO became a Specialised Agency in December 1974, and is responsible for the promotion, through cooperation among member states, of worldwide protection of Intellectual Property which the Organisation defines as inventions, trademarks, designs and copyrights. The agency is also responsible for the administration of various 'Unions' comprising groups of states which are parties to a particular Convention, e.g. the Berne Convention on Copyright. A substantial part of the activities and resources of WIPO is devoted to assistance in developing countries, particular emphasis being laid on the transfer of technology. The headquarters of the organisation are in Geneva, where an annual Conference of all member states is held to plan the next year's activities and budget, and also where the majority of the almost daily technical meetings are held. The conference is normally a joint one with the General Assembly of those states party to the Berne or Paris 'Unions'.

## WORLD METEOROLOGICAL ORGANIZATION

The WMO seeks to maintain and improve international cooperation and coordination in the field of meteorological services, in particular the exchange and standardisation of weather data and the establishment of a worldwide network of meteorological stations. It encourages research and training in meteorology, and furthers the study of the application of meteorology to shipping, water usage, agriculture, and other human activities. It has its headquarters and Secretariat in Geneva and is controlled by the World Meteorological Congress composed of the heads of the meteorological services of member states meeting every four years and an Executive Committee of 36 meeting annually.

# SUBSIDIARY ORGANISATIONS

As the United Nations has developed, the General Assembly has found it necessary to establish several new organisations in order to fulfil its obligations satisfactorily. All vary considerably in scope and constitution, but all depend ultimately on the General Assembly.

## HUMAN RIGHTS

International intervention in support of human rights has existed for a very long time and in a wide variety of forms; and the term 'human rights' has widely different interpretation depending on religion, values, and culture, which has rendered precise definition problematical and has limited the ratification of Conventions: for some, it is a life-or-death matter of freedom from want and freedom from fear, whilst for others, more fortunate, it is a delicate matter of finding an acceptable balance between liberty and license. It received a major impetus with the adoption of the Covenant of the League of Nations and the subsequent establishment of the International Labour Organization in 1919, but human rights in the widest sense became a definitive factor in international relations with the adoption of the *Universal Declaration of Human Rights* by the General Assembly on 10 December 1948. The Assembly called upon all member countries to publicise the text and 'to cause it to be disseminated, displayed, read and expounded principally in schools and other educational institutions, without distinction based on the political status of countries or territories'.

On the basis of the Declaration, two major international instruments have been drawn up:

*   the *International Convention on Economic, Social and Cultural Rights* which came into effect on 3 January 1976 and which has been ratified or acceded to by eight-four states; and
*   the *International Covenant on Civil and Political Rights* and the *Optional Protocol* which came into force on 23 March 1976. Other major agreements falling broadly within the category of 'Human Rights' are the 1949 Geneva Conventions, the Convention on the Rights of the Child, the 1951 Geneva Convention relating to Refugees, the 1954 Convention relating to the Status of Stateless Persons and the 1967 New York Protocol relating to the Status of Refugees; whilst regional arrangements include the Council of Europe Convention for the Protection of Human Rights and Fundamental Freedoms, the African Charter on Human and People's Rights and the American Convention on Human Rights.

It is the responsibility of the Economic and Social Council, in terms of article 62 of the Charter, to 'make recommendations for the purpose of promoting respect for, and observance of, human rights and fundamental freedoms for all', and such matters are normally dealt with by the Council's Second (Social) Committee. The Council has also established the *Commission on Human Rights* and the *Commission on the Status of Women.*

*The Commission on Human Rights* meets annually for a period of approximately six weeks and may concern itself with any matter relating to human rights. It is composed of representatives of forty-three member states, and its subsidiary bodies include the Sub-Commission on the Prevention of Discrimination and Protection of Minorities, and various working parties.

*The Commission on the Status of Women* is composed of representatives of thirty-two member states of the United Nations and meets twice a year for periods of three weeks. Its main task is to prepare draft resolutions and decisions for consideration by the Economic and Social Council, and on 18 December 1979 the General Assembly adopted the *Convention on the Elimination of All Forms of Discrimination against Women* which entered into force on 3 September 1981. This establishes, *inter alia*, a twenty-three-member Committee on the Elimination of Discrimination against Women which reports annually to the General Assembly.

*The Human Rights Committee* was established in 1977 under the provisions of the International Covenant on Civil and Political Rights in order to monitor the progress of member states in the implementation of human rights. It consists of eighteen members of high moral character and recognised competence in the field of human rights, elected by states which are party to the Convention from among their nationals and who act in a personal capacity for a four-year term. The Committee may receive complaints from states and also, in respect of those states signatories of the Optional Protocol, from individuals. It normally holds three sessions annually, and reports to the General Assembly.

The task of enforcing human rights under the direction of the UN High Commissioner for Human Rights is constantly to the forefront of United Nations activities, and in addition to the formal framework established under the Charter, the General Assembly and its specialised agencies have from time to time agreed Declarations and resolutions on pressing issues such as Apartheid and all forms of racial discrimination, Victims of Torture and Migrant Workers, as well as on situations arising in specific countries.

## INTERNATIONAL LAW COMMISSION

The ILC was set up by resolution of the UN General Assembly in November 1947. The body consists of thirty-four distinguished international lawyers, who are elected by the General Assembly for a five-year period of office, and exists to encourage 'the progressive development of international law and its codification'. The members of the Commission are not government representatives but are elected on a personal basis and sit in their personal capacity as experts. The ILC conducts its sessions in Geneva.

## INTERNATIONAL RESEARCH AND TRAINING INSTITUTE FOR THE ADVANCEMENT OF WOMEN

INSTRAW was established by the General Assembly and the Economic and Social Commission in 1976 and seeks to stimulate and assist, through research, training and the collection and exchange of information, the efforts of inter-governmental, governmental and non-governmental organisations aimed at the advancement of women in development both as participants and beneficiaries. The Institute is funded by voluntary contributions and is situated in Santo Domingo, Dominican Republic.

## OTHER CONSULTATIVE BODIES

Of the special committees and commissions set up by the General Assembly from time to time for specific purposes those listed above have acquired a permanent or semi-permanent nature; others, equally dependent on the General Assembly, have not become institutionalised to the same extent. In addition to those with a purely organisational or administrative function they deal with peace-keeping and security, political matters, decolonisation and questions relating to trusteeship, legal, scientific, and educational matters; they include:
Commission for the Unification and Rehabilitation of Korea
Committee on the Peaceful Uses of Outer Space
Conciliation Commission for Palestine
Scientific Committee on the Effects of Radiation
Working Group on Direct Broadcasting Satellites
United Nations University (Tokyo)
World Food Council
Commission for the prevention of Armament in Space
Scientific Commission for the Effects of Radiation

## UN CONFERENCE ON DISARMAMENT AND THE DISARMAMENT COMMISSION

The Conference on Disarmament stems from an agreement by the USA, the then USSR, France and the UK in 1959 to set up a Ten Nation Committee on Disarmament to include representatives of their four countries together with Bulgaria, Canada, Czechoslovakia, Italy, Poland and Romania. In 1961 it was expanded into an Eighteen Nation Disarmament Committee, and again in 1969 to twenty-six members, when it was renamed the Conference of the Committee on Disarmament (CCD). At the first UN Special Session on Disarmament (UNSSD) in 1978 it was increased to forty members, and its name was changed back to the Committee on Disarmament (CD). Its name was changed again to the Conference on Disarmament in 1984. The Conference meets once a year, usually during the period when the General Assembly is not in session, in Geneva. It is the only multilateral negotiating body of the international community as a whole in the field of disarmament.

The UN Disarmament Commission (UNDC), in contrast, is a deliberative body. It was first formed under the Security Council in 1952 with a membership of eleven states, subsequently increased to twenty-five in 1957 and then a year later it was increased to comprise all members of the UN. The UNDC did not meet from 1965 until 1979, but following its revival by the first Special Session on Disarmament substantive sessions of the UNDC are held once a year in New York.

## UNITED NATIONS CHILDREN'S EMERGENCY FUND

UNICEF provides aid and welfare to children throughout the world. It assists specific projects in the fields of health, nutrition, family and child welfare, education and vocational training; provides basic equipment for maternal and child health centres, and training and stipends for their staff; helps campaigns against endemic diseases; encourages increased production and consumption of protective foods; provides aid for basic social services for children in developing countries, and emergency help to children who are victims of floods, earthquake, drought or other disasters. It comes under the aegis of ECOSOC and obtains its funds in the form of donations from governments and private sources. The Executive Director is appointed by the UN Secretary-General in consultation with the Board of thirty-one members which meets annually to determine policy. The Fund is based in the UN Secretariat in New York, with regional officers in Abidjan, Bangkok, Bogota, Copenhagen, Kathmandu, Sydney and Tokyo.

## UNITED NATIONS CONFERENCE ON TRADE AND DEVELOPMENT

UNCTAD originally met in 1964 as a Conference convened by the General Assembly in order to help restructure the traditional patterns of international trade in the interests of developing countries. It became institutionalised as an organ of the General Assembly, and reports to the General Assembly through the Economic and Social Council. Its purpose is to obtain fair and stable prices for primary commodities, to facilitate trade and development, and in particular to enable developing countries to gain access to the markets of developed countries. It has its headquarters and Secretariat in Geneva, and is controlled by a Conference of its members meeting every four years and a Trade and Development Board elected by the Conference and meeting annually. It has seven main Committees: Shipping; Manufactures; Commodities; Invisibles and Financing related to Trade; Economic Cooperation among Developing Countries; Transfer of Technology and the special Committee on Preferences; also various sub-committees, working parties and *ad hoc* committees of experts. Among the major achievements of UNCTAD are the Generalised System of Preferences and the concept of solidarity and cooperation among developing countries. A major concern currently is the strategic options available to developing countries in view of the globalisation of the world economy. UNCTAD in cooperation with the World Trade Organization has also established the International Trade Centre, with headquarters in Geneva, as the United Nations focal point for technical cooperation in trade promotion. The ITC works with developing countries and countries with economies in transition to set up trade promotion programmes to expand their exports and improve their import operations. Technical cooperation programmes are funded by UNDP and voluntary contributions.

## UNITED NATIONS ENVIRONMENT PROGRAMME

The UNEP was established as a result of the United Nations Conference on the Human Environment held in Stockholm in 1973. Its major purpose is to encourage and coordinate policies for the reduction of pollution in its various forms, and to carry out research and relevant studies. It assesses the state of the world's environment and identifies issues requiring international cooperation; helps formulate international environmental law; and helps to integrate environmental principles in the social and economic policies and programmes of the United Nations system. Its headquarters and Secretariat are in Nairobi, with regional offices in Bahrein, Bangkok, Cairo, Geneva, Mexico City and New York.

## UNITED NATIONS FUND FOR POPULATION ACTIVITIES

The UNFPA was established in 1967 and comes under the direction of the Administrator of the UNDP. The Fund considers the wider aspects of population activities including the status of women. It concentrates on monitoring population trends and evaluating national policies, and reports at intervals to the Economic and Social Council on its findings. A major objective was the holding of a population census by member countries between 1975 and 1985. Since 1994 its focus has been on the needs of the individual.

## UNITED NATIONS HIGH COMMISSION FOR REFUGEES

The origins of the UNHCR are to be found in the aftermath of the First World War and the establishment by the League of Nations of the principle that the international community of states has a duty to provide refugees with protection and find solutions to their problems. Following the Second World War, the UN established the International Refugee Organisation in order to continue the work of the League, and this was superseded in 1951 by the UNHCR, with the task of 'providing international protection … and … seeking permanent solutions for the problems of refugees'.

The activities of UNHCR and the obligations of the signatories were specified in the 1951 Convention Relating to the Status of Refugees and the subsequent 1967 Protocol (126 states subscribing to the former and 118 to the latter) which clarifies and extends the definition of the term 'refugee' and establishes the social and legal status of refugees. Regional definitions and principles have been adopted to meet special circumstances, in particular the 1969 Organisation of African Unity Convention Governing the Specific Aspects of Refugee Problems in Africa and the 1984 Cartagena Declaration on Refugees.

The UN High Commissioner for Refugees is elected by the UN General Assembly on the nomination of the Secretary General. The General Assembly and ECOSOC provide policy directives, and the Executive Committee composed of forty-seven member-government representatives supported by two sub-committees put them into effect.

## UNITED NATIONS INDUSTRIAL DEVELOPMENT ORGANISATION

UNIDO was established by the General Assembly in 1966 for the purpose of encouraging and implementing United Nations efforts in the field of industrial development, particularly by carrying out research studies on behalf of developing countries. Its governing body, the Industrial Development Board, is elected by the General Assembly and reports to the Assembly through ECOSOC; and its Secretariat is at the UN City in Vienna.

## UNITED NATIONS INSTITUTE FOR TRAINING AND RESEARCH

UNITAR seeks to contribute to the process of modernisation and development through the better use of the training of human resources. It carries out training programmes in diplomatic practice, international organisation and technical and economic cooperation, and has as a major objective the creation of a corps of personnel of the highest calibre, particularly from the developing countries, equipped to serve in assignments within the United Nations or with national services connected with the work of the UN. A Board of Trustees determines policy, and the Executive Director and headquarters are in Geneva, with an Office in New York.

## UNITED NATIONS RELIEF AND WORKS AGENCY FOR PALESTINE REFUGEES AND THE NEAR EAST

UNRWA provides aid and assistance to Palestine refugees in the Near East, and endeavours to arrange for their permanent settlement; it was originally established as an *ad hoc* committee by the United Nations General Assembly, and is supported by donations from governments and private sources. Its main concern is the provision of food, clothing and shelter, education and health services. It is controlled by an Advisory Committee, and the Commissioner-General has his headquarters in Vienna.

# INTERNATIONAL ORGANISATIONS AND AGREEMENTS OUTSIDE THE UNITED NATIONS

Multilateral negotiation is increasingly conducted through the medium of international organisations, and these require a specialised form of diplomacy as well as a specific legal concept, namely the law of international organisations. In addition to the United Nations, which is the supreme institution of world order and co-operation, the following are of major significance:

## AFRICAN UNION

The AU is succesor to the Organisation for African Unity. Its members are: Algeria, Angola, Benin, Botswana, Burkina Faso, Burundi, Cameroon, Cape Verde, Central African Republic, Chad, Comoros, Democratic Republic of the Congo, Republic of the Congo, Côte d'Ivoire, Diibouti, Egypt, Equatorial Guinea, Eritrea, Ethiopia, Gabon, Ghana, Guinea, Guinea-Bissau, Kenya, Lesotho, Liberia, Libya, Madagascar, Malawi, Mali, Mauritania, Mauritius, Mozambique, Namibia, Niger, Nigeria, Rwanda, Sahrawi Arab Democratic Republic, Senegal, Seychelles, Sierra Leone, Somalia, South Africa, Swaziland, São Tomé and Príncipe, Tanzania, The Gambia, Sudan, Togo, Tunisia, Uganda, Zambia and Zimbabwe.

The principal objectives of the Union are: to achieve greater unity and solidarity between the African countries and the peoples of Africa; to defend the sovereignty, territorial integrity and independence of its Member States; to accelerate the political and socio-economic integration of the continent; to promote and defend African common positions on issues of interest to the continent and its peoples; to encourage international cooperation, taking due account of the Charter of the United Nations and the Universal Declaration of Human Rights; to promote peace, security, and stability on the continent; to promote democratic principles and institutions, popular participation and good governance; to promote and protect human and peoples' rights in accordance with the African Charter on Human and Peoples' Rights and other relevant human rights instruments; to establish the necessary conditions which enable the continent to play its rightful role in the global economy and in international negotiations; to promote sustainable development at the economic, social and cultural levels as well as the integration of African economies; to promote co-operation in all fields of human activity to raise the living standards of African peoples; to coordinate and harmonize the policies between the existing and future Regional Economic Communities for the gradual attainment of the objectives of the Union; to advance the development of the continent by promoting research in all fields, in particular in science and technology and to work with relevant interational partners in the eradication of preventable diseases and the promotion of good health on the continent.

The major organs of the Union are the Assembly of Heads of State or Government; the Executive Council; the Comission, the Permanent Representatives Committee, the Peace and Security Council, the Pan-African Parliament, the Economic, Social and Cultural Council and the Court of Justice. The financial institutions consist of the African Central Bank, the African Monetary Fund and the African Investment Bank; and there are seven Specialised Technical Committees. The Secretariat is in Addis Ababa.

## ARAB LEAGUE/THE LEAGUE OF ARAB STATES

The League of Arab States is an association of countries having a common heritage and mutual interests, based on the Cairo Pact of the League of Arab States in 1945, supplemented by the 1959 Treaty of Mutual Defence and Cooperation. The objects of the League are to strengthen the bonds between member countries; to coordinate their political activities so as to ensure their independence and sovereignty, and to promote the interests of Arab countries. It also seeks close collaboration in the fields of culture, health, social welfare, transport and communications, passports, visas and nationality laws, and economic and financial matters including trade, customs, currency, agriculture and industry; and provides that in the event of aggression or a threat of aggression a member state may request a meeting of the Council of the League. In 1997 it was agreed that a greater Arab Zone of Free Trade should be established. The members are Algeria, Bahrain, Comoros, Djibouti, Egypt, Iraq, Jordan, Kuwait, Lebanon, Libya, Mauritania, Morocco, Oman, Palestine, Qatar, Saudi Arabia, Somalia, Sudan, Syria, Tunisia, United Arab Emirates, and Yemen. The League of Arab States has observer status in the General Assembly and in its subsidiary organisations; and the Secretariat and Headquarters of the League are in Cairo.

## ASIA-PACIFIC ECONOMIC COOPERATION

The Asia-Pacific Economic Cooperation (APEC) was formed in 1989 in response to the growing interdependence among Asia-Pacific economies. Its objectives are to sustain economic growth of the APEC region and of the world; to enhance positive gains by encouraging the flow of goods, services, capital and technology; to develop and strengthen the open multilateral trading system and reduce those barriers to trade in goods and services that are inconsistent with the World Trade Organization principles. The three pillars of APEC are trade and investment liberalisation; trade and investment facilitation; and economic and technical cooperation, the latter aiming to assist the developing member countries in enhancing their economic progress so that they will be in a position to take part in the trade and investment liberalisation process. A specific objective is to achieve free trade and investment in the Asia-Pacific area by the year 2020, with industrialised countries achieving this goal by 2010. Special emphasis is also placed on increasing the role of the private sector in the development of the area.

Ministerial Meetings are held every year, and subjects discussed have included education; energy; the environment and sustainable development; finance; human resources development; science and technology cooperation; small and medium enterprises; the telecommunication and information industry; trade; and transportation. In addition, there are ten Working Groups, namely fisheries; human resources development; industrial science and technology; marine resource conservation; regional energy cooperation; telecommunications; tourism; trade and investment data; trade promotion; and transportation.

The APEC members are Australia, Brunei, Canada, Chile, China, Hong Kong China, Indonesia, Japan, Republic of Korea, Malaysia, Mexico, New Zealand, Papua New Guinea, Peru, Philippines, Russia, Singapore, Chinese Taipei, Thailand, the United States of America, and Vietnam. A 10-year moratorium on new members is now in force. The ASEAN Secretariat, the Pacific Economic Cooperation Council (PECC) and the South Pacific Forum (SPF) have observer status. The Secretariat of APEC, headed by the Executive Director, is in Singapore.

## ASSOCIATION OF SOUTH-EAST ASIAN NATIONS

ASEAN was established in Bangkok on 8 August 1967, founding members being Indonesia, Malaysia, Philippines, Thailand and Singapore. Brunei Darussalam joined in 1984, Vietnam in 1995, Laos and Myanmar in 1997 and subsequently Cambodia. The aims of the Association are primarily to accelerate the economic growth, social progress and cultural development in the region and to promote regional peace and stability.

Areas of cooperation include political, security, economic, functional and external relations. ASEAN's major political initiatives include the Declaration on the Zone of Peace, Freedom and Neutrality (ZOPFAN) of 1971, the Treaty of Amity and Cooperation in South-East Asia (TAC) in 1976 and the Treaty on the South-East Asia Nuclear Weapon-Free Zone (SEANWFZ) of 1995. The ASEAN Regional Forum (ARF), established in 1994, aims to promote political and security dialogues in the Asia-Pacific region.

Economic cooperation includes trade and investment; industry; food, agriculture and forestry; financial and banking services; transport and communications, tourism, minerals and energy; and private sector participation. In 1992, ASEAN entered into a Common Effective Preferential Tariff (CEPT) scheme for the ASEAN Free Trade Area (AFTA). All manufactured products, including capital goods, and processed and unprocessed agricultural products are included in the CEPT scheme. ASEAN is also undertaking trade facilitation measures such as elimination of non-tariff barriers, harmonisation of tariff nomenclature, customs procedures and valuation. Other functional areas involve cooperation in science and technology; environment; culture and information; social developments and drugs and narcotics control. A major initiative is the establishment in 1995 of the *ASEAN Mekong Basin Development Corporation* to assist in the development of countries in the basin and Kunming in China.

ASEAN's external relations are focused on two organisations:

*The ASEAN Regional Forum*

The ASEAN Regional Forum (ARF) was established in 1992 in order to promote external dialogue on enhancing security in the region. This is in addition to the ongoing dialogue on Asia-Pacific security. Members of the ARF are the ASEAN members, the ASEAN observer Papua New Guinea, and ASEAN Dialogue Partners namely, Australia, Canada, China, India, the EU, Japan, New Zealand, the Republic of Korea, Russia and the United States of America. The Forum endorsed the purposes and principles of the Treaty of Amity and Cooperation in South-East Asia as a code of conduct governing relations among states in the region; agreed to concentrate on Confidence Building Measures in order to develop a more predictable and constructive pattern of relations for the Asia Pacific region, to concentrate on Preventive Diplomacy and to establish the mechanism for conflict resolution.

*Asia–Europe Meeting*

The Asia–Europe Meeting (ASEM) was conceived as ASEAN's initiative with a view to redressing the 'missing link' between Asia and Europe. The members of ASEM are China, Japan, Republic of Korea, the member states of the European Union and the President of the European Commission, and the member states of ASEAN.

*Organisational structure of ASEAN*

The Meeting of Heads of Government is the highest decision-making body of ASEAN, and there are thirteen sectoral Ministerial Meetings including the annual meetings of the Foreign Ministers and of the Economic Ministers. The ASEAN Secretariat, headed by the Secretary-General, is in Jakarta.

# BANK FOR INTERNATIONAL SETTLEMENTS

The BIS was founded as a result of an intergovernmental Convention dated 20 January 1930. It is a Central Banking Institution which makes its services available to central banks and intergovernmental institutions. It is also a centre for economic and monetary research and consultations, and acts as technical agent for the execution of certain specific agreements with, for example, the OECD and the ECSC. It cooperates with other institutions such as the IMF, and since 1982 has been particularly instrumental in resolving liquidity problems of debtor countries by providing short-term bridging loans. Its membership of thirty-two comprises nearly all European central banks, as well as the monetary authorities of a number of non-European countries including Japan and the USA; and although some of the shares are held by the public, all rights of voting and representation in respect of the shares are vested in the central bank of each country in which the shares were issued. Under its statutes the BIS may only undertake operations that are in conformity with the monetary policy of the central banks concerned, and its operations are essentially short term. There are 50 central bank members of the BIS, and the headquarters of the Bank are in Basel.

# BLACK SEA ECONOMIC COOPERATION

BSEC is a regional organisation of eleven states established in accordance with the Summit Declaration on Black Sea Economic Cooperation signed in Istanbul on 25 June 1992. The objective is to promote peace, stability and prosperity in the region, on the basis of shared values such as multi-party democracy, social justice, human rights, the rule of law, fundamental freedoms, a free market and economic prosperity. Members of BSEC are Albania, Armenia, Azerbaijan, Bulgaria, Georgia, Greece, Moldova, Romania, Russia, Turkey and Ukraine. Observer status is accorded to Austria, Egypt, Israel, Italy, Poland, Slovakia and Tunisia.

The institutions of BSEC are the Annual Meetings of Heads of State or Government, a Parliamentary Assembly, the Black Sea Trade and Development Bank in Thessaloniki and the Coordination Centre for the Exchange of Statistical Data in Ankara. The BSEC Council is the organ of the business communities of the member states for the purpose of developing initiatives and cooperation in the private sector, and the Secretariat is in Istanbul.

# CARIBBEAN REGIONAL ORGANISATIONS

## THE ASSOCIATION OF CARIBBEAN STATES

The ACS was established in 1995 primarily as a coordinating body to enhance the status and bargaining power of the region in political and economic negotiations. It provides a forum for consultation, cooperation and concerted action in areas of mutual cultural, economic and technical concern, especially transport and tourism. Membership consists of the islands of the Caribbean, together with the mainland states of Colombia, Mexico, Surinam and Venezuela; also six Observer members. The Secretariat is in Port of Spain, Trinidad and Tobago.

*The Caribbean Community* (CARICOM) is the major regional economic organisation in the Caribbean. Its main function is the creation of a Caribbean Common Market but its activities extend to a wider sphere and include the harmonisation of economic and related policies. Members are Antigua and Barbuda, Barbados, Belize, Dominica, Grenada, Guyana, Jamaica, Montserrat, St Kitts-Nevis, St Lucia, St Vincent and the Grenadines, Trinidad and Tobago, Turks and Caicos Islands, and the British Virgin Islands.

The Heads of Government Conference is responsible for the policy of the Community, and the Common Market Council of Ministers is responsible for the Common Market. The Secretariat is in Georgetown, Guyana.

*The Organisation of Eastern Caribbean States* (OECS) consists of Antigua and Barbuda, Dominica, Grenada, Montserrat, St Kitts-Nevis, St Lucia and St Vincent and the Grenadines, all of which have in the past shared certain common services such as a common currency and judiciary. These common services are being extended to include, *inter alia*, harmonisation of foreign policies and joint overseas diplomatic representation. A major objective is to increase bargaining power in inter-governmental negotiations.

# CENTRAL AMERICAN COMMON MARKET

The members of MCCA are Costa Rica, El Salvador, Guatemala, Honduras and Nicaragua. In terms of the 1960 treaty of Managua and the Guatemala Declaration on Monetary Integration the parties aim to eliminate tariffs on nearly all intra-regional trade, and eventually to create a customs union. They envisage the harmonisation of policies relating to taxation, customs classification, monopolies, dumping and unfair trade practices; the acceptance of the principles of coordinated industrial development and of freedom of transit, and the establishment of a Central American Bank of Economic Integration. The institutions of MCCA are the Central American Economic Council composed of Ministers of each of the parties, and an Executive Council on which each party is represented. The Secretary-General and the Secretariat are in Guatemala City.

# CENTRAL EUROPEAN INITIATIVE

The CEI was founded in 1989 with the objective of contributing to the stability and economic development of Central Europe, increasing the scope of dialogue and co-operation between member-states, with the aim of increasing economic and political cooperation, developing cross-border infrastructure and providing a forum for the discussion of regional problems. Its major purpose now is to facilitate the process for those members who are not yet members of the European Union, within a framework of parliamentary democracy, and the maintenance of human rights. Members of CEI are Albania, Austria, Belarus, Bosnia and Herzegovina, Bulgaria, Croatia, Czech Republic, Hungary, Italy, Macedonia (FYR) Moldova, Poland, Romania, Slovakia, Slovenia and Ukraine. The *Land* government of Bavaria participates in some activities as an observer.

The organisational structure of the CEI is flexible and is based on a series of regular forums: the annual Heads of Government Meeting, the annual meeting of Ministers of Foreign Affairs, the Committee of National Coordinators which meets on a regular basis, the Special Meetings of Sectoral Ministers, and the Parliamentary Conference attended by delegates representing national Parliaments. In addition, cooperation and dialogue relationships exist with the European Union, the Organisation for Security and Cooperation in Europe, the Council of Europe, the European Bank for Reconstruction and Development, the Council of Baltic Sea States, the Black Sea Economic Cooperation, the Community of Alps Adriatic and the Community of the Danubian Region.

The CEI Secretariat is in Trieste, and the Chairmanship is held by member countries in rotation.

## COMMON MARKET FOR EASTERN AND SOUTHERN AFRICA

COMESA was established in 1994 as a successor organisation to the Preferential Trade Area for Eastern and Southern Africa (PTA). As with the Southern African Development Community and the Southern African Customs Union between South Africa, Namibia, Swaziland, Lesotho and Botswana (SACU) it seeks to create a momentum towards economic integration, and in addition provides a clearing-house with its own unit of account for financial transactions between member states, namely Angola, Burundi, Comoros, Democratic Republic of the Congo, Djibouti, Egypt, Eritrea, Ethiopia, Kenya, Lesotho, Madagascar, Malawi, Mauritius, Mozambique, Namibia, Rwanda, Seychelles, Somalia, Sudan, Swaziland, Tanzania, Uganda, Zambia and Zimbabwe. The Secretariat of COMESA is in Lusaka.

## THE COMMONWEALTH

The Commonwealth is an association of states all but two of which at one time formed part of the British Empire or were Protected States in treaty relations with the Crown. Intra-Commonwealth cooperation and consultation are maintained by institutional and personal contact in cultural and educational matters; and meetings of heads of governments or their representatives are held normally every two years for the exchange of views on matters of common concern. Aid and development are featured in the initiation of the Colombo Plan and in the Commonwealth Fellowships; and trade, in preferential tariff and quota arrangements, now mainly incorporated in the Lomé Convention. Her Majesty Queen Elizabeth II is Head of the Commonwealth, and the Commonwealth Secretariat and its Secretary-General are situated in London. The following states are full members of the Commonwealth: Antigua and Barbuda, Australia, Bahamas, Bangladesh, Barbados, Belize, Botswana, Brunei, Cameroon, Canada, Cyprus, Dominica, Fiji, The Gambia, Ghana, Grenada, Guyana, India, Jamaica, Kenya, Kiribati, Lesotho, Malawi, Malaysia, Maldives, Malta, Mauritius, Mozambique, Namibia, Nauru, New Zealand, Nigeria, Pakistan, Papua New Guinea, St. Kitts and Nevis, St Lucia, St Vincent and the Grenadines, Samoa, Seychelles, Sierra Leone, Singapore,

Solomon Islands, South Africa, Sri Lanka, Swaziland, Tanzania, Tonga, Trinidad and Tobago, Tuvalu, Uganda, the United Kingdom of Great Britain and Northern Ireland, Vanuatu, Zambia and Zimbabwe. The Commonwealth Parliamentary Association provides a focus for the mutual interests of the legislatures of the Commonwealth; those member states which fail to maintain the concept or practice of parliamentary government being suspended from membership of the Association.

## THE COMMONWEALTH OF INDEPENDENT STATES

The Commonwealth of Independent States – like the British Commonwealth and the French Community – is engaged in developing an institutional structure within which its former component parts can continue to cooperate in those aspects of government that they consider to be to their advantage; and like other similar institutions, it is in a state of evolution, as the original economic interdependence decreases and the sense of national identity among those states that have seceded from the Soviet Union becomes stronger.

The CIS is based on the 1991 Minsk Agreement between Russia, Belarus and Ukraine. These former Republics of the Soviet Union, having concluded that the USSR 'had ceased to exist as a subject of international law and a geographical reality', declared that 'cooperation between the members of the Commonwealth would be carried out in accordance with the principle of equality through coordinating institutions'. Areas of cooperation were defined as foreign policy; forming and developing a united economic area and a common European and Eurasian market in the area of customs policy, transport and communications, the environment, migration and organised crime.

Other former Republics – Armenia, Azerbaijan, Georgia, Kazakhstan, Kyrgyzstan, Moldova, Tajikistan, Turkmenistan and Uzbekistan – acceded to the Declaration, and also signed the Agreement on Strategic Forces whereby they 'recognised the need for joint command of strategic forces and for maintaining unified control of nuclear weapons', and the Agreement on Armed Forces and Border Troops which formed the basis for subsequent bilateral peace-keeping arrangements. Proposals for the creation of a unified CIS military command were abandoned in favour of a military coordinating committee, and Russia has offered to assist in the defence of the borders of the Central Asian and Trans-Caucasian Republics if so requested. Other fields of cooperation include the creation of a CIS Bank, a Petroleum and Gas Council, moves towards free trade and an economic union, and a structure to regulate inter-state financial transactions together with an Economic Court.

The organisational structure is based on the Council of Heads of State and the Council of Heads of Governments and various consultative and coordinating bodies; and the Secretariat is in Minsk.

# COUNCIL OF EUROPE

The Council of Europe was the first international organisation established in Europe after the 1939–45 war, and in terms of its Statute, signed on 5 May 1949 by the ten founder countries, its objective is to work for greater European unity, to uphold the principles of parliamentary democracy, to promote human values, and to improve living conditions. Currently its major concerns are human rights, education, culture and sport, social questions, youth unemployment, public health, environment and architectural heritage, local and regional authorities and legal affairs. In particular it aims to achieve a greater unity between its members for the purpose of safeguarding and realising the ideals and principles which are their common heritage and facilitating their economic and social progress: in short 'to promote European Cultural Identity continent-wide'.

Major achievements of the Council have been the European Convention on Human Rights, and the establishment of the European Commission and Court of Human Rights, whose jurisdiction has now been accepted as compulsory by thirty-four member states, and the European Convention on the Suppression of Terrorism, which *inter alia* defines those offences that shall *not* be regarded as political offences or as offences connected with a political offence or as offences inspired by political motives. Other conventions of major significance include the Convention on the protection of human rights and human dignity concerning the application of biology and medicine and the Supplementary Protocol forbidding the cloning of human beings.

The institutions of the Council are the Committee of Ministers of all member states which meets twice a year, a series of specialised committees, and the Parliamentary Assembly, which is a consultative body and which meets three times a year.

Membership consists of Albania, Andorra, Armenia, Austria, Azerbaijan, Belgium, Bosnia Herzegovina, Bulgaria, Croatia, Cyprus, Czech Republic, Denmark, Estonia, Finland, France, Georgia, Germany, Greece, Hungary, Iceland, Ireland, Italy, Latvia, Liechtenstein, Lithuania, Luxembourg, Macedonia (FYR), Malta, Moldova, Netherlands, Norway, Poland, Portugal, Romania, Russia, San Marino, Serbia and Montenegro, Slovakia, Slovenia, Spain, Sweden, Switzerland, Turkey, Ukraine and the United Kingdom. The Secretariat-General is in Strasbourg.

# ECONOMIC COOPERATION ORGANIZATION

The Economic Cooperation Organization is a regional group for economic cooperation, consisting of Afghanistan, Azerbaijan, Iran, Kazakhstan, Kyrgyzstan, Pakistan, Tajikistan, Turkey, Turkmenistan and Uzbekistan. Subjects of special concern are transport, communications, trade, energy and the establishment of a regional payments system. The Headquarters and Secretariat are in Tehran.

# EURASIAN ECONOMIC COMMUNITY

The Eurasian Economic Community is the successor to the C.I.S. Customs Union and seeks to promote closer economic co-operation between Belarus, Kazakhstan, Kyrgystan, Russia and Tajikistan. It also has a border cooperation agreement with Mongolia. Armenia, Moldova and Ukraine have observer status, and the Secretariat is in Moscow and Astana.

# EUROPEAN FREE TRADE ASSOCIATION/
# EUROPEAN ECONOMIC AREA

EFTA was founded in terms of the 1960 Stockholm Convention by seven Western European states which did not elect to join the EEC, with the principal objective of creating a free trade area in industrial goods, with agreed rules of origin. This was achieved in 1966, and in 1972/73 free trade agreements were concluded with the EC, creating the Western European Free Trade System. In 1992 agreement was reached between EFTA and EU member states for the creation of the *European Economic Area* establishing a system (with certain exceptions) for the free movement of industrial goods, services, capital and people; and with the member countries adopting relevant EU rules. The institutions of EFTA – the Council of Ministers, the Standing Committee, the Committee of Members of Parliament, the Consultative Committee and the Court – are supplemented by the creation of joint EFTA/EU institutions. Membership of EFTA is Iceland, Liechtenstein, Norway and Switzerland, and the Secretariat-General is in Geneva. The EEA consists of the members of the European Union together with Norway, Iceland and Liechtenstein.

# EUROPEAN UNION

The EU consists of 25 member states: Austria, Belgium, Cyprus, Czech Republic, Denmark, Estonia, Finland, France, Germany, Greece, Hungary, Ireland, Italy, Latvia, Lithuania, Luxembourg, Malta, The Netherlands, Poland, Portugal, Slovakia, Slovenia, Spain, Sweden and the United Kingdom. The accession of Bulgaria and Romania is anticipated in 2007/2008, and applications from Turkey and Balkan states are under consideration.

The members are signatories of, or have subsequently acceded to, the 1957 Treaty of Rome, the 1986 Single European Act, the 1992 Maastricht Treaty, the 1997 Amsterdam Treaty, the 2001 Treaty of Nice and the various Treaties of Accession; and on 18 June 2004 reached agreement on the text of a Constitutional Treaty for the European Union. This treaty, once ratified, will in many ways be the culminating act in the process of European integration that started with the Conference of Messina in 1955 and the Treaty of Rome of 1957, and it consolidates the subsequent treaties designed to achieve 'ever closer Union'. The Treaty stipulates *inter alia*, that the

European Union has a legal personality, and confirms the general primacy of European law over national law. It creates the post of full-time President of the European Council for an extended period, and a Minister for Foreign Affairs supported by a world-wide network of Diplomatic Missions; and it increases the powers of the European Parliament. Qualified Majority Voting in the Council of Ministers is extended, and an affirmative vote is to be based (except in specific circumstances) on the approval of at least 55% of the members representing 65% of the Union's population. The European Court of Justice has the potential to acquire increased competence in the interpretation of the Charter of Fundamental Rights; and the right of members to secede is confirmed.

Association Agreements covering limited facilities have been entered into with a wide range of countries, and the E.U., together with Iceland, Liechtenstein and Norway have created the European Economic Area with free movement of manufactured goods, capital, services and individuals. It has also entered into a Free Trade Area with Turkey, and has undertaken a Euro-Mediterranean dialogue with twelve states of the region on the basis of the 1996 Barcelona Conference.

The objective of the original six members of the Treaty of Rome was to remove barriers to trade and to create a process leading to 'ever closer union' (preamble to the Treaty); and this was to be achieved principally by 'establishing a common market and progressively approximating the economic policies of member states' (Article 2). In the words of Jean Monnet, architect of the Community, 'We are not creating an association of states: we are creating a union of peoples', and the administrative and decision-making procedures of the European Economic Community were accordingly structured so as to create a process leading towards the goal of unification.

This political purpose was spelled out in 1969 in The Hague where the objective of 'paving the way for a united Europe' was recognised, and was reaffirmed in 1983 in the 'Stuttgart Solemn Declaration'; and in 1986 in the Single European Act, member states undertook 'to transform relations as a whole among their states into a European Union' (preamble), and stipulated that 'the European Communities and European Political Co-operation (i.e. harmonisation of foreign policies) would have as their objectives to contribute together to making concrete progress towards European Unity' (Article 1). A major provision of the Act designed to further the process of unification was the diminution of the blocking veto powers of individual member governments by the extension of the system of qualified majority voting in the Council of Ministers.

The process of creating an economic involvement and dependence that would go far to meet most member states' ultimate goal of European unity was carried a major stage further in 1992 with the signing at Maastricht of the Treaty on European Union, which set as its objective the establishment of 'a European Union . . . a new stage in the process of creating an ever closer union among the peoples of Europe'. Provision was made for the Union to become a reality through, *inter alia*, the establishment of economic and monetary union, including the creation of a single currency, and the introduction of Union citizenship. Moreover, the Union would 'assert its identity in the international scene, in particular through the implementation of a common foreign and security policy'.

The Maastricht Treaty, unlike the American Constitution, did not list the specific functions that would be transferred to a central authority, on the assumption that the European Court of Justice would determine what responsibilities such an authority should assume in order to fulfil its agreed objective of creating the Union. It specified, however, that the goal of member states – namely a political union – constituted a binding obligation. The Treaty introduced a dynamic concept into the process of integration: it obliged governments to take further steps towards the goal of union, and it constituted a source of European Union Law, and an operative text.

Since the signing of the Treaty of Rome, an increasing degree of cooperation has taken place between the countries of Western Europe in general, and within the Union in particular, where a high degree of standardisation and conformity has been achieved. The aim of establishing the 'Four Freedoms of Movement' – of manufactured goods, services, capital and people – was, in the main, completed by the target date of January 1993, and non-tariff barriers to trade have been largely eliminated. Agriculture is centrally regulated and remains more a matter of politics than economics. However, substantial progress has been made in the transfer of resources from industrialised to agriculturally-dependent countries and in the tranfer of financial assistance to the less developed regions of the Union (the 'cohesion' policy), thus encouraging the stated aim of 'economic convergence'. Freedom of movement has been largely achieved by the adhesion of most of the member-states to the Schengen Agreement, and 12 countries – Austria, Belgium, Finland, France, Greece, Germany, Ireland, Italy, Luxembourg, The Netherlands, Portugal and Spain have created a single currency – the Euro.

In the implementation of the Common Foreign and Security Policy, the European Council determines the principles and the general guidelines relating not only to defence, but also to such matters as the safeguarding of European Values, and promoting democracy, human rights and the rule of law. It also determines *common strategies* in areas where member-states have important common interests e.g. the Balkans; and if a member opposes a decision taken in the Council of Ministers for reasons of important national policy, the matter can be referred to the European Council where the basis of unanimity will apply.

In its task of formulating and implementing the C.F.S.P. guidelines set by the European Council, the Council of Ministers works in close co-operation with the Commission, and with the advice of the Political Committee of political directors of member-states and various correspondents and working groups, and with the concurrence of the European Parliament. The current (and, where necessary, following) Presidency of the E.U. also plays an important role in the implementation of policy with the close co-operation of the High Representative for the C.F.S.P. who is, at the same time, Secretary-General of the European Council. Foreign Trade policy and 'dialogue' relations with e.g. ASEAN and the Group of Rio are among the Commission's foreign policy responsibilities, and an extensive network of diplomatic representation abroad has been established.

In the 'third pillar' of Justice and Home Affairs, immigration, asylum, visa policy (and the eventual abolitian of frontiers) are dependent on a unanimous vote in the Council.

The Institutions and major decision-making bodies are:

*The Commission* of the European Communities which consists of up to a maximum of 27 members nominated by the governments of each of the member states but acting independently of them. It acts as the Executive of the Union and has the sole right of initiating measures to be adopted by the Union, though in some instances the Council asks the Council to initiate specific measures. Each Commissioner is appointed by her or his member state for five years, and their responsibility for a particular function of administration is allocated by the President of the Commission.

*The European Council* (or 'Summit') which consists of Heads of State or government of member states accompanied by their Ministers for Foreign Affairs who meet together with the President of the Commission at least twice a year in order to determine overall policy.

*The Council of the European Union*, which consists of Ministers nominated by, and representing, each of the member states, and can veto or amend proposals from the Commission. Decisions are in most cases taken by qualified (i.e. weighted) majority vote, but in some unanimity is required. Voting is weighted on the following basis: Austria 10, Belgium 12, Bulgaria 10, Czech Republic 12, Cyprus 4, Denmark 7, Estonia 4, Finland 7, France 29, Greece 12, Germany 29, Hungary 12, Ireland 7, Italy 29, Latvia 4, Lithuania 7, Luxembourg 4, Malta 3, The Netherlands 13, Poland 27, Portugal 12, Romania 14, Slovakia 7, Slovenia 4, Spain 27, Sweden 10 and the United Kingdom 29. An additional population-related qualification remains under consideration.

*The European Parliament* which consists of 686 members (rising to 738 when Bulgaria and Romenia become members of the European Union) is elected by direct franchise on the following basis: Austria 17, Belgium 20, Bulgaria 17, Czech Republic 20, Cyprus 6, Denmark 13, Estonia 6, Finland 13, France 74, Greece 20, Germany 99, Hungary 20, Ireland 12, Italy 74, Latvia 8, Lithuania 12, Luxembourg 6, Malta 5, The Netherlands 25, Poland 52, Portugal 20, Romania 35, Slovakia 13, Slovenia 7, Spain 52, Sweden 18 and the United Kingdom 74. The Parliament has three fundamental powers: legislation, supervision of the executive and ultimate control of the annual Budget. It is also the body to which the European Central Bank is accountable. Parliamentary 'co-decision' with the Commission is necessary for legislation relating to the free movement of workers, the creation of the internal market, research and technological development, consumer protection, education, culture and health; and for the admission of new members to the EU. In matters of taxation and the annual farm prices review Parliaments function is limited to consultation; and with regard to the Common Foreign and Security Policy, the Council Presidency ensures that its views are taken into consideration.

*The European Court of Justice*, which consists of sixteen independent judges, is the supreme Court in all matters relating to the Union and generally in the interpretation of the Union Treaties. It is also the custodian of 'a new legal order' and interprets the law in such a way as 'to make concrete progress towards European unity'. It has the power to levy fines on the recommendation of the Commission on states which have 'failed to fulfil an obligation' of the Treaty of Rome (Article 171).

In addition to the Economic and Social Committee and the Council of the Regions there are:

*The General Affairs Council* which is composed of the Mininsters for Foreign Affairs of all member-states.

*The Presidency of the Council*, which rotates every six months between member states. Whichever member has the Presidency presides also over all the various Council and committee meetings and determines their agenda, and its Foreign Minister delivers the opening speech to the European Parliament.

*The Committee of Permanent Representatives* (COREPER), which consists of two committees: one of the Permanent Representatives (i.e. Ambassadors) of the member states accredited to the European Union, and the other comprising the deputy permanent representatives. Both meet every week, their main task being to process and prepare material for discussion and decision by the EU Council. They also carry out functions delegated by the Council.

A special relationship was established between members of the Community and their former dependent territories through the Yaoundé, Arusha and subsequently Lomé Conventions. The Lomé IV Convention expired in the year 2000, and the new convention between the EU and the 71 member-states will continue until 2020. Benefits in trade and aid for the A.C.P. countries will accompany a *quid pro quo* extending into the fields of democracy, human rights and investment protection. The institutions of the Convention are the ACP–EU Council of Ministers which meets annually, the ACP–EU Ambassadors Committee which meets every six months, and the EU–ACP Joint Assembly composed of delegates of ACP countries and members of the European Parliament in equal numbers, which meets once a year.

## FREE TRADE AREA OF THE AMERICAS

Proposed free trade area of 34 states signatories of the Common Market Convention of 2001 providing for open markets and adherence to commitments relating *inter alia* to democracy, the environment and the prevention of drug smuggling by the year 2005.

# GULF COOPERATION COUNCIL

The Gulf Cooperation Council was founded in 1981 and its policy was set out in its Charter which was ratified in 1982. The member states are: Bahrain, Kuwait, Oman, Qatar, Saudi Arabia and the United Arab Emirates. The essential purpose is to achieve coordination, cooperation and integration in all economic, social and cultural affairs. Comparable regulations have been established in economic and financial affairs; commerce, customs and communication; education and culture; social and health affairs; media and tourism, and legislative and administrative affairs; whilst agreement has been reached on stimulating scientific and technological progress in industry, agriculture and water resources. In terms of the Unified Economic Agreement, tariff barriers between the six will be abolished, and Gulf nationals will be free to set up industries and to enter into contracts in any state with equal rights. In addition, plans are in place for a Joint Defence Force for Rapid Deployment.

The institutions of the Gulf Cooperation Council are the Supreme Council of Heads of State which meets annually, the Advisory Commission for the Supreme Council consisting of 30 members drawn in equal numbers from each of the member-countries, and the Council of Ministers which meets every three months. The Secretariat-General is in Riyadh, Saudi Arabia.

# GUUAM

Regional organisation consisting of Georgia, Ukraine, Uzbekhistan, Azerbaijan and Moldova whose objectives were set out in a Statement of Presidents signed in Washington on 24 April 1999. Based on participation in the process of integration into European and Euro-Atlantic structures, these cover a wide range of areas of co-operation including the non-proliferation of weapons of mass destruction, the strengthening of international organisations and forums, the development of Europe-Caucasus-Asia transport and the implementation of the results of the International Conference on the Restoration of the Historic Silk Route held in Baky in 1998.

# INDIAN OCEAN RIM ASSOCIATION FOR REGIONAL COOPERATION

The principal aim of the IOR-ARC is to facilitate trade and investment in the region. Members are Australia, Bangladesh, India, Indonesia, Iran, Kenya, Madagascar, Malaysia, Mauritius, Mozambique, Oman, Singapore, South Africa, Sri Lanka, Tanzania, Thailand, United Arab Emirates and Yemen. Dialogue Partners are China, Egypt, France, Japan and the United Kingdom. The Secretariat is in Port Louis, Mauritius.

# LATIN AMERICAN ECONOMIC ORGANISATIONS

*The Latin American Integration Association* (LAIA or ALADI) was established in 1980 by the new Treaty of Montevideo, which superseded the 1960 Treaty which created the Latin American Free Trade Area (LAFTA). The purpose of the new treaty is to pursue the integration process in order to promote the harmonious and balanced socio-economic development of the region; the long-term objective of such a process being the gradual and progressive establishment of a Latin American common market (article I). The scope of the new treaty is greater than that of the original one, but the methods of achieving closer cooperation are more flexible, and in the form of a framework for pragmatic development, rather than a fixed timetable for achieving specific objectives. The treaty makes provision for regional tariff preferences, regional and sub-regional cooperational agreements, assistance to less-developed member states, and the establishment of relations with other regional economic organisation. The Secretariat is in Montevideo, and the member states are the same as for the previous treaty, namely Argentina, Bolivia, Brazil, Chile, Colombia, Ecuador, Mexico, Paraguay, Peru, Uruguay and Venezuela. Policy is determined by the Council of Ministers for Foreign Affairs of each of the member countries which meets when appropriate, whilst the Committee of Representatives is the permanent executive body. LAIA is essentially an 'umbrella' organisation which oversees and helps to coordinate the various sub-regional organisations of Latin America.

Complementary organisations are the *Sistema Económico Latino-americano* (SELA) which meets at intervals in order to coordinate economic planning and policies and whose membership includes nearly all Latin American countries; and the *United Nations Economic Commission for Latin America and the Caribbean* which is a centre for economic research and a source of economic and social information. The seat of the Commission is Santiago, Chile.

*The Andean Integration System* envisages the creation of an Andean Community, and is the successor to the Andean Group (Grupo Andino) which was formed in 1969 as a sub-regional group in order to provide a more cohesive economic unit within the Latin American Free Trade Area – now the Latin American Integration Association.

The aim is freedom of movement of goods, services and capital transfers, and the establishment of a Free Trade Area with MERCOSUR. Members are Bolivia, Ecuador and Colombia, Peru and Venezuela.

*MERCOSUR/MERCOSUL* was established in 1991 by the Treaty of Asunción for the purposes of establishing, by the year 2006, a Customs Union including the free movement of goods, services, capital and labour, and for promoting regional investment. Member states are Argentina, Brazil, Paraguay and Uruguay, with Chile as an Associate Member. By 1995, 85 per cent of tariffs had been eliminated, with some exceptions permitted for Paraguay and Uruguay. Free Trade Agreements have been entered into with Chile and Bolivia.

*Group of three* – G3 is a forum for political discussion on the promotion of economic integration with a view to the creation of a Free Trade Area. Members are Colombia, Mexico and Venezuela, and the Secretariat is in Bogotá.

## MAGHREB ARAB UNION

The UMA was founded in terms of the 1993 Treaty of Marrakesh as a regional organisation for stability, security and economic coordination. Membership consists of Algeria, Libya, Mauritania, Morrocco and Tunisia; and the Secretariat is in Rabat. Its activities are temporarily restricted owing to the Western Sahara dispute.

## NEW PARTNERSHIP FOR AFRICAN'S DEVELOPMENT

NEPAD is a Declaration of Commitment by African leaders to the peoples of Africa to pursue a policy of democratic government and sound economic development, and to promote peace and security. It was approved by the members of the (then) O.A.U. in 2001, and was subsequently endorsed by members of G.8 who undertook to respond to the initiative with financial assistance and debt reduction.

## NILE BASIN INITIATIVE

Association of riparian states of the river Nile designed to foster co-operation, and to research and promote economic development. Members are Burundi, Congo (Democratic Republic), Egypt, Eritrea, Ethiopia, Kenya, Rwanda, Sudan, Tanzania and Uganda.

## NORTH AMERICAN FREE TRADE AGREEMENT

NAFTA, signed in 1992 by Canada, Mexico and the United States of America, seeks to establish a Free Trade Area by the phased removal of tariffs and quotas on industrial and agricultural goods in the area within ten years (for agriculture and motor vehicles, fifteen years), and by freedom to establish services. The objectives of the Agreement are set out more specifically in the Preamble which states that the contracting parties are resolved to:

> strengthen the special bonds of friendship and cooperation among their nations; contribute to the harmonious development and expansion of world trade and provide a catalyst to broader international cooperation; create an expanded and secure market for the goods and services produced in their territories; reduce distortions of trade; establish clear and mutually advantageous rules governing their

trade; ensure a predictable commercial framework for business planning and investment; build on their respective rights and obligations under the World Trade Organization and other multilateral and bilateral instruments of cooperation; enhance the competitiveness of their firms in global markets; foster creativity and innovation, and promote trade in goods and services that are the subject of intellectual property rights; create new employment opportunities and improve working conditions and living conditions and living standards in their respective territories; undertake each of these objectives in a manner consistent with environmental protection and conservation; preserve their flexibility to safeguard the public welfare; promote sustainable development; strengthen the development and enforcement of environmental laws and regulations, and protect, enhance and enforce basic workers' rights.

Special provisions apply in respect of the 1973 Convention on the International Trade in Endangered Species of Wild Fauna and Flora, the 1987 Montreal Protocol on Substances that deplete the Ozone Layer; the 1989 Basel Convention and the 1986 US, Canada, Mexico Agreement on the Control of Transboundary Movements of Hazardous Wastes and their Disposal; and the 1983 US, Mexico, Agreement on Cooperation for the Protection and Improvement of the Environment in the Border Area.

In January 1996 Chile became associated with NAFTA as a prelude to the projected 'Free Trade Area of the Americas from Alaska to Tierra del Fuego'.

# NORTH ATLANTIC TREATY ORGANISATION

NATO was founded in 1949, with the objective of providing the military means of containing the expansionist policies of the then Soviet Union. The essence of the North Atlantic Treaty is that an armed attack against one or more of the signatories is considered as an attack against them all (Article 5); in which event each member-state will assist the Party or Parties so attached by taking ... such action as it seems necessary, including the use of armed force ... . Since the dissolution of the Soviet Empire NATO has evolved and adapted to changing circumstances, and has re-defined its role by consensus, in accordance with the foreign policy objectives of its member-states; and for the first time in NATO's history Article 5 was invoked following the 9/11 attack on the U.S.A. Since that event, the international fight against terrorism has become a major focus of the Alliance, and has significantly influenced both the evolution of policy and the conduct of its work, in particular with regard to the accession of new member countries and the development of cooperation with partner and other non-member countries.

Signatories of the Treaty are: Belgium, Bulgaria, Canada, Czech Republic, Denmark, Estonia, France, Germany, Greece, Hungary, Iceland, Italy, Latvia, Lithuania, Luxembourg, the Netherlands, Norway, Poland, Portugal, Romania, Slovakia, Slovenia, Spain, Turkey, the United Kingdom and the United States of

America. NATO will review the enlargement process and consider applications for membership from other European emerging democracies whose admission would fulfil the objectives of the Treaty.

The area of application of the treaty extends to the territory of any of the parties in Europe and North America; an attack on the forces of any party in Europe, on the islands under jurisdiction of any party in the North Atlantic area north of the Tropic of Cancer, or on the vessels or aircraft of any parties in this area. Out-of-area operations for the purpose of conflict prevention, peace enforcement and peace-keeping have subsequently evolved without prejudicing the terms of Article 5. The prime concern of NATO, acting in a defensive capacity, continues to be to safeguard the security, sovereignty and territorial integrity of its members, maintaining security at the lowest possible level of forces consistent with the requirements of defence. In a more positive role it seeks, through dialogue, partnership and cooperation, a new and more peaceful order, based on the conviction that stability and security in the Euro-Atlantic area will increasingly be built on a framework of interlocking and mutually reinforcing institutions.

In 1991, in response to the changed political and military situation in Europe, the member countries of NATO, together with the former members of the Warsaw Pact, agreed to create the *North Atlantic Cooperation Council* (NACC). This initiative was followed in 1994 by a system of *Partnership for Peace* (PfP) whereby member countries of NACC and OSCE were invited to take part in dialogue and mutually confidence-building measures, with a view to ensuring transparency in national defence planning and expenditure; democratic control of defence forces; the maintenance of the capability and readiness (subject to constitutional constraints) to contribute to operations under the authority of the UN or the OSCE; the development of cooperative military relations with NATO; and the development, over the longer term, of armed forces that are better able to operate with those of NATO member countries. Members of PfP are Albania, Armenia, Austria, Azerbaijan, Belarus, Croatia, Finland, Georgia, Ireland, Kazakhstan, Kyrgyz Republic, Macedonia, Moldova, Russia, Sweden, Switzerland, Tajikistan, Turkmenistan, Ukraine and Uzbekistan.

In 1997 the NACC was succeeded by the *Euro-Atlantic Cooperation Council* (EACC), which provides a multilateral framework for the enhanced efforts within PfP concerning an expanded political dimension of partnership and practical cooperation. It complements the respective activities of the OSCE and other relevant institutions such as the European Union and the Council of Europe, and it provides the overarching framework for consultations among its members on a broad range of political and security-related issues. PfP in its enhanced form will be a clearly identifiable element within this flexible framework. The enhanced political dimension of consultation and co-operation which the EAPC offers allows Partners to develop a direct political relationship individually or in smaller groups with the Alliance. The Council is inclusive, in that opportunities for political consultation and practical co-operation are open to all Allies and Partners equally. It also maintains self-differentiation, in that Partners are able to decide for themselves the level and areas of co-operation with NATO, for example in political and security related matters; crisis management; regional matters; arms control issues; nuclear, biological and chemical (NBC) proliferation and defence issues; countering international terrorism; defence planning and budgets and defence policy and strategy, and security impacts of economic developments. There is also scope for consultations and cooperation on issues such as civil emergency and disaster preparedness; armaments cooperation under the aegis of the Conference of National Armaments Directors (CNAD); nuclear safety; defence related environmental issues; civil-military co-ordination of air traffic management and control; scientific co-operation, and issues related to peace support operations.

In parallel with NATO's enlarged membership and its increasing role as a major factor in the process of creating a 'European' identity it has undertaken a developing strategic partnership with the European Union, and has established the *NATO-Russia Permanent Joint Council* in order to provide a forum for consultation and cooperation between the two partners on matters of mutual concern including conflict prevention, peace-keeping and security policies. The 'Founding Act on Mutual Relations, Cooperation and Security between NATO and the Russian Federation' expressed *inter alia*, the resolve to reinforce the role of the OSCE as the major Pan-European organisation, and reiterated the commitment in the Helsinki Final Act to respect the sovereignty, independence, and territorial integrity of states, and to settle disputes peacefully. A special Charter with Ukraine was also established in 1997, and a Mediterranean Dialogue on a regular basis was agreed.

NATO's role in conflict limitation resulted in the operation undertaken in 2001 at the request of the Macedonian President in order to prevent conflict in Macedonia, which continued until the end of March 2003 when responsibility for this mission was handed over to the European Union; in restoring stability by its involvement in the former Yugoslavia (IFOR/SFOR) and in its military intervention in Kosovo in March 1999 and the subsequent deployment of the NATO-led Kosovo Force (KFOR) in June 1999; and whilst the European Union will resume assume responsibility for the NATO-led SFOR mission in Bosnia-Herzegovina towards the end of 2004, NATO is committed to maintaining a presence in the country. It is also committed to the International Security Assistance Force in Afghanistan and to the creation of the NATO Response Force by the year 2006.

The basic organisational and decision-making structure of NATO consists of the North Atlantic Council on which all member countries are represented by a Permanent Representative with the rank of Ambassador. The Council is supported by a number of subordinate committees and agencies. Its work is prepared and followed up by the International Staff, of which the Secretary General is the head. As Chairman of the Council and other senior decision-making bodies, the Secretary General is responsible for guiding the process of concensus-building among the member countries on which all NATO decisions are based. The work of the Council is also supported by the Millitary Committee and its Chairman, and by the International Millitary Staff under the guidance of its Director. Following a major reorganisation of the NATO International Staff undertaken in 2003, six substantive divisions were created to support the work of the North Atlantic Council and its subordinate bodies under the overall direction of the Secretary General. The organisation of the divisions reflects the principal roles and responsibilities of the organisation. They are the Division of Political Affairs and Security Policy, the Division of Defence Policy and Planning; the Operations Division; the Division of Defence Investment; the Division of Public Diplomacy and the Executive Management Division.

The NATO Military Structure is headed by the Military Committee on which all member states are represented. It is the primary source of military advice to the North Atlantic Council, Defence Planning Committee and Nuclear Planning Group and is responsible to these bodies for the overall conduct of the millitary affairs of the Alliance. It is divided into two Strategic Commands , the one operational and the other with more functional responsibilities relating to the transformation and development of NATO's military capabilities to bring them into line with the new challenges and tasks facing the Alliance. Allied Command Operations is located at Mons, Belgium and comes under the command of the Supreme Allied Commander Europe (SACEUR). Allied Command Transformation is under the command of the Supreme Allied Commander Transformation (SACT) and is located in Norfolk, Virginia, USA.

The NATO Headquarters and Secretariat, which also houses the Diplomatic representatives from the Alliance's Co-operation Partners, is in Brussels, and the NATO Defence College is in Rome. A number of other NATO civilian and military agencies are located in other Alliance member countries.

## ORGANISATION FOR ECONOMIC CO-OPERATION AND DEVELOPMENT

The OECD was established as a successor to the Organisation for European Economic Cooperation (OEEC) and came into being on 30 September 1961. Its objectives are to promote economic and social welfare throughout the OECD area by assisting its member governments in the formulation of policies designed to this end, and by co-ordinating these policies; and to stimulate and harmonise its members' aid efforts in favour of developing countries. The supreme body of the organisation is the Council, composed of one representative from each member country. It meets at permanent representative level (normally ambassadorial) approximately once a week under the chairmanship of the Secretary-General, and at ministerial level usually once a year under the chairmanship of a Minister elected annually. Decisions and Recommendations are adopted by mutual agreement of all members of the Council. The Council is assisted by an Executive Committee composed of fourteen of its members designated annually.

The major part of the Organisation's work is prepared and carried out in specialised committees and working parties of which there are about 200. These include Committees for economic policy; economic and development review; development assistance (DAC); trade; invisible transactions; financial markets; fiscal affairs; restrictive business practices; consumer policy; tourism, maritime transport; international investment and multinational enterprises; energy policy; industry; steel; scientific and technological policy; education; manpower and social affairs; environment;

agriculture; fisheries, etc. Four autonomous or semi-autonomous bodies also belong to the Organisation: the International Energy Agency (IEA); the Nuclear Energy Agency (NEA); the Development Centre; and the Centre for Educational Research and Innovation. In 1990 the Centre for Cooperation with the European Economics in Transition (CCEET) was established to act as the point of contact between the OECD and Central and Eastern European countries seeking guidance in moving towards a market economy.

Members of the OECD are Australia, Austria, Belgium, Canada, Czech Republic, Denmark, Finland, France, Germany, Greece, Hungary, Iceland, Ireland, Italy, Japan, Republic of Korea, Luxembourg, Mexico, The Netherlands, New Zealand, Norway, Poland, Portugal, Slovakia, Spain, Sweden, Switzerland, Turkey, the United Kingdom, and the United States of America. The Commission of the European Communities generally takes part in the work of the OECD. The Secretariat, headed by the Secretary-General, is in Paris.

# ORGANIZATION FOR SECURITY AND CO-OPERATION IN EUROPE

The OSCE (until 1994 the Conference on Security and Cooperation in Europe) has its roots in the Cold War confidence-building process based on the 1975 Helsinki Final Act, and developed its present form following the Charter of Paris for a New Europe in 1990, the Helsinki Summit of 1992 and the Budapest Summit of 1994. The current objectives of OSCE include conflict anticipation and prevention; arms control; human rights; the establishment of a Code of Conduct relating to military transparency and the role of the armed forces in democratic societies; and crisis management, in which connection it supervised the 1996 elections in Bosnia and Herzegovina in furtherance of the Dayton Accord.

The institutions of the OSCE are the OSCE Summit of Heads of State or Government which meets every two years; the Foreign Ministers Council which meets annually; the Senior Council of Political Directors which meets in Prague, and the Permanent Council of Delegates which meets in Vienna weekly. The OSCE Parliament Assembly meets annually and its Secretariat is in Copenhagen. The Office for Democratic Institutions and Human Rights, which is situated in Warsaw, is concerned specifically with human rights and the process of national elections; the office of the High Commissioner on National Minorities is in The Hague, and the Court of Conciliation and Arbitration is in Geneva. The Forum for Security Cooperation meets weekly in Vienna.

The factor which gives the OSCE especial significance is the composition of its membership, including as it does all the participants of the Cold War; and since it operates on the basis of unanimity it is the only regional organisation which provides a forum for creating a New European Order continent-wide with the participation of the USA. The significance of this special relationship between the former 'East' and 'West' was underlined in the 1997 Founding Act on Mutual Relations, Cooperation and Security between NATO and Russia which in the preamble defines the role of the OSCE as 'the inclusive and comprehensive organisation for consultation, decision-making and cooperation in its area' and as a Regional Arrangement under Chapter VIII of the UN Charter which makes provision for 'regional arrangements or agencies . . . dealing with . . . matters relating to the maintenance of international peace and security as are appropriate for regional action'. The two signatories agreed to 'help strengthen the OSCE in Europe', including developing further its role as a primary instrument in preventive diplomacy, conflict prevention, crisis management, post-conflict rehabilitation and regional security cooperation, as well as in enhancing its operational capabilities to carry out these tasks.

On this basis the OSCE has deployed Missions in several countries in the OSCE area including Bosnia and Herzegovina, Croatia, Estonia, Georgia, Latvia, Macedonia, Tajikistan, Moldova and Ukraine; and has established an Assistance Group in Chechnya acting on behalf of the Council of Europe. Apart from its role in supervising elections, and monitoring human rights, the OSCE also serves as a framework for conventional arms control and confidence-building measures. The 1994 Vienna Document obliges States to show transparency and predictability in their military activities; and a recently adopted military Code of Conduct sets out principles to guide the role of armed forces in democratic societies. Several mechanisms for settling disputes have also been developed.

The OSCE's Parliamentary Assembly meets once a year to discuss issues pertinent to OSCE affairs and consider declarations, recommendations and proposals to enhance security and co-operation in the OSCE area. The Assembly's Secretariat is located in Copenhagen. The organization has also established a Court of Conciliation and Arbitration in Geneva. Participating States, which are signatories to the Convention on Concilation and Arbitration, may submit a dispute to the Court for settlement by the Arbitral Tribunal or the Conciliation Commission. The OSCE is also the repository of the EU-initiated Pact on Stability.

Membership of the OSCE is Albania, Andorra, Armenia, Austria, Azerbaijan, Belarus, Belgium, Bosnia and Herzegovina, Bulgaria, Canada, Croatia, Cyprus, Czech Republic, Denmark, Estonia, Finland, France, Georgia, Germany, Greece, Hungary, Iceland, Ireland, Italy, Kazakhstan, Kyrgyzstan, Latvia, Liechtenstein, Lithuania, Luxembourg, Macedonia, Malta, Moldova, Monaco, The Netherlands, Norway, Poland, Portugal, Romania, Russia, San Marino, Slovakia, Slovenia, Spain, Sweden, Switzerland, Tajikistan, Turkey, Turkmenistan, Ukraine, United Kingdom, United States of America, Uzbekistan, Vatican City, Serbia and Montenegro. Partners for Cooperation are Japan and Korea; Mediterranean Partners are Algeria, Egypt, Israel, Morocco and Tunisia; and the Secretariat is in Vienna.

# ORGANIZATION OF AMERICAN STATES

The OAS has inherited a long tradition of cooperation in North, Central and South America and is today the supreme regional coordinating body for all matters affecting inter-state relations in this region. It is based on the 1948 Charter of the Organization of American States as amended by the 1967 Protocol of Buenos Aires, the 1985 Protocol of Cartagena de Indias, the 1992 Protocol of Washington and the 1993 Protocol of Managua.

The members of the Organization are: Antigua and Barbuda, Argentina, Bahamas, Barbados, Belize, Bolivia, Brazil, Canada, Chile, Colombia, Costa Rica, Cuba (suspended), Dominica, Dominican Republic, Ecuador, El Salvador, Grenada, Guatemala, Guyana, Haiti, Honduras, Jamaica, Mexico, Nicaragua, Panama, Paraguay, Peru, St Kitts and Nevis, St Lucia, St Vincent and the Grenadines, Surinam, Trinidad and Tobago, the United States of America, Uruguay and Venezuela. Permanent Observer status is accorded to thirty-seven states, and to the European Union.

Policy matters are determined by the General Assembly which meets annually and in occasional special sessions, and Consultative Meetings of Ministers of Foreign Affairs which are held when necessary. Three Councils, each composed of one representative of each member state, meet in Washington, where the General Secretariat is situated. These are the Permanent Council which supervises the work of the Organization and deals with matters of a political nature; the Inter-American Economic and Social Council; and the Inter-American Council for Education, Science and Culture. In addition, there are the Inter-American Judicial Committee, the Inter-American Commission on Human Rights and the Inter-American Development Bank (IDB).

# ORGANISATION OF THE ISLAMIC CONFERENCE

The OIC was founded in 1969 with the objective of strengthening Islamic Solidarity among member states; enhancing cooperation in the political, economic, social, cultural and scientific fields and promoting the struggle of all Muslim people to safeguard their dignity, independence and national rights. It coordinates action to safeguard the Holy Places and in supporting the struggle of the Palestinian people and assisting them in recovering their rights and liberating their occupied territories. In addition it will work to eliminate racial discrimination and all forms of colonialism, and to create a favourable atmosphere for the promotion of cooperation and understanding between member states and other countries. The Charter is based on full equality among member states; observation of the right to self-determination and non-interference in the internal affairs of member states; observation of sovereignity, independence, and territorial integrity of each state; the settlement of disputes between member states by peaceful means such as negotiations, mediation conciliation and arbitration and the pledge to refrain, in relations among member states, from resorting to force or threatening to resort to the use of force against the unity and territorial integrity or the political independance of any of them. Institutions of the Organisation are the OIC Summit and Ministerial Conferences, the Al-Quds Committee, the Islamic Commission on Economic, Cultural and Social Affairs and

Standing Committees for Information and Cultural Affairs; for Economic and Trade Cooperation and for Scientific and Technical Cooperation.

Members of OIC are Afghanistan, Albania, Azerbaijan, Bahrein, Bangladesh, Benin, Brunei, Burkina Faso, Cameroon, Chad, Comoros, Côte d'Ivoire, Djibouti, Egypt, Gabon, The Gambia, Guinea, Guinea-Bissau, Guyana, Indonesia, Iran, Iraq, Jordan, Kazakhstan, Kuwait, Kyrgyzstan, Lebanon, Libya, Maldives, Mali, Mauritiana, Morocco, Mozambique, Niger, Nigeria, Oman, Pakistan, Palestine, Qatar, Saudi Arabia, Senegal, Sierra Leone, Somalia, Sudan, Surinam, Syria, Tajikistan, Togo, Tunisia, Turkey, Turkmenistan, Uganda, United Arab Emirates, Uzbekistan and Yemen. Observer states are Bosnia and Herzegovina, Central African Republic and Thailand; and the Secretariat is in Jeddah.

# ORGANIZATION OF THE PETROLEUM EXPORTING COUNTRIES

OPEC was founded in 1960, and member states are Algeria, Indonesia, Iran, Iraq, Kuwait, Libya, Nigeria, Qatar, Saudi Arabia, the United Arab Emirates and Venezuela.

OPEC's prime objective is to ensure fair and stable petroleum prices for producers and a regular and efficient supply for consumers, and pricing policies have a considerable influence on those of most other oil-exporting countries. Regular meetings of OPEC Oil Ministers are held at intervals of six months, with provision for extraordinary meetings. The Secretariat of OPEC is in Vienna.

# SHANGHAI COOPERATION ORGANISATION

The main purposes of SCO are strengthening mutual trust and respect for each other's independence; cooperation in political social and economic affairs, and fostering democracy, justice and rationality. Members are China, Kazakhstan, Kyrgyzstan, Russia, Tajikistan and Uzbekistan, and the Secretariat is in Beijing.

# SOUTH ASIAN ASSOCIATION FOR REGIONAL COOPERATION

The South Asian Association for Regional Cooperation comprising Bangladesh, Bhutan, India, Maldives, Nepal, Pakistan and Sri Lanka was inaugurated at the first Summit meeting of the Heads of State and Heads of Government held in Dhaka, Bangladesh, in December 1985.

Institutionally, SAARC has four tiers: the annual Meetings of Heads of State or Government which constitute the supreme authority; the Council of Foreign Ministers which meets twice a year or additionally in extraordinary sessions and is responsible for the review and formulation of policy; the Standing Committee of Foreign Secretaries responsible for the overall coordination of policies and for identifying new areas of cooperation; the Programming Committee of senior officials responsible for organisation and administration; the Technical Committees, responsible for formulating programmes and projects, and Action Committees responsible for their implementation.

Areas of special cooperation are agriculture, communications, environment, health, population, meteorology, drug trafficking and abuse, rural development, science and technology, tourism, transport, and women in development. The initiative of special significance is the SAARC Audio Visual Exchange Programme which encourages the exchange of radio and television material in order to promote people-to-people understanding. Economic cooperation takes the form of the South Asian Development Fund and the formation in 1993 of the SAARC Preferential Trading Arrangement designed to liberalise, on a step-by-step basis, intra-regional trade and to make provision for the least developed countries in the region.

Decisions at all levels are taken on the basis of unanimity; bilateral and contentious issues are excluded from SAARC deliberations; regional cooperation is not held as a substitute for bilateral or multilateral cooperation, but as complementary to them; and cooperation is based on respect for the principles of sovereign equality, territorial integrity, political independence, and non-interference in internal affairs of other states.

Despite its diversity, SAARC provides a forum for cooperation, active collaboration and mutual assistance among the countries of the South Asian region in the economic, cultural, technological and scientific fields. It also highlights the objective of strengthening cooperation in international forums on matters of common interest and of enhancing mutual trust, understanding and appreciation of one another's problems. The Secretariat is in Kathmandu.

## SOUTH PACIFIC REGIONAL ORGANISATIONS

*The South Pacific Forum* (successor to the South Pacific Bureau for Economic Cooperation (SPEC)) is the major regional organisation in the South Pacific. It is an informal organisation concerned with a wide range of economic matters relating to cooperation within the South Pacific region, and equally with the region's external relations through meetings with 'dialogue partners': in particular, commodity marketing, industrial development, security, tourism, shipping, civil aviation, transfer of technology, oil prospecting and environmental protection. Membership is restricted to sovereign and self-governing states in the South Pacific (including Australia and New Zealand). It consists of an annual meeting of Heads of Governments at which political, as well as economic, matters are discussed and determined by consensus; the Forum Officials Committee consisting of one representative from each member state who implement overall policy, and the Secretariat which is based in Suva.

*The South Pacific Commission* (SPC) is concerned principally with rural development, youth and community development, *ad hoc* expert consultancies, cultural exchanges, training facilities and marine resource development and research. It consists of twenty-seven sovereign states and self-governing territories in the South Pacific including Australia and New Zealand, the United Kingdom and the United States of America. The Secretariat is in Noumeia, New Caledonia.

*The South Pacific Organisations Coordinating Committee* (SPOCC), as its name implies, seeks to enhance cooperation and avoid duplication of effort in the South Pacific region.

## SOUTHERN AFRICAN DEVELOPMENT COMMUNITY

The SADC was established by Treaty in 1992 and developed as a post-apartheid regional organisation of countries with common values and objectives. Its major aim is to create a momentum towards economic integration and close cooperation in the fields of security, conflict resolution, transport and the maintenance of democratic institutions. Military forces from Angola, Namibia and Zimbabwe have participated in the Democratic Republic of the Congo under the auspices of SADC.

Heads of State meet annually and Foreign Ministers twice yearly; and member countries are Angola, Botswana, Congo Democratic Republic Lesotho, Malawi, Mauritius, Mozambique, Namibia, Seychelles, South Africa, Swaziland, Tanzania, Zambia and Zimbabwe. The Secretariat of SADC is in Gaborone.

## VISEGRÁD GROUP

The Visegrád Group is a regional organisation for the coordination of mutual inter- ests: the members being the Czech Republic, Hungary, Poland and Slovakia. The major initiative was the Central European Free Trade Area, joined subsequently by Slovenia and Romania.

## WEST AFRICAN INTER-GOVERNMENTAL ECONOMIC GROUPINGS

There are over thirty inter-governmental economic groupings in West Africa. To a large extent they are the product of the historical differences within the region, and most have the same objectives of economic harmonisation and eventual integration. The most important are:

*The Economic Community of West African States*, created at Lagos on the 28 May 1975 to promote economic development in West Africa by establishing a common market (based on the progressive elimination of all discrimination between national boundaries) and harmonising a variety of economic policies including agricultural policies, industrial development plans and monetary policies, co-operation for the development of energy and mineral resources and for the joint development of infra-structure. In addition it agreed to add 'Political Cooperation' to its objectives in 1993, and has accepted responsibility for organising military peace-keeping forces in the area in terms of the 1981 Protocol of Mutual Assistance and Defence; the ECOWAS Monitoring Group (ECOMOG) being established for this purpose.

ECOWAS is the 'umbrella' organisation for the various economic integration groupings in West Africa consisting, as it does, of sixteen members: five are anglophone – The Gambia, Ghana, Liberia, Nigeria and Sierra Leone; eight are francophone – Benin, Burkina Faso, Côte d'Ivoire, Guinea, Mali, Niger, Senegal and Togo; two are Lusophone – Cape Verde and Guinea Bissau, and one arabic-speaking – Mauritania. ECOWAS operates on the basis of an annual Conference of Heads of State, meetings of the Council of Ministers at least once a year, a Tribunal which interprets the provisions of the Treaty and resolves disputes, a Fund for Cooperation and Development, the ECOBANK, six Specialised Commissions and an Executive Secretariat based in Abuja.

*The Council of the Entente States* is one of the oldest groupings, founded in 1959 by Benin, Burkina Faso, and Côte d'Ivoire and joined by Togo on 3 June 1966. It is an informal organisation for the coordination of economic policies among member states, and has a Mutual Aid and Guarantee Fund for economic cooperation.

*The River Niger Commission or the River Niger Basin Authority* (RNC) was established in October 1983 by Benin, Burkina Faso, Cameroon, Côte d'Ivoire, Mali, Niger and Nigeria for promoting, encouraging and coordinating studies and programmes related to the development of the Niger Basin.

*The Organisation for the Development of the Senegal River* was established in 1972 in Nouakchott by Mali, Mauritania and Senegal, and is open to all states through which the river flows provided that they accept the spirit and letter of the Convention.

*The Economic and Monetary Union of West Africa* (UEMOA) through its central bank, the Banque Centrale des Etats de l'Afrique de l'Ouest (BCEAO), undertakes the linkage of member states' currencies. It consists of Benin, Burkina Faso, Côte D'Ivoire, Mali, Mauritania, Niger, Senegal and Togo, and the aim is regional economic cooperation for their development through free trade in products of local origin (such as livestock, agricultural products, fish and mineral products) that have not undergone industrial processing (i.e. raw materials); a special preferential import duty regime (the regional cooperation tax) for traded manufactured products that originate in member states; and the establishment of a common external tariff.

WEST AFRICAN CURRENCY UNION

Proposed single currency system for West African countries that meet specified convergence criteria, particularly relating to inflation, budget deficits and debt GDP ratio. Members are The Gambia, Ghana, Guiné, Liberia, Nigeria and Sierra Leone.


# WORLD TRADE ORGANIZATION

The WTO, which is the successor to the General Agreement on Tariffs and Trade (GATT), was established on 1 January 1995, and is the legal and institutional basis of the multilateral trading system. It now has 147 member-states, and provides the principal contractual obligations determining how governments frame and implement domestic trade legislation and regulations, and it is the platform on which trade relations among countries evolve through collective debate, negotiation and adjudication. The essential functions of the WTO are: administering and implementing the multilateral and plurilateral trade agreements which together make up the WTO; acting as a forum for multilateral trade negotiations; seeking to resolve trade disputes; overseeing national trade policies, and cooperating with other international institutions involved in global economic policy-making.

In accordance with the 'most favoured nation' (MFN) clause, members are bound to grant to the products of other members no less favourable treatment than that accorded to the products of any other country. The commitment to 'national treatment' requires that once goods have entered a market, they must be treated no less favourably than the equivalent domestically produced good. Quotas are generally outlawed, but tariffs or customs duties are legal in the WTO. Tariff reductions made by over 120 countries in the GATT Uruguay Round are contained in national tariff schedules which are considered an integral part of the WTO. The Tariff reductions, for the most part phased in over five years, will result in a 40 per cent cut in industrial countries' tariffs on industrial products, from an average of 6.3 per cent to 3.8 per cent.

Members have also undertaken an initial set of commitments covering national regulations affecting various services activities. These commitments are, like those for tariffs, contained in binding national schedules. In addition, the WTO extends and clarifies previous GATT rules that laid down the basis on which governments could impose compensating duties on two forms of 'unfair' competition: dumping and subsidies. The WTO Agreement on agriculture is designed to provide increased fairness in farm trade; that on intellectual property will improve conditions of competition where ideas and inventions are involved, and another will do the same for trade in services. GATT provisions intended to favour developing countries are maintained in the WTO, in particular those encouraging industrialised countries to assist trade of developing nations. Developing countries are given transition periods to adjust to the more difficult WTO provisions. Least-developed countries are given even more flexibility, and benefit from accelerated implementation of market access concessions for their goods.

The highest WTO authority is the Ministerial Conference which meets every two years, whilst the day-to-day work falls to a number of subsidiary bodies, principally the General Council, which also convenes as the Dispute Settlement Body and as the Trade Policy Review Body. The General Council delegates responsibility to three other major bodies – namely the Councils for Trade in Goods, Trade in Services and Trade-Related Aspects of Intellectual Property Rights. Four other bodies established by the Ministerial Conference report to the General Council: the Committee on Trade and Development, the Committee on Balance of Payments, the Committee on Trade and Environment, and the Committee on Budget, Finance and Administration. The plurilateral agreements of the WTO – those on civil aircraft, government procurement, dairy products and bovine meat – have their own management bodies which report to the General Council.

The WTO is headed by its Director-General and four Deputy Directors-General. The Secretariat is responsible for servicing WTO delegate bodies with respect to negotiations and the implementation of agreements. It has a particular responsibility to provide technical support to developing countries, and especially the least-developed countries. WTO economists and statisticians provide trade performance and trade policy analyses, while its legal staff assist in the resolution of trade disputes involving the interpretation of WTO rules and precedents. Other Secretariat work is concerned with accession negotiations for new members and providing advice to governments considering membership. The WTO budget is calculated on the basis of shares in the total trade conducted by members. Part of the budget also goes to the International Trade Centre. The Secretariat is located in Geneva.

# INTERNATIONAL LAW AND PRACTICE

'A law dependent for its existence on the consent of its subjects, without legislature for its creation or alteration, lacking effective machinery of enforcement, difficult to ascertain and regularly disregarded is no law at all.' Discuss.*

## DEFINITION AND GENERAL PRINCIPLES

International law is the outcome of man's endeavours to extend into the field of inter-state relations the rule of law and the respect for order which (ideally) exists within the state. The period since the end of the Cold War, however, has not been an encouraging one for its advocates. Whether in the field of recognition, extradition or the use of force, international law has been ignored, contravened or perhaps worse, abused in the political interest.

Basically – and traditionally – international law is defined as the body of rules governing the relations between states. However, since the rapid evolution of the concepts of social and interstate responsibilities resulting from postwar factors and events (e.g. the creation of new states and increased involvement of the individual) and reflected in the development of the United Nations, a wider definition of the term has become necessary. The following is J.G. Starke's definition as contained in his *Introduction to International Law*.

International law may be defined as that body of law which is composed for its greater part of the principles and rules of conduct which states feel themselves bound to observe, and therefore, do commonly observe in their relations with each other, and which include also:
(a) the rules of law relating to the functioning of international institutions or organisations, their relations with each other and their relations with states and individuals; and
(b) certain rules of law relating to individuals and non-state entities so far as the rights or duties of such individuals and non-state entities are the concern of the international community.

---

* Tutorial essay question set by Professor Maurice Mendelson Q.C. to members of the Oxford University Foreign Service Programme.

Although international law is the subject of much debate and opposing viewpoints, there are certain areas of almost complete agreement (e.g. piracy on the high seas and the immunities of diplomats), just as at the other end of the spectrum there are areas of considerable disagreement. It cannot thus be claimed that it is a subject merely for academic lawyers; but on the other hand it could be argued that 'international law' was, in some respects, a contradiction in terms. It is something of a paradox, attracting both disciples and sceptics: those who, with missionary zeal, see it as the path to world peace and righteousness; and those who maintain that without legislature or international sanctions there can be no international law. Both views are to some extent valid, and its relevance in diplomatic relations lies in the fact that considerations of international law do in fact influence governments and provide standards of international behaviour which they acknowledge as being the ideal, even though they may not always manage to live up to them, and even though they often use it as a basis of criticism of other states even if they do not always comply scrupulously themselves. But like all good causes, international law is liable to be the subject of evil designs, and politicians the world over are not slow to invoke and if necessary distort its principles when it suits their purposes, or to disclaim them if they should prove to be embarrassing. It is thus a subject that diplomats must be acquainted with, but handle with care. The sources of international law are, in brief: treaties, custom, general principles of law, judicial precedents and the writings of leading authorities.

The following topics have been selected as being of interest to diplomats and as a basis for further study; it is not pretended that issues of international law can be effectively reduced to simple generalisations and to imprecise non-legal terminology.

# TREATIES AND TREATY-MAKING

## GENERAL PRINCIPLES

States enter into treaty relationships when they agree with each other or with a group of other states to undertake certain commitments. Treaties invariably take the form of documents, though a verbal undertaking could be claimed to have the same validity as a written one.

Treaties (to use the general term) may be made in different forms, such as between Heads of State; between states; between governments (to some extent in the order of their importance and formality, but often depending on whim or custom). Such treaties are equally binding on the states concerned even though they may be expressed as agreements between Heads of State or governments.

## TYPES OF TREATIES

The instruments recording international agreements have various titles, such as agreement, arrangement, convention, declaration, exchange of notes, general act, *modus vivendi, procès-verbale*, protocol, or statute. All have equal validity but vary in form and wording; and as far as practice in the USA is concerned ratification by the Senate is required for treaties, but 'executive agreements' can be concluded either following Congressional approval or upon constitutional authority. Generally speaking, bilateral instruments take the form of a treaty, agreement, exchange of notes or *modus vivendi* (in the order of their importance and formality); and multilateral instruments take the form of treaty or convention unless they are on a grand scale when such terms as general act or statute apply. A Final Act is a series of agreements or treaties resulting from a conference, each one of which requires specific approval.

A *protocol of signature*, which is rarely used, has a particular function in that it may be used as a sort of 'postscript' to a treaty. It is considered by the negotiators to be part of the treaty but is written and signed as a separate document. It is less formal than the treaty it accompanies and may record reservations by certain signatories, clarification of points in the treaty, or other subsidiary considerations. It may be used after a short period to record a further point of agreement.

A *'protocol'*, which is often used, is an international agreement that is usually supplementary to, or amends, a treaty. An *exchange of letters* may be attached to a treaty for roughly similar purposes, but these are a rather less formal record of intentions and are not necessarily signed by the negotiators. However, an *exchange of notes* (or letters) is more normally made independently of a treaty, as a less formal means of recording agreement between states.

## THE PROCESS OF TREATY-MAKING

### (a)  Accreditation and full powers

Heads of State, Heads of Government and Foreign Ministers (as well as, in certain circumstances, Ambassadors) are presumed to have the power to commit their state by virtue of their Office. The process of treaty-making requires that other persons who conduct the negotiations on behalf of the states concerned should be able to prove that they are authorised to do so; that is to say that they should be able to establish their *credentials.* These usually take the form of a letter signed by or on behalf of the Minister for Foreign Affairs.

If a treaty or other international instrument is to be concluded and signed at bilateral negotiations or at a multilateral conference, representatives must be provided with *full powers*.

A typical example of full powers issued to a delegate to a plenipotentiary conference would be as follows:

Whereas, for the better treating of and arranging certain matters which may come into discussion between the Government of ... and the Governments of certain other Powers and States represented at the forthcoming Conference [name of Conference] to be held at ... on ... it is expedient that a fit person should be invested with Full Power to conduct the said discussion on the part of the Government of ... : I, [name in full] Minister for Foreign Affairs, do hereby certify that

[name in full, decorations and official designation of the leader of the delegation]

is by these Presents named, constituted and appointed as Plenipotentiary and Representative having Full Power and Authority to agree and conclude with such Plenipotentiaries and Representatives as may be vested with similar Power and Authority on the part of the Governments aforesaid any Treaty, Convention, Agreement, Protocol or other Instrument that may tend to the attainment of the above-mentioned end, and to sign for the Government of ... everything so agreed upon and concluded. Further, I do hereby certify that whatever things shall be so transacted and concluded by the said Plenipotentiary and Representative shall, subject if necessary to Ratification by the Government of ... be agreed to, acknowledged and accepted by the said Government of ... in the fullest manner. In witness whereof I have signed these Presents and affixed hereto my Seal. Signed and sealed at the Ministry of Foreign Affairs (place) ... the ... day of ... Two thousand ... ...

*Seal*                                                    Signature of Minister
                                                            for Foreign Affairs

At conferences in which a large number of states are participating, it is customary for a Credentials or a Full Powers Committee to be established for the purpose of confirming the powers and authenticity of the delegates.

*(b)  Negotiation*
The negotiation of a treaty is normally preceded by an understanding between the states concerned – sometimes a *letter of intent* – as to the general purpose and likely outcome of its proceedings. In the case of multilateral negotiations an *agenda* is usually agreed in advance. In the case of bilateral treaties it is usual for the governments to outline the pattern of negotiations and to subdivide them under specific *heads of agreement*. It may then be found advisable to refer certain heads to technical or specialist subcommittees so that their conclusions can be considered by the negotiators at a plenary session. The art of negotiation needs no elaboration: it is the skill and patience of the marketplace elevated to a higher plane. Negotiators, however, are usually limited in their conduct by written instructions from their government – their 'brief' – and by the availability of the telephone, fax or e-mail which enables them to refer back all major problems for decision.

### (c) *Authentication and signature of the text*

When a document has been agreed it is either initialled, signed, or signed *ad referendum* by the negotiating representatives. Initialling normally signifies merely the establishment of an authentic text, and further action is required to signify the consent of the states to be bound. Signature *ad referendum* requires confirmation by the state concerned to constitute full signature. If the treaty is 'subject to ratification', signature is of limited significance. In other cases, whether the signature of the properly accredited delegate makes the treaty binding on his state or not depends on the intention as shown by the terms of the treaty, e.g. with regard to its entry into force; as agreed during the negotiations, or as otherwise indicated, e.g. by the terms of the relevant full powers. Multilateral treaties may in most instances be signed with reservations if these are not excluded by the terms of the treaty or incompatible with its object and purpose.

### (d) *Ratification*

Where ratification is stipulated (or understood) a treaty is referred to the governments of the negotiating parties for confirmation. Ratification in the international law sense is an executive act: whether or not this is effected before the national legislature gives it approval or legislates to implement the treaty being a matter of domestic law and practice. A state is under no legal obligation to ratify a treaty agreed by its own delegate, but its choice of action is usually limited to acceptance or complete rejection – though in exceptional cases, ratification may be made with reservations, these being usually of a procedural rather than substantive nature. It cannot normally ask to reopen negotiations with a view to introducing amendments. Ratification is not retroactive to the date of the signature of the treaty (unless special provision is made to this effect).

### (e) *Acceptance*

In some instances provision may be made for the 'acceptance' of treaties as an alternative to ratification, accession or adherence. The practice is a new one, intended to meet constitutional difficulties of certain states; it mainly relates to United Nations Conventions, some of which contain an acceptance formula clause. Acceptance is effected by the deposit of an instrument of acceptance.

### (f) *Accession or adherence*

Provision may be made in treaties (normally multilateral) for subsequent accession or adherence (occasionally adhesion) by states which did not originally sign the treaty. The two terms are generally considered to be synonymous, but it is sometimes held that 'accession' is used to apply to the whole treaty, and 'adherence' to only part of it. Accession or adherence can take place only with the consent of all signatories of the treaty, and where it is considered to be acceptable a permissive clause to this effect is usually included in the treaty.

*(g) Exchange or deposit of ratifications*

The signature of an instrument of ratification on behalf of a state has in itself little significance in international law; it is only the exchange of instruments of ratification that gives them effect – or, as is usual in the case of multilateral conventions, their being deposited with the depositary. (The depositary may be a government or the secretariat of an organisation.) The exchange or deposit of ratification is usually effected and recorded by means of a *procès-verbale*. Instruments of ratification are signed by the Head of State, by the head of government or by the Minister for Foreign Affairs, depending on the importance of the issue.

*(h) Registration and publication*

Article 102 of the United Nations Charter stipulates that all treaties and international agreements entered into by member states shall be registered with the Secretariat and published by it. Failure to do so (on either part) does not invalidate the treaty; but it has the consequence that the treaty may not be invoked before the International Court of Justice or any other organ of the United Nations.

THE FORM AND CONTENT OF TREATIES

Treaties can normally be divided into three parts:

1. *The preamble*, somewhat formal in style, setting out the names of the parties to the agreement, the names of the plenipotentiaries and the object of the agreement, e.g.

> The Republic of X and the Kingdom of Y
> Desiring to facilitate ...........................................................................
> Having in mind ................................................................................
> Having resolved to conclude a Treaty of ...........................................
> and have appointed as their Plenipotentiaries for this purpose:
>
> > The Republic of X: The Hon. A.B.C.
> > The Kingdom of Y: His Excellency D.E.F.
>
> Who, having communicated their respective full powers, found in good and due form, have agreed as follows . . .

2. *The terms or substance of the agreement*, known as the substantive clauses.

3. *The administrative clauses* or final clauses (sometimes known as the *clauses protocolaires*) which include provision for some or all of the following:

> The date or method of entry into force of the treaty
> The duration and method of termination of the treaty
> Definition of terms

The method of settlement of any dispute
Reservations
Accession to the treaty by other states
Amendment or review
The languages of the treaty which are to be authoritative
Ratification, and deposit of instruments of ratification
Registration with the United Nations

and invariably:

Date and place of signature
Signature (and sometimes seal) of plenipotentiaries.

## THE VALIDITY OF TREATIES

A treaty is essentially a contract between states, and its validity may theoretically be challenged by one or more of the parties concerned on various grounds, which are specified in Articles 48–53 of the Vienna Convention on the Law of Treaties in particular. These are:

*Error* relating to a fact or situation which was assumed by the state concerned to exist at the time when the treaty was concluded and which formed an essential basis of its consent to be bound by the treaty (except if that state contributed by its own conduct to the error or if the circumstances were such as to put the state on notice of a possible error).

*Fraud*, i.e. when a state has been induced to conclude a treaty by the fraudulent conduct of another negotiating state.

*Corruption of a representative* of a state.

*Coercion of a representative* of a state.

*Coercion of a state* by the threat or use of force.

Breach of *jus cogens*: i.e. treaties conflicting with a peremptory norm of general international law. A 'peremptory norm' in this context is one accepted and recognised by the international community of states as a whole as a norm from which no derogation is permitted and which can be modified only by a subsequent norm of general international law having the same character. Such norms are rare: examples are the prohibition of genocide, slavery and aggression.

No general rule can be given to cover the case where a treaty which is signed in good faith proves to be incompatible with the terms of an earlier treaty – a situation capable of arising as between a bilateral agreement and a multilateral agreement possibly through the oversight of an archivist. So far as the provisions of the United Nations Charter are concerned, article 103 stipulates that obligations under the Charter shall have precedence over all others in the event of conflict.

## THE TERMINATION OF TREATIES

A treaty may legitimately come to an end by the agreement of the parties concerned; at the expiry of the time limit provided in the treaty, or by parties making use of a termination clause provided in the treaty. Varying degrees of legitimacy can be claimed for such unilateral action in the event of:

(a) a fundamental change having taken place in the circumstances which existed at the time the treaty was drawn up;

(b) the extinction of the other contracting party as a state (in a bilateral treaty) in such a way that the successor state does not inherit rights or obligations under this treaty;

(c) the outbreak of war;

(d) the denunciation of a multilateral treaty by such a number of the parties as to render the treaty inoperative;

(e) a material breach of the treaty by another party to it.

The other major source of International Law is Customary International Law. Treaties normally derogate from customary rules, unless they conflict with a rule of *jus cogens* (see above). But there remain quite a few areas of International Law where treaties have made only limited in roads into Customary International Law (e.g. the law of state responsibility). Essentially the constant and uniform practice of States gives rise to an obligation (or right, as the case may be) – usually for all States – to conform to that practice. The details are somewhat complicated, but are usefully set out in the International Law Association's London Principles on the Formation of Customary International Law.*

## POLITICAL ASYLUM AND THE EXTRADITION OF CRIMINALS

There are two categories of political asylum: *territorial asylum* (i.e. granted by a state to an alien in its territory) and *diplomatic asylum* (i.e. in the premises of a diplomatic mission or other such premises entitled to inviolability). Instances of the former are many, and groups of 'political refugees' are to be found in most states; but because they are living in a different country they are no great embarrassment to their own government.

---

\* International Law Association, International Committee on the Formation of Customary (General) International Law, *Final Report of the Committee, including London Statement of Principles relating to the Formation of General Customary International Law*, Sections 28-32, in International Law Association, *Report of 69th Conference* (2000), 712-777: also on internet at http://www.ilahq.org/html/layout_committee.htm.

A different situation arises in instances of diplomatic asylum, when the political offender is able to live protected and unmolested in his own country and in the midst of his fellow-countrymen whom he is presumably attempting to turn against their government.

As a general principle, a state has the right and the duty in cases covered by the Refugee Convention to grant asylum to aliens within its own territory ('territorial asylum'), and the onus is on the state wishing to extradite them to show why they should be given up. If on the other hand a state has given refuge in one of its missions to a national of the state in which it is situated it is up to the head of that mission, or his government, to justify the action.

## DIPLOMATIC ASYLUM

The inviolability of the premises of a diplomatic mission has traditionally rendered them liable to be sought as a place of refuge. The question of the existence and validity of this right of asylum from political persecution (it is not normally applicable in ordinary criminal cases) remains dormant for long periods, only to be the subject of acrimonious discussion from time to time. In Europe the practice is nearly extinct. It is a situation that can, in the end, be resolved only by negotiation, if only because the Vienna Convention on Diplomatic Relations, whilst ensuring the inviolability of the premises of a diplomatic mission (and thus of those within it) makes no provision for the departure under safe conduct of any person not covered by the Convention. In some regions, local usage sanctions its continuation even though diplomatic asylum is not recognised as existing in terms of Customary International Law. The Latin American practice, which may usefully serve as a practical approach to an evolving problem of humanitarian application, may be summarised on the basis of the Convention on Diplomatic Asylum drawn up by the Tenth Inter-American Conference held in Caracas in 1954, as follows:

1. Every state has the right to grant asylum, and to determine for itself the nature of the offence or the motives for the persecution of the person seeking asylum.
2. In the context of the granting of asylum, a legation includes not only the seat of a regular diplomatic mission and the residence of the head of mission, but also any other premises provided by the mission for the asylees when their number exceeds the normal capacity of the buildings.
3. Asylum may not be granted except in urgent cases and for the period of time strictly necessary for the asylee to depart from the country with the guarantees granted by the government of the territorial state.
4. Urgent cases are understood to be those, among others, in which the individual is being sought by persons or mobs over whom the authorities have lost control, or by the authorities themselves, and is in danger of being deprived of his life or liberty because of political persecution and cannot, without risk, ensure his safety in any other way. It shall rest with the state granting asylum to determine the degree of urgency of the case.

5. It is not lawful to grant asylum to persons who, at the time of requesting it, are under indictment or on trial for common offences or have been convicted by competent regular courts and have not served the respective sentence, nor to deserters from land, sea, and air forces, save when the acts giving rise to the request for asylum are clearly of a political nature.

6. Immediately asylum is granted the fact must be reported to the Minister for Foreign Affairs of the state of the person who has secured asylum, or to the local administrative authorities if the act occurred outside the capital.

7. The government of the state has the right to require that the asylee be sent out of the national territory within the shortest possible time; and the diplomatic agent of the country which has granted asylum in turn has the right to require that the asylee be permitted to leave the territory; and in both instances the necessary guarantee of safe conduct and inviolability must be provided.

8. Asylees enjoying safe conduct may not be deposited at any point in or near the national territory from which they have sought asylum.

9. While enjoying asylum, refugees shall not be allowed to perform acts contrary to the public peace.

10. If, as a consequence of a rupture of diplomatic relations, the diplomatic representative who granted asylum has to leave the territorial state, he must be allowed to leave with the asylees, or if this is not possible, he may surrender them to the diplomatic mission of a third state.

11. The fact that the government of the territorial state is not recognised by the state granting asylum does not prejudice the application of the general principles set out above; nor does their application imply recognition.

## EXTRADITION

Extradition is the forcible removal of a person from one state to another to stand trial or suffer imprisonment for an alleged offence; and requests for extradition arise when a person who is accused or convicted of a criminal offence seeks refuge (or is at the time resident) in another state. Normally the alleged crime will have been committed in the state seeking extradition or aboard a ship flying its flag. Applications for extradition are made through diplomatic channels, and are reasonably straightforward where both states have agreed to specific principles in advance through the medium of an Extradition Treaty. The following principles are normally embodied in such treaties and are applied even where no treaty exists, though practice varies to a considerable extent between countries:

(a) The person whose extradition is sought must be a national of the state seeking his extradition, or a national of a third state. It is not normally the practice for a state to hand over one of its own nationals at the request of another state, though the United Kingdom and the United States of America are exceptions to this general rule.

(b) The alleged offence for which extradition is sought must be a grave one, it must normally be an offence in both states involved, and adequate details of the individual's implication must be provided. Offences for which extradition is not normally applicable include political offences, military offences such as desertion (unless this comes within the scope of the legislation of the host state, e.g. a Visiting Forces Act), and religious offences.

The Council of Europe *European Convention on Extradition* contains the following more specific circumstances in which extradition shall *not* be applicable:
(a)  if the offence in respect of which it is requested is regarded by the requested party (i.e. state) as a political offence *or as an offence connected with a political offence*;
(b)  if the requested party has substantial grounds for believing that a request for extradition for an ordinary criminal offence has been made for the purpose of prosecuting or punishing a person on account of his race, religion, nationality or political opinion ...

These provisions are qualified to the extent that the taking or attempted taking of the life of a Head of State or a member of his family shall not be deemed to be a political offence for the purposes of the Convention. Other principles are common in both bilateral and multilaterals e.g. the principle of speciality (prosecution for an offence other than that specified) or *ne bis in idem* (no double jeopardy).

Special provision relating *inter alia* to extradition has been made in respect of crimes against internationally protected persons in the United Nations Convention on the Prevention and Punishment of Crimes against Internationally Protected Persons, including Diplomatic Agents of 14 December 1973 (the New York Convention).

# RECOGNITION OF STATES AND GOVERNMENTS

## STATES

The question of recognition of states arises when a state undergoes a fundamental change; it may change territorially, or disappear altogether or a new state or states may emerge as a result of cession, amalgamation, federation, secession or subdivision. There are two main schools of thought in international law concerning recognition of states: one is that recognition makes the state, legally speaking; the other that recognition is merely the formal acceptance of an established fact. In the practice of many states recognition of a new state is essentially a political decision; but it is generally accepted that a state must have a defined territory, a permanent population and a sovereign government which commands the obedience of the populace and has the capacity to enter into relations with other states.

## GOVERNMENTS

Governments also are capable of radical and unconstitutional change, but recognition of a new government in such circumstances is usually granted provided that it is in effective control of much the greater part of the state territory and has the obedience of the mass of the population, and that its control has a reasonable prospect of permanency.

Until recently it was the policy of the British government to make a formal announcement when it had decided to 'recognise' a new government of doubtful legitimacy, but, in company with several others, has now desisted from this practice mainly on the grounds that 'recognition' can be mistaken for 'approval'. Its present attitude on whether or not a new regime should be treated by the British Courts as a government is that it is left to be inferred from the nature of its dealings with it; and in particular whether or not it is dealing with it on a normal government-to-government basis.

*De facto* recognition of governments enables them to exercise the normal international functions of a sovereign state with reciprocal responsibilities in international law, but usually does not enable them to conclude and formally sign bilateral treaties, establish formal diplomatic relations or issue Consular *exequaturs*: these acts are considered to imply or require recognition *de jure*. Recognition *de facto* is generally accepted as an indication that recognition *de jure* will, if all goes well, be accorded in due time. It is often used when there is an element of doubt as to the permanency or legitimacy of the government so recognised. In the event of civil war, the situation may arise in which a substantial part of the territory of a state is held and administered by an administration other than that of the *de jure* government. Practice, in these rare circumstances, varies between countries, but it is possible for the rebel administration to be granted *de facto* recognition in that part of the territory that it administers. A state's international obligations and rights are not affected by a change of government.

# THE EXTENT OF STATE SOVEREIGNTY AND JURISDICTION

## SOVEREIGNTY

The territorial sovereignty of a state extends over the land within the state frontier and the air space above it, but not to the upper air (outer space). In the case of maritime states, sovereignty also extends, with certain limitations, over the internal waters and the territorial sea; and the state has a measure of control over the contiguous zone, the exclusive economic zone and the continental shelf. The international regime for determining maritime legality is based mainly on the 1958 Geneva Convention and the 1982 Law of the Sea Convention.

The major provisions of the Conventions include:

Coastal states exercise sovereignty over their *territorial sea* up to twelve nautical miles in extent, but foreign vessels are allowed 'innocent passage' through these waters for purposes of peaceful navigation, and permission to overfly is subject to the approval of the coastal state.

All ships and aircraft of all countries are entitled to 'transit passage' through *straits used for international navigation*, as long as they proceed without delay and without threatening the coastal states. States bordering the straits will be able to apply generally accepted international regulations and pollution control, but may not hamper or impede transit.

*Archipelagic states*, made up of a group or groups of closely related islands and interconnecting waters, have sovereignty over the sea area enclosed by straight lines drawn (subject to some limitations) between the outermost points of the islands. Ships and aircraft of all other states enjoy the right of passage through sea lanes designated by the archipelagic state.

Coastal states have sovereign rights in a 200-nautical-mile *exclusive economic zone* (EEZ) with respect to natural resources and most economic activities, and are also entitled to have a certain degree of jurisdiction over scientific research and environmental protection. All other states have freedom of navigation and overflight in the zone, as well as freedom to lay submarine cables and pipelines. When coastal states cannot fully utilise the resources available, they should provide access for other states, with a certain preference for specified categories of states.

Delimitation of overlapping economic zones is to be effected by agreement on the basis of international law in order to achieve an equitable solution.

Coastal states have sovereign rights over the *continental shelf* for the purpose of exploring and exploiting it without affecting the legal status of the water or air space above. The shelf extends at least to 200 nautical miles from the shore, and further where there is an actual physical prolongation. A Commission on the Limits of the Continental Shelf makes recommendations to states on the shelf's outer boundaries. Coastal states are to share with the international community part of the revenue they derive from exploiting oil and other resources from any part of their shelf beyond 200 nautical miles. The 1982 Convention provides for delimitation of overlapping shelves in terms identical with those relating to the EEZ.

All states enjoy the traditional freedoms of navigation, overflight, scientific research and fishing on the *high seas*. They have the obligation to adopt, or cooperate with other states in adopting, measures to manage and conserve living resources.

The territorial sea, the exclusive economic zone and the continental shelf of islands are to be determined in accordance with rules applicable to land territory, but rocks which cannot sustain human habitation or economic life will have no economic zone or continental shelf.

States bordering enclosed or semi-enclosed seas are expected to cooperate on the management of living resources and on environmental and research policies and activities.

Land-locked states have the right of access to and from the sea, and enjoy freedom of transit through the territory of transit states by all means of transport, subject to agreement.

A 'parallel system' (as amended in 1994) provides for the exploration and exploitation of *the international sea-bed area*. All activities in the area are deemed to be under the control of the International Sea-Bed Authority, which is responsible for supervising the recovery of minerals from the sea-bed, and which has its headquarters in Kingston, Jamaica.

All marine scientific research in the exclusive economic zone and on the continental shelf is subject to the consent of the coastal state, but such states shall, in normal circumstances, grant consent to foreign states when pure scientific research is to be conducted for peaceful purposes as laid down in Article 246 of the Convention. A coastal state can deny permission for such research or insist on its cessation, but only under circumstances defined in the Convention. In the event of a dispute, the researching state can require the coastal states to submit the matter to international conciliation on the grounds that it is not acting in a manner compatible with the Convention.

States are bound to promote the development and *transfer of marine technology* on fair and reasonable terms and conditions. This will be done with proper regard for all legitimate interests, including the rights and duties of holders, suppliers and recipients of technology.

States are obliged to settle by peaceful means their *disputes over the interpretation or application of the Convention*. When they cannot agree on the means of settlement, they have to submit most types of disputes to a compulsory procedure entailing decisions binding on all parties. They have four options: an International Tribunal for the Law of the Sea, established under the Convention; the International Court of Justice; arbitration; and special arbitration procedures for special types of dispute. Certain types of disputes have to be submitted to conciliation, a procedure whose outcome is not binding on the parties.

## JURISDICTION

The jurisdiction of a state is generally recognised as extending over all persons, property, acts and events within its territory; and for this purpose its territory includes the Territorial Sea. However, it is customary for a state to exercise restraint in applying jurisdiction in respect of offences committed on board foreign ships by foreign nationals, provided that the general peace is not disturbed and that the crime is not a grave one; and particularly if the consular representative of the country concerned is seen to be in control of the situation. Jurisdiction also relates to aircraft registered in, and ships flying the flag of, a state and to a state's nationals abroad, as well as universal jurisdiction over pirates and war criminals.

However, even where a state has jurisdiction to *prescribe* laws for persons (e.g. its nationals) or things (e.g. aircraft) abroad, it does not normally have jurisdiction to *enforce* those laws in a foreign territory without the consent of that territory's government.

# NATIONALITY

The possession of a nationality grants privileges to an individual and correspondingly imposes obligations:

> 'It is for each state to determine under its own law who are its nationals. This law shall be recognised by other states in so far as it is consistent with international conventions, international custom, and the principles of law generally recognised with regard to nationality.
>
> Any question as to whether a person possesses the nationality of a particular state shall be determined in accordance with the law of that state.'

These fundamental principles set out in the Hague Convention of 1930 on the Conflict of Nationality Laws have been modified by a subsequent principle that when a state grants nationality to a person whose association with that state is so tenuous as not to constitute a 'genuine link', other states are not bound to recognise that grant of nationality; otherwise they continue to apply.

Nationality is normally acquired by birth in the territory *(jus soli)* or as the descendant of a national *(jus sanguinis)*; occasionally by naturalisation or marriage, and on rare occasions as a consequence of conquest, cession or other change in the nature of a state. It is often forfeited on the acquisition of a different nationality and may be lost by renunciation, specific state legislation or, in some cases, marriage to an alien or or prolonged absence. Dual nationality may occasionally result from an overlap of two countries' legislation on the subject or from exceptional circumstances. A person becomes stateless when he is deprived of his nationality and does not acquire an alternative.

The laws relating to nationality are complicated and varied, but they are very relevant to diplomats in general and to consular officers in particular. For example, a state has the right to accord diplomatic protection to its nationals while abroad but not to others; a person usually has the right to be granted re-entry into the state of which he is a national (and therefore *prima facie* entitlement to a transit visa through an adjacent state in the direction of that state); or he may be liable to military service or subject to extradition. A duly authorised passport is generally accepted as *prima facie* evidence of nationality.

# CONFERENCES

International negotiation is a specialised form of bargaining: when it takes the form of bilateral negotiation it may be relatively informal, but multilateral negotiation is normally conducted on a formal conference basis. As the range of international business has increased over recent years, so has *conference practice and procedure* become to a greater extent refined and standardised: that is a sort of science; and *conference diplomacy*, which is rather more an art, has, like diplomacy in all its forms, adapted to changing situations.

Conference practice and procedure are concerned with the commonly accepted rules designed to ensure the most successful possible outcome of a conference and the greatest degree of satisfaction to all participants; whereas conference diplomacy is the expertise practised by the individual delegate who seeks to gain the maximum advantage for his country. It may be said that the chairman or president of a conference requires a high degree of diplomacy to ensure a successful outcome of a conference, but as he also needs to be well acquainted with practice and procedure his skill can best be summed up in the term *conference management*.

International conferences can be classified in a number of ways. They may be:
- bilateral or multilateral;
- single-subject or multi-subject;
- *ad hoc* or regular;
- those with a permanent secretariat and those without.

International conferences may also be classified in terms of the objectives that they set out to achieve. These may be:
- to serve as a forum for the general discussion of a subject or subjects;
- to make non-binding recommendations to governments or international organisations;
- to make decisions binding on governments (in most instances *ad referendum*);
- to make decisions giving guidance or instructions to the secretariat of an intergovernmental organisation, or on the way in which a programme financed by governments should be administered, e.g. the standing or executive committees of international organisations in the interim between plenary sessions;
- to negotiate and draft a treaty or other formal international instrument;
- to provide an international exchange of information, e.g. UN Conference on the Peaceful Uses of Atomic Energy;
- to provide for the pledging of voluntary contributions to international programmes, e.g. UN High Commission for Refugees; World Food Programme.

# CONFERENCE PRACTICE AND PROCEDURE

## RULES OF PROCEDURE

The first requirement of every formal conference is a set of written rules that guide and determine the activities of the participants and to which the chairman can refer in cases of doubt or dissent. These must either be standing rules which, having been approved by a previous session, are accepted as standard procedure by subsequent sessions, e.g. the rules of procedure of the United Nations General Assembly; or they must be submitted to, and approved by, the conference. In the latter instance they would be circulated in draft form in advance, and would include the date and place of the meeting, adequate advance notice of which must always be given.

## THE AGENDA

The agenda of a conference lists the items of business that will be raised and the order in which each item will be considered. A draft or provisional agenda is normally prepared and circulated by the convenors or secretariat of the conference and will, in the case of regular meetings, include (i) obligatory items (e.g. the approval of the minutes of the previous meeting); (ii) items of business left over from the previous session; and (iii) new submissions for consideration. The agenda must be circulated sufficiently far in advance of the conference to give participants time to study the various items of business. Similarly, items to be included on the agenda must be sent to the secretariat/convenors sufficiently early for them to be processed and the participants notified. For certain conferences (e.g. the UN General Assembly) it is obligatory for an explanatory memorandum to be circulated in respect of each substantive item on the agenda.

## COMPOSITION OF DELEGATIONS

The composition of delegations is normally provided for in the Rules of Procedure. The United Nations recognises representatives (maximum five) and alternate representatives (maximum five), and as many advisers, experts, etc., as are required.

## CREDENTIALS

Credentials are provided in a document identifying a representative and authorising him or her to act; they are usually verified by a credentials committee which reports to the plenary meeting for approval. Credentials must be issued by the proper authority and comply with the requirements of the conference rules of procedure. Full powers are required in certain instances, e.g. for adopting the text of a treaty. Paragraph 29 of the General Assembly rules of procedure allows for the provisional admission of a representative against whom objections have been raised.

## OBSERVERS

The admission and status of observers depend on the rules of procedure of the conference, but they do not in any circumstances have a vote. In the UN General Assembly it is exceptional for observers to be permitted to join in the discussions, but in the Security Council it is a common practice.

## OFFICIAL LANGUAGES AND WORKING LANGUAGES

Official languages are those in which texts and resolutions are published and in which discussions are held. Working languages are those languages used in discussion and from and into which interpretation is provided.

## PUBLICITY

Conferences can be divided into three general categories: those that are completely open and to which the public and media are invited; those that are completely closed, the public and the media being provided with a final communiqué agreed by the participants; and those that are limited to the participating members, the public and the media being informed by individual participants by means of press conferences, television interviews and other forms of publicity. In practice there is a spectrum of *ad hoc* arrangements between the closed and the open conference (e.g. some sessions may be open to the public and others not).

## RECORDS

A fundamental requirement of any conference is that there should be no doubt as to what has, and what has not, been agreed. For this purpose records of the proceedings are invariably kept and are agreed as correct by the participants. The records kept can be divided into three categories:
(a) verbatim records (manual or audio);
(b) summary records, usually prepared by the secretariat, and supervised by a *rapporteur*;
(c) the texts of resolutions only.

Participants normally have the right and opportunity to make minor alterations to improve the presentation but not the substance of a report of their intervention when it is circulated in draft form; this applies particularly in respect of verbatim reports.

## THE RIGHTS OF PARTICIPANTS

The rights of participants as well as the limitations on their activities are usually specified in the rules of procedure; and are subject always to the proviso that it is the task of the presiding officer to ensure that the conference reaches a satisfactory conclusion, and that the business of the meeting is not deliberately or needlessly obstructed. These rights are usually: the right to speak once on each question under discussion, the right to make a *point of order* (usually an objection to the remarks of a participant which are considered offensive or irrelevant); the right to make a *procedural motion* (a procedural motion relates to the conduct of the meeting and must immediately be put to the vote by the presiding officer); and the right to reply to another speaker.

## MAKING PROPOSALS AND TAKING DECISIONS

Decisions at conferences are normally taken on the basis of written proposals submitted for consideration by one or more participants: these are referred to as draft resolutions. In the UN they take the form of a preamble and an operative section; and they are normally required to be submitted with an explanatory memorandum.

Amendments and sub-amendments to draft resolutions may be proposed (and may subsequently be withdrawn) before voting takes place. Voting is firstly on sub-amendments; secondly on 'the amendment furthest removed in substance from the original proposal' (UN General Assembly rule 92) when two or more amendments relate to the same text; and finally on the draft resolution as amended. Amendments cannot negate the substance of a resolution: they must add to, delete from or revise part of a proposal. *Explanations of vote*, i.e. a verbal statement given by a participant explaining why his vote has been cast in a particular way, are normally permitted, as are *motions for division*, which provide for separate voting on separate sections of a resolution in the event of this being specifically provided for.

## VOTING QUORUMS AND MAJORITY REQUIREMENTS

Voting is usually on the basis of a simple majority (i.e. over half) of the representatives *present and voting*; in certain instances (often for important questions) the rules of procedure may specify a two-thirds majority (i.e. two-thirds or more) of the representatives *present and voting*; or alternatively a simple or two-thirds majority of *total membership*.

Normally each country has one vote, but systems of *weighted voting* exist in, for example, the ILO and the IMF (in accordance with their rules of procedure), whereby certain categories of participants or certain countries having a greater financial or practical stake in the matter in question have more votes than others.

Rules of procedure normally provide for two specific *quorums*:
(a) the minimum number of members or participants who must be present for a vote to take place;
(b) the minimum number required to be present for business to proceed.

Voting in the Security Council is on the basis of two categories of representatives: permanent members and non-permanent members. In the General Assembly, where each country has one vote, a resolution on which there is an equally divided vote is voted on at a second meeting held within forty-eight hours, and is rejected if the votes are again equal. This procedure does not apply to the elections of officers.

Votes may be counted in various ways: by a show of hands, a roll call, by members standing or pressing a button, by secret ballot or by postal ballot.

## DETERMINING PROPOSALS BY CONSENSUS

It is unnecessary to go to the extent of casting votes on certain proposals – for example that the Conference should adjourn for lunch: the president decides that there is a consensus of opinion among the representatives that they are feeling hungry, and accordingly proposes that they should do so. This is a *consensus decision without a resolution*: it is based on an assumption by the presiding officer of what is sufficiently self-evident not to warrant taking up the time of the meeting on preparing a resolution, and is particularly applicable to procedural decisions. It is also a device that may be adopted by the presiding officer if he judges that the absence of a resolution is the best political solution to a particularly delicate situation and would be accepted as such by the participants.

A *consensus decision with a resolution* falls within the same category but is slightly more formal. It is for routine and non-controversial items, and for those items to which a minority of representatives object, but would rather not be seen to object through the publicity of a vote. The term 'consensus' is also used to an increasing extent in various inter-governmental organisations as an extension of the term 'unanimity'; implying that:

(a) all delegates have had an opportunity of expressing their point of view before final approval is given, and
(b) although they may not be entirely in favour of a draft resolution, all delegates consider it advisable, on balance, not to force the issue by opposing it.

## SUBCOMMITTEES AND WORKING PARTIES

It is common practice for conferences to resolve themselves into subcommittees or working parties in order to deal with separate issues of a problem, and then to consider their reports at plenary sessions. They may also provide a useful means of making recommendations on highly specialised subjects; and in cases where a conference meets at lengthy intervals are a means whereby business can be continued during the intervening periods.

## THE ELECTION OF THE OFFICIALS

The president, vice-president(s) and, where applicable, the rapporteur assume their functions either by election (as is the case in the majority of conferences) or by rotation (as the chairmanship of the Security Council). In an *ad hoc* conference the representative of the country in which the conference is being held is normally the provisional chairman.

## SEATING, PROTOCOL, ORDER OF PRECEDENCE, ETC.

In *bilateral* conferences normal diplomatic protocol is customarily observed. In *multilateral* conferences precedence is normally based on the alphabetical order of name of country (in English or French). In the UN General Assembly the point of seniority in the alphabetical order is varied for each session.

# CONFERENCE MANAGEMENT

## THE ROLE OF PRESIDING OFFICERS

There is a close parallel between the role of the presiding officer and that of the football referee. Each has the lonely and responsible task of supervising the interplay of skills and techniques between professional players each seeking to gain the maximum advantage; and within a given space of time he has to ensure that the game is played according to the rules and that the final decision is accepted by all the participants. He is provided with a book of rules (the rules of procedure) but his authority, though theoretically supreme, can have no substance unless he is able, by his sensitivity and diplomacy, to persuade those concerned that it is in their own interests to accept it and abide by his decisions. Both need fairness, firmness, knowledge of the rules and very sensitive antennae; not to mention monumental patience and, at times, self-restraint.

The functions of the presiding officer fall into two categories: procedural and substantive.

*1. Procedural functions*
(a) Opening, closing and adjourning meetings.
(b) Calling on representatives to speak.
(c) Limiting the length of speeches if necessary, or if the rules so require.
(d) Giving rulings on points of order and points of procedure.
(e) Clarifying points where necessary.
(f) Calling for the termination of irrelevant remarks.
(g) Ensuring that the business of the meeting is carried out.

*2. Substantive functions*
(a) Carrying out *ad hoc* functions which the meeting entrusts to the Presiding Officer's discretion (e.g. the appointment of countries/members to new committees).
(b) Acting as mediator, and assisting the conference to reach a conclusion. This may take the form of:
  • permitting time for informal discussions;
  • promoting informal discussions in which he does not participate;
  • promoting informal discussions and participating in them;
  • holding discussions with individual representatives to see if he can find sufficient common ground to overcome an *impasse*.

The increasing impact of multilateral organisations on international relations has resulted in the need – and opportunity – for the Presiding Officer to play a much more active role than previously. Delegates gather not so much to play an adversarial role as to seek solutions – not all of which will meet the objectives of their individual countries, but which provide the most satisfactory result for the members of the organisation as a whole. They undertake an exercise in *Positive Diplomacy*, and the Presiding Officer, aware of this sense of purpose, is, to an increasing extent, able to submit a draft resolutions for initial consideration and – with the blessed invention of the computer as wordprocessor – to proceed virtually without interruption to sponsor a whole series of amended drafts until a final version is produced of which nobody may really approve wholeheartedly but one to which nobody is prepared to object: a process of consensus-building and eventually of *nemine contradicente*.

## THE SECRETARIAT

The secretariat provides the administrative backing to a conference; not only to the presiding officer and representatives during the conference, but in preparation for the conference and on its conclusion. If the secretariat is a permanent one it also continues its administrative functions between meetings, when it may assume a largely executive role, acting on the general or specific guidance of its governing body.

Before a conference, and assuming that the place of meeting has been determined, the secretariat will be mainly concerned with invitations, protocol, reception and hospitality, transport, liaison with local authorities, and the arrangement of the conference hall down to the last microphone, pencil and cup of coffee; but above all it will be concerned with the preparation and distribution of the agenda (or draft agenda) and the agenda papers, together with the rules of procedure for the conference where applicable.

While the conference is in progress the secretariat will be responsible for its entire administration, including the provision of translators and the keeping of such records of the proceedings as may be specified by the rules of procedure or required by the presiding officer. A considerable number of documents is invariably required for circulation at all stages of the proceedings – draft resolutions in particular – and typists are normally available at all reasonable hours. After the close of the conference there are two major tasks apart from the general clearing-up operations: the circulation of the Report of the Proceedings (the minutes or *procès-verbale*): these are often circulated in draft in the first instance (and nearly always so in the case of verbatim reports) so that participants may correct minor errors of punctuation, spelling or grammar (but not change the substance of their intervention); and putting into effect the various decisions that have been reached at the conference.

The head of the secretariat in many instances has certain specific functions that he is required to perform and these are usually set out in the rules of procedure. These may relate to the submission of periodic reports, the presentation of accounts, and matters relating to the staff.

# CONFERENCE DIPLOMACY

The object of conferences is to discuss problems and find solutions that are so far as possible acceptable to all participants, and this process is carried on by the traditional methods of diplomacy. However, the flourishing of multilateral diplomacy since the foundation of the United Nations has resulted in a proliferation of international organisations, conferences and committees, and has brought with it an additional dimension to traditional diplomacy: the phenomenon of group voting. Group interest does not normally override national interest, but where the national interest is not strong the group policy will be followed, mainly on the reasoning that strength lies in numbers and in unity, but also because many states with the right to vote do not have the staff to research every issue that comes before them. It is also a particularly useful system for prearranging the election of officers and generally exchanging information on matters of mutual concern.

The fundamental types of group are:
Political and cultural,
Economic development,
Regional,
Economic treaty-linked states.

Among the major groups at the present time are:
* African group
* Asian group
* The European Union
* Group of Arab States
* Group of 77 (developing countries of Africa, Asia and Latin America, now over a hundred in number)
* Latin-American group

There are in addition *ad hoc* groups which form to protect their common interests in specific matters. For example in the law of the sea conferences members of the same political or regional group opposed each other in the Continental Shelf group, the group of territorialists (200 mile territorial sea), the fishing states group and the various other *ad hoc* groups that came together on this particular issue.

For a comprehensive study of conference practice and procedure, conference management and conference diplomacy see *Conference Diplomacy* by Johan Kaufmann (Martinus Nijhoff Publishers).

# THE DIPLOMAT AND THE MEDIA

*'We began the 19th century with the choice: whether or not to spread our nation from coast to coast. We began the 20th century with a choice: to harness the Industrial Revolution to our values. At the dawn of the 21st century we must now choose how to shape the forces of the Information Age and the Global Society.'*

These are the words of President Clinton on the occasion of his inauguration as President of the United States for a second term of office: a historical survey of the two major issues that faced his country in the 19th and 20th centuries, and his view of the major challenge that would face his country in the coming century – namely the advent of the Information Age and the Global Society. And what may be deduced from his observation is that the relationships between the existing units of the Global Society – the sovereign independent states – will require management with ever-increasing skills and perception, as well as constant adaptation and an awareness of how the by-products of the Information Age – in particular the television – can be used or abused in the service of diplomacy.

The basis of diplomacy throughout the ages has been person-to-person communication through the medium of envoys or ambassadors. But the term 'diplomacy' relates to the study of documents; and when considering the evolution of the various media of communication throughout history, it is evident that the written word – through the medium of the Press in particular – has had a significant influence on the formulation of foreign policy and on the processes of diplomacy; and a wary but mutually advantageous relationship has developed between diplomats and journalists and their counterparts in radio broadcasting. Now, in the age of the satellite dish and digitalisation, it is the impact of the audio-visual image that demands the diplomat's attention.

The television revolution, which has burst upon the world with unexpected speed and as yet unpredictable effect, is a revolution affecting men's minds. The increased availability of television has created a global awareness, motivating the mass of the world's population to new visions and new ideas. The hundreds of millions who hitherto have concerned themselves essentially with the survival of the family and the local community, now see themselves as part of a social and political unit with a voice in their country's domestic and foreign policies. Moreover, the impact of the television revolution on policy formulation is both national and international.

Nationally, the television can influence the government's foreign policy agenda by the selection and intensity of its news coverage. Every country has three elements to its foreign policy formulation: the rational, which is what the Minister for Foreign Affairs, on the advice of his or her diplomats considers to be in the best interests of the country; the political, which is what the government considers to be possible and appropriate; and the emotional, which is what the public expects, based to a very large extent on what they have seen on the television. Until recently, the formulation of foreign policy was primarily the concern of a literate, politically-conscious élite: now, the principal medium of information – the television – being ubiquitous and no longer elitist, or requiring literacy, has the power to arouse emotions and create uninformed opinion throughout all strata of society.

Internationally – and it is a little more than a decade since coverage by satellite became effectively international – television has brought about a structural revolution: the creation of the 'Global Society'. It has:

(a) enhanced the sense of global involvement and responsibility by the immediacy of its news coverage;
(b) created an increased awareness of humanitarian needs and concern for the environment;
(c) created for diplomats a new dimension to traditional Public Diplomacy which has two major components: it enables a country to influence another country's foreign policy by appealing directly to that country's public opinion over the head of the government; and it provides scope for Media Diplomacy which may be described as a process of negotiation whereby governments utilise the medium of television in order to make public statements of policy relating to other countries, with a view to influencing the outcome of a dispute. Above all, it has had a profound effect on the development of *Disinformation Diplomacy* and *Media Management* both in domestic politics and in the conduct of inter-state relations.

The situation has now been reached where international television companies not only seek interviews with diplomats to help fill their daily 'news hole' – a joint venture to the advantage of both parties; they also welcome, to an increasing extent, the Video News Release. This is a professionally produced video cassette which has three characteristics: it is suitable and attractive for television presentation; it can be produced and put into storage and brought out when its timing would produce the greatest impact; and it carries a message that the instigator wishes to put across to as wide an audience as possible. There are more than a hundred firms engaged in the production of Video News Releases in the UK alone. Customers are mainly governments and Non-governmental Organisations, and the VNRs often provide a sporting event or touristic attraction as a foreground to the real message that they wish to put across. Major NGO users of VNRs are environmental organisations, charities aid organisations and other special interest groups, and they rely for their success on the profound observation that 'Man has a natural craving to be distracted and entertained'. The Video News Release is essentially entertainment but with a hidden message.

These developments are all relatively innocent, and reflect the ability of governments and others to adapt their processes of diplomacy and persuasion to the changing possibilities of the times; but this advance of technology can bring dangers as well as benefits, in the form of disinformation and misinformation. Disinformation is a form of deliberate deceit – a practice which is by no means new to diplomacy, and can normally be detected (provided that it is not subliminal) and countered.

Misinformation is also the provision of a false image, but in this case without evil or deliberate intent, and often without the producer's awareness of his or her own deception. It is, however, a real danger on account of the impact that it has on the emotional input into the formulation of foreign policy. The major components of Misinformation are:

*Technical Limitations.* Camera crews cost money, and are only sent where there is likely to be the most action and excitement. Hence the saying 'News is where the camera is'.

*Selective perception and subjectivity.* However objective producers may be, they inevitably have a personal perception of what is important and what is not; what is right and what is wrong. Moreover, they do not just want to be reporters of events: they want to make an impact on society.

*Cultural limitations.* These are an important factor because people of different regions and cultures become accustomed to judging certain countries or situations from a fixed viewpoint: and what is more they are not readily receptive to a change. When President Bush, standing on the steps of the White House, put his arm around the then President de Klerk of South Africa soon after the end of Apartheid and said 'who would have thought, a year ago, that we two would be standing here' he exemplified the fact that reports from South Africa were expected to accord with the American perception of the time. But apartheid did not end suddenly – it had been disappearing gradually for several years – but no journalist and very few diplomats dared to say so because it was contrary to conventional wisdom – to what people at home had wanted to believe and had grown accustomed to believing.

*Personal political commitment* is something that all producers will have; and perhaps without realising it and certainly not intending it, they will allow it to influence their work.

*Dramatised reporting* marks a stage in the evolution of the theatre and the concept of 'Art for Art's sake', and is a major distorting factor. All television producers aim to create good viewing, good theatre. They want the praise of their fellow producers for being good at their job; and if that involves a little exaggeration or the manipulation of facts in order to produce an exciting and stimulating effect it can be justified on the grounds that all television – the 'docudrama' as an example – is an extension of the theatre, an emotional experience and thus a legitimate contribution to the entertainment industry.

*Post-fabricated reporting.* Camera crews can rarely be on the spot when an event occurs, just as the fire brigade can rarely be there when the fire breaks out – but they can be there soon after. The consequence is that many of the events seen on television are replays of what took place earlier on: faithful replays – but post-fabricated nevertheless.

*The Media Law of Demand and Supply* is based on the fact that the demand for news is constant and relentless, and producers may sometimes be forced to broadcast whatever they can find: which is where the Video News Release comes into its own. It is no good announcing 'This is the 9 o'clock news – oh sorry we haven't got any news today: here is a Western instead'. News creation is at times inevitable.

*The Magnifier Effect* comes into play when minor incidents are magnified out of all significance. Crowd scenes can be manufactured on the basis of a small gathering, and impressions are created by generalising from the particular.

*The need to simplify, personalise and demonise.* An audience can often more easily identify with an individual politician than with a country; and if there is a conflict situation they need to be able to identify the Good Guy from the Bad Guy.

This new situation has imposed an obligation on diplomats to become proficient in the skill of *Media Presentation*, both nationally and internationally: nationally because a country's foreign policy, in order to be effective, requires a high degree of popular support – or at least understanding – and a diplomat should be prepared to explain and justify his government's policy to his own people in the most effective manner which is the wide-reaching, audio-visual medium of the television; and internationally by diplomats *en poste* because every opportunity should be taken of improving the country's image abroad to as wide an audience as possible, and to explain and justify its actions. They may or may not seek it, but it will catch up with them one day. Appearing on television is a grave responsibility, with serious consequences if it is handled badly, a benefit for their country if handled well; and since television is in many ways a modern method of 'Diplomatic Representation' supplementing influence with the political élite by influencing the public, they must react positively and professionally to the opportunities that are offered to them.

## THE TELEVISION INTERVIEW

A television interview requires careful preparation and analysis, and the diplomat must consider ('him' being 'him/her' throughout):

*The interviewers' objective*: why should they go to the trouble of interviewing him: what are they trying to achieve? The answer is a story to help fill the daily 'news hole': that is their job.

*The diplomat's objective*: why should he agree to be interviewed: what is he trying to achieve? On the negative side, if an interviewer says that a diplomat has 'declined to be interviewed' on a particular subject, it can be made to appear that there must be some sinister reason behind the refusal; whilst on the positive side an interview provides the opportunity to reach out to millions of viewers and to provide a tele-visual 'representation' of his country and so enhance its image. It also provides an opportunity for countering a *cumulative public perception* of a negative nature that another country may be trying to create for its own foreign policy purposes. An interview should be seen as a joint venture between interviewer and diplomat: both have something to gain from it.

*The circumstances of the interview*: in order to work out a strategy it is essential to know whether the interview will be live or recorded; whether or not it will be one-on-one or if others will take part and if so who they are; will it form part of the news, a documentary, a chat-show or be in front of an audience? At what time will it be shown and will the audience be popular or serious? Most important of all, will it be shown as a whole, or will a sentence or two be extracted and used as a contribution to a 'docudrama' which the producer is putting together in accordance with his script, but where the diplomat will be unaware of the denouement. Whether arrangements are being prepared for the diplomat himself or for one of his visiting Ministers, it is important to ensure that the seating and lighting are satisfactory, and that the camera is at eye-level; and ideally that the interview takes place at a specified time and on 'home' ground. Impromptu interviews, for example at airports or receptions, should be avoided if at all possible.

*The strategy of the interviewer* may be to obtain information and explanation; it may be sensation-seeking, or it may be to create a theatre-piece or docudrama. The diplomat's strategy must be adapted accordingly.

*The strategy of the diplomat* is to leave the audience with a good impression of himself and of his country – bearing in mind that there are nearly 200 countries in the world, some with confusing names, and that the interview may be the only way that the audience has of gaining an impression of a country, which it does by associating the diplomat with the country. Geographical Fatigue is a malady that even the most enlightened may suffer from.

What does the public expect of a diplomat? He should be composed, confident, reliable, credible, honest, reasonable, trustworthy and warm: he should not appear to be ill-at-ease, hesitant, confused, dogmatic or superior. To sum up, a diplomat's strategy will be influenced by the occasion, the audience, the culture of the country and the interviewer's choice of strategy – gentle treatment or rough. To some extent, it is a matter of playing out time without conceding a goal, whilst taking every opportunity of proving that his country plays attractively and according to the rules.

*The tactics of the interviewer* vary according to the individual: each one normally has a particular style, objective and *modus operandi*, and the diplomat should know the host country well enough to be familiar with its television personalities. Those who want to provide an exciting, provocative piece of entertainment may seek to:
- destabilise the diplomat, unsettle him
- provoke an indiscretion
- lead him towards subjects he wishes to avoid
- get him talking man-to-man, from his heart rather than from his head
- get him on the defensive
- use any trick within reason (such as pretending that the interview is over when in fact the camera is still running) in order to produce good theatre

*The tactics and techniques of the diplomat*: these are limited by the fact that the producer of the programme controls the cameras, and that the viewing audience identifies with the interviewer; but the diplomat has an advantage in that the interviewer must maintain his audience's interest and produce 'good theatre', and has only a strictly limited time for his act. The diplomat's tactics are – inevitably – mainly reactive, but if a question put to him is one that he wishes to avoid he can take advantage of the fact that the interviewer does not normally ask a question without first putting it in its context by providing some background information: his audience wants to feel involved and to identify with the questioner; and it is perfectly legitimate to pick on one of the background assumptions for an answer, and ideally to provide a key phrase for the interviewer to continue his questioning on another tack rather than reverting to his main question. What the interviewer is seeking to achieve is a harmonious flow of question and answer, and he will not wish to break the sequence. Moreover, if a person looks, speaks and behaves like a diplomat he/she will be treated as one.

The diplomat's techniques may be divided into *content* and *presentation*: content being what he says, and presentation being the way that he says it in terms of body language, appearance and voice; and it is perhaps surprising that a diplomat's presentation impresses the viewer far more than what he says.

## CONTENT

For diplomats, the major rules of content are:

Analyse your audience and shape the content accordingly.

Make sure you know what you are allowed to say: remember that you are speaking for your country – not yourself.

Go prepared, and therefore unhurried.

Have a central message and look for an opportunity to put it across to the audience.

Before the interview, write down a few impressive phrases that can fit in easily and try to get them in.

Anticipate the questions that you will be asked and prepare the answers.

Always try to set out your ideas in a logical and easy – to – follow sequence.

Try not to let the interviewer determine the course of the interview; have your own plan of campaign, and do not just accept his topics and his assumptions.

Do not only talk about the negative points that the interviewer may bring up: put an emphasis on the positive aspects.

How lengthy should your answer be? Long enough to maintain the flow of conversation, but not so long as to be tedious or to give the impression that you are wasting the interviewer's – and thus the audience's – time.

What if an argument develops? Do not argue back: look hurt at the interviewer's bad manners.

Do not quote figures unless they are essential: it confuses the audience.

Do not specify the number of points that you are going to mention: you may forget one.

Write down any personal names, quotations or initials (e.g. OSCE, ECSC) that you may wish to mention, to make sure that you do not get them wrong (or don't just go blank).

Remember that your opening phrase and your closing phrase are particularly important. It is the first impression that you give that sets the stage, and your exit lines
that leave the most lasting impression of you.

Never admit that your government is in the wrong.

Never deviate from the fundamental sequence: Listen, Pause, Think, Answer.

If there is a pause in the conversation do not think that is up to you to fill it: you may
say something un-rehearsed aud unintended.

## PRESENTATION

The major rules of presentation are:

*1. Voice*

The importance of the voice is greatly underestimated in all aspects of personal communication. One's voice can immediately put someone on the defensive; it may
even result in a hostile response to a simple query; on the other hand it may immediately establish a rapport wavelength.

Learn how to breathe properly and learn how to control your breathing: start off taking a deep breath. Make your voice interesting – vary the pitch, the volume and
the speed.

Speak clearly, softly rather than loudly, slowly rather than quickly. Avoid saying 'um',
'er', or 'well' (silence is better, or slow down).

Pitch your voice up slightly at the beginning of a sentence, and indicate to the interviewer that your reply has come to an end by lowering your voice (if in English).

*2. Facial expression and body language*

The major element of body language is facial expression, and it is essential to strike
an appropriate balance between looking too animated on the one hand and too 'wood-
en' on the other: local perceptions and expectations may influence the balance, but
diplomats generally are expected to be 'heavyweight' rather then 'lightweight'. They
should normally face the interviewer and listen intently, bearing in mind that *listen-
ing is a positive form of communication*, rather than face the camera: those who wish
to impose their personality on the viewers may do so, but that is not the role of a
diplomat. Apart from facial expression, body language is also expressed in the way a
person sits and moves: he may slouch in his chair and give the impression that he is
doing the interviewer (and thus his audience) a great favour by deigning to be interviewed; he may sit awkwardly and give the impression of being inadequate and ill-at-
ease, or he may move his eyes and head and wave his arms around in a distracting
manner. It is a rather alarming thought that whenever you are sitting, walking or even
standing still you are making a statement; and if there is a television camera nearby
(say, within half a mile) it will be able to pick it up and magnify it to your advantage
or otherwise.

## 3. Appearance

Appearance is expected to be formal rather than casual, neat rather than scruffy, and appropriate to the occasion. If spectacles are likely to obscure the eyes they should, if possible, be removed five minutes before the interview; and ladies should avoid jewellery or a hair style that is distracting, or clothes that are of a dramatically contrasting pattern: it is advisable to check in advance the colour of the background of the interview room.

## CONCLUSION

The advances in television technology and in presentation techniques have outstripped the viewers' ability to appreciate the extent to which they are being manipulated by what they see and hear, and to make the necessary mental adjustment. There is always a cath-up period involved between invention and utilisation, and it was a decade before the Nazi government with its propaganda and President Roosevelt with his Fireside Chats to the American people took advantage of the medium of radio for political purposes. Now it is the turn of television which is being fully exploited for foreign policy purposes.

It is no exaggeration to say that we have arrived at a watershed – a point of no return – in international relations where there is potentially worldwide transparency, with everybody being able to see – with very few exceptions – what is going on in their neighbours' back gardens. And it is inevitable that the technical developments that are taking place with such rapidity in Information Technology in general and in television viewing in particular will present governments with opportunities and problems in the future that are as yet unforeseeable. Misinformation and disinformation in the future may cause misunderstandings and arouse hatreds; but on the other hand the Global Society may produce a younger generation that sees violence and conflict as being barbaric and outdated. The media may perhaps give diplomats the opportunity through media diplomacy to develop the skill of mediation to the point where existing inter-cultural animosities can be overcome.

The majority of situations that call for mediation have their roots in the displacement of peoples, whether forced or voluntary; the imposition of alien rule or other fundamental contradictions: in Europe alone, millions of people live on the wrong side of their linguistic or cultural frontier, and elsewhere peoples with irreconcilable values live in conditions of passive hostility within the same state. Nevertheless, it is often the case that a very limited number of individuals play a decisive role in any conflict situation, and the psychological impact of 'media attention' – even of 'media pressure' – on their reasoning and responses should not be underrated. Moreover, since diplomats are trained to appreciate the importance of words, they can use their influence to discourage weasel words which have an emotional appeal and produce a mass response, but which create a false impression, distort reality and result in dashed expectations.

The essential requirement is that diplomats, with the encouragement of their governments, should be aware of the media revolution that is going on around them, and that they should think positively how they can utilise it for the benefit of their country's interest, and for the betterment of the Global Society of which they are part. They should take a positive interest in the subject and understand the progress of information technology revolutions and realise the speed of change in the technologies that will affect their work. Diplomats have adapted to working in the Computer Age: they now have to adapt to the Information Age and the Global Society.

# APPENDICES

# ENTERTAINING

In multilateral organisations, entertainment is usually of a fairly overt nature, and commonly takes place in the somewhat formal atmosphere of a restaurant or institutional surroundings. For the diplomat *en poste*, however, entertaining has a genuine element of hospitality and of cameraderie that enables members of the diplomatic community to enjoy themselves more openly in the company of like-minded friends and members of the local community. The more elevated the diplomat, of course, the greater the degree of formality; but events nevertheless usually take place in the diplomat's residence and are of a relatively domestic nature. And however junior a diplomat may be, he or she may find themselves suddenly thrust into Ambassadorial circles in order to fill a last-minute gap in the seating plan or to balance the male/female ratio: hence this rather old-fashioned section on a traditional and potentially embarrassing subject.

The primary purpose of entertaining is to afford the maximum pleasure and enjoyment to one's guests. But for diplomats it has a rather more serious purpose, and may in addition have the following objectives:
(a)  to improve the public image of their country;
(b)  to obtain opinions and information from local residents and from other diplomats;
(c)  to make friends and contacts which may prove useful;
(d)  to enable spouses to meet and make friends with other wives so that they may share and discuss matters of mutual interest.

Also, and this is equally important, it enables heads and senior members of missions informally to 'sound out' members of the Ministry of Foreign Affairs (and to a lesser extent politicians, businessmen and other diplomats) regarding proposals they would like to make, but would rather not put into writing or raise officially lest the result should be a definite, and possibly irreversible, negative.

It would be unrealistic to pretend that hard and fast rules of conduct are universally applicable, because practice varies considerably from country to country, and the range of gradations between formality and informality is great. Nevertheless, it is possible to make certain generalisations, and the following deliberately err on the side of formality, on the grounds that it is safer to be too formal rather than too informal, just as it is safer for a lady to be over-dressed than under-dressed, though in both instances a telephone call to a friendly colleague is often the best way of resolving any doubts.

# OFFERING HOSPITALITY

When offering hospitality in the form of lunch or dinner, there are two tasks to be undertaken apart from organising the food and drink and making sure that the date selected does not coincide with a major national day or local religious festivity: the seating plan and invitations.

## THE SEATING PLAN

Before invitations are despatched for a lunch or dinner, a seating plan is worked out. The guests are selected, and it is essential first to ensure as far as possible that none are likely to clash (politically, personally or socially); and secondly that none are likely to object to the precedence that has been accorded to them.

The world community of states has grown rapidly in the past quarter of a century, and new social and cultural patterns have become established. Diplomatic interaction therefore is more complex, and the customs and practices of various communities need to be taken into account in diplomatic entertainment. Local custom and practice should generally prevail, with allowances being made appropriately for the sensitivities of individual guests. The essence of good diplomatic hospitality is the right atmosphere, and the compatibility of the guests is all important.

If diplomats only are present, the seating plan should cause no problems, given the absolute nature of their order of precedence (attachés being a possible complication); but if non-diplomats of the host country are present problems could easily arise, as their order of precedence is not so definite. In this latter instance senior diplomats and members of a Ministry of Foreign Affairs have a high degree of precedence, while among non-officials social status and age are major factors. In cases of doubt it is common practice to seek the advice of the Protocol Department; and it is normally found that a youthful guest will not resent giving way to age, particularly if the hostess adds a quiet word of apology.

Seating plans where only the host or the hostess is present and guests are all male or all female are based essentially on the principle that the senior guest sits on the host's right and the next senior on his left; the third senior on his right but one, the fourth senior on his left but one, and so on (in some Nordic countries, contrary to normal practice, seniority is on the left). The following examples may be adapted to circular tables without basic change:

*All male/female seating plan: host/hostess and seven guests*

If a host were holding a luncheon or dinner in honour of a specific guest he might adopt the following plan:

When both host and hostess are present the principle is extended as follows:

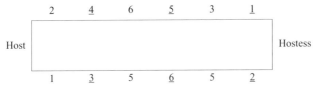

*Mixed seating plan: host, hostess and six couples (men underlined)*

The same rules apply when the host and hostess sit opposite each other in the centre of the long sides of the table. This arrangement has many advantages, but tends to leave those at the ends of the table rather out in the cold: a situation aggravated if, as sometimes happens, the end places are not filled.

The hostess normally sits facing the door leading to the kitchen, so that she may more effectively control her staff.

It is not normally the practice in European countries for wives to be placed next to their husbands, nor do two ladies or two gentlemen normally sit next to each other, but in this respect the custom of the country should be adhered to. It will be found that tables of 6, 10 and 14 work out satisfactorily if the host and hostess are at opposite ends of a rectangular table, whereas 8 and 12 do not permit host and hostess to sit at opposite ends. However 14 is risky, because if one person drops out the hostess is left with – to some – an unlucky 13.

It may sometimes happen that a couple drop out, or that one of the partners is unable to attend at the last minute. In these instances members of one's own mission or friendly colleagues may be asked to help out. When members of an ambassador's or a high commissioner's staff include their head of mission and his wife in the guest list for a lunch or dinner it is customary for the latter to be seated as though they were the hosts in the same way as a Foreign Minister or a Head of State does when visiting one of his own missions.

## INVITATIONS

These should be sent out two or three weeks before the event: shorter notice might not give the host time to invite an alternative guest if it is refused, and longer notice might embarrass a guest who, for some reason, might wish to refuse on some fictitious grounds, e.g. that he had a prior engagement.

Invitations are written in the third person and normally in the following style:

*The Ambassador of ........................................................................ and Mrs 'X'*
*Request the pleasure of the company*
*of*
*Mr and Mrs 'Y'*
*at Lunch*
*on Thursday 17 September at 1.15 p.m.*

Address                                                                                    R.S.V.P.

In certain instances (e.g. if inviting the Minister for Foreign Affairs) one would request 'the *honour* of the company'. An alternative method (the current practice for the particular post should always be followed) is to issue the invitation by telephone, if appropriate through secretaries. If the answer is in the affirmative, the host or hostess then sends an invitation card with the necessary details and with the initials 'p.m.' or the words 'to remind', and encloses a list of guests giving their titles and function. This ensures that all those invited know in advance who the other guests are and what they do – an obvious aid to successful entertaining.

An invitation to dinner would include the type of dress: e.g. 'Black Tie' or Lounge suit or for ladies 'Long dress' where appropriate.

## A DINNER PARTY

Should one arrive with a gift for the hostess? In most countries it is customary to do so, and a small, attractively wrapped gift perhaps related to one's own or the host country is a courteous gesture. Flowers are traditional, but should be sent in advance rather than delivered personally, otherwise the hostess – unless she has a large domestic staff – will not have time to deal with them.

It is customary at a gathering of ten or more for a table plan to be displayed so that guests may know their table places in advance; otherwise it is the task of the hostess to indicate to guests where they sit when they enter the dining-room. When ten or more are invited all places should have name cards: even for smaller gatherings these can be an attractive contribution to the table decoration.

If the time of the dinner is stated as 7.30 for 8 p.m. it is expected that guests will arrive soon after 7.30 p.m. (never before); they will be introduced to the other guests and will drink fruit juice or aperitifs until about 8 p.m. (or later if any of the guests have been late in arriving), after which time dinner will be served.

Guests will be welcomed by the host and hostess and introduced to the other guests present. If guests arrive late and the host and hostess are not awaiting them on their entry into the room, they must seek them out, apologising for their lateness, whereupon they will be introduced to those already present.

The following are usually served as aperitifs together with others customarily served in the region:

Sherry, dry
White wine
Gin and tonic water, with preferably a slice of lemon peel (the 'zest')
Whisky (Scotch) and soda; alternatively Bourbon
Fruit juice

When all the members of the party are assembled and when the hostess has been told by a member of the staff that dinner is ready, she will lead the guests into the dining-room. On very formal occasions the gentlemen will be asked to escort specific ladies to their places, but such a procedure is rare. It is, however, a courtesy to help the lady on one's right to seat herself at the table by pulling out her chair for her. (It is also a nice introduction.)

The choice of menu will depend on personal taste and circumstances, but dietary restrictions of guests on account of health or religion have always to be taken into account.

During the meal it is the duty of the host and hostess – and indeed of all the guests – to ensure that no individual or group monopolises the conversation to the exclusion of any one of the company. The men, in particular, should engage the ladies on either side of them in conversation, irrespective of their charm or vivacity, to an equal extent throughout the meal. At some time during the meal it will be appropriate for the host to say a few words of welcome, and for the senior guest to reply.

At the end of the meal, when all have finished, the hostess catches the eye of the senior lady present to ensure that she is ready to leave the table, and will then rise from her seat; that being a signal for all to rise. If it is the practice for the men to remain at the table to discuss matters of business after the ladies have left (a rare relic of former days) they will normally congregate at one end for their coffee, cigars and liqueurs. If lady diplomats are present, and wish to join in the discussions, it is the responsibility of the host to ensure that they feel welcome to do so. It is not advisable to smoke during a meal, as this may cause offence to others; nor should cigars be lit until after the toast (where appropriate) has been given or the port has been circulated (customarily clockwise). In order to bring the evening to a close drinks may be served around 10.30 p.m. (the time depending on local custom), after which the senior guest will leave followed by the others. If an Ambassador is present as a guest and also a member of his staff, the latter should not leave before his head of mission. Ambassadors and other particularly important guests are normally escorted to their cars.

After an interval of two or three days it is customary in some countries for guests to send a visiting card marked 'p.r.' *(pour remercier)*, to say 'thank you' for the dinner or, more personally, to write a 'thank-you' letter.

## A BUFFET DINNER

In recent times a popular method of entertaining has been the Buffet Dinner. It provides an opportunity to offer a variety of dishes to meet various tastes and dietary restrictions, and it enables the host and hostess more effectively to move among their guests. There are many variations. Guests may be formally seated at tables of six or eight where the first course is served, with guests subsequently helping themselves at the Buffet Table. In rather formal Buffet Dinners it would not be unusual for the second course to be served, and also the dessert. A slightly less formal buffet would be to arrange table placings by name at round or card tables, but no courses would be served: guests would help themselves. An informal Buffet Dinner would be one without place settings, but with tables for guests to sit where they will. And finally a Buffet Dinner organised by a diplomat in a small house or apartment could be quite informal with guests sitting wherever seats are available or – as a last resort – standing.

## A LUNCH PARTY

The invitation, seating plan and other arrangements (including the leaving of cards, *p.r.*) are the same as for a dinner, but the meal will be lighter and the general atmosphere of the party is likely to be less formal. Ladies (guests) may or may not wear hats, according to the custom of the country (the hostess never wears a hat). Guests are normally invited at 1 o'clock for 1.15 p.m., in which case they would leave between 2.15 and 2.30 p.m. They will be offered aperitifs or fruit juice on arrival and, after the meal, coffee and liqueurs.

## A VIN D'HONNEUR

When there is a specific cause for celebration or for honouring an individual or a group of people – for example when a Head of Mission has presented his credentials, an agreement has been signed or a delegation has arrived – a Vin d'Honneur is commonly offered. Drinks, both alcoholic and non-alcoholic – often champagne – are served, and the occasion, which is quite formal, usually lasts for about an hour.

## GENERAL OBSERVATIONS

For Muslims and people of the Judaic faith, pork or pork products are unacceptable, and orthodox Muslims and Jews will not eat other meats unless they are halal or kosher respectively. If one has guests of the Hindu faith, it would be improper to serve beef, but it would not be unreasonable to serve a vegetarian meal, making particular provision for one's vegetarian guests. It would therefore be a thoughtful gesture to enquire about any dietary restrictions your guests may have when inviting them to a function, making appropriate arrangements to meet particular sensitivities.

In East Asia, the preferred implements for eating are chopsticks. In South-East and South Asia and in West Asia one uses knives, forks and spoons or one's fingers, but it is taboo to use the left hand. When in doubt the rule is to do as one's host or hostess does.

In many non-European societies it is considered impolite to hand or receive anything with the left hand; also in some societies it is impolite to point with the index finger or to sit in a manner where the soles of your feet or shoes are visible to your host or guests.

In many Asian societies it is customary to remove one's shoes before entering a home. Moreover, more orthodox Muslims do not shake the hand of a person of the opposite sex. In all such situations it would be wise to be guided by local custom and practice.

It is also useful to bear in mind that smoking is actively discouraged by some hosts and hostesses. Smokers should look out for signs: the non-availability of ashtrays being a clear signal that smoking is not welcome.

## ACCEPTING HOSPITALITY

Invitations in writing should be answered promptly, preferably within twenty-four hours. If they are not answered promptly and the answer is in the negative, the hostess will not have an opportunity to find a suitable substitute. The reply is in the third person, and on the following lines:

> Mr and Mrs X thank Mr and Mrs Y for their kind invitation to dinner on Thursday 3rd May at 7.30 p.m. and have much pleasure in accepting.
> *or*
> Mr and Mrs X thank Mr and Mrs Y for their kind invitation to dinner on Thursday 3rd May at 7.30 p.m. but very much regret that they will be unable to accept as they will be away from .......................... on that date (or 'owing to a previous engagement').

If a husband and wife are invited to lunch or dinner and only one can attend, it is usual to decline on behalf of both. If, however, a verbal understanding is reached, or if the occasion does not involve a seating arrangement (e.g. a reception), then the one may accept for himself (occasionally herself) alone, the reply being on the following lines:

Mr and Mrs X thank Mr and Mrs Y for their kind invitation to a reception on Thursday 3rd May at 9 p.m. Mrs X very much regrets that she will be unable to attend, but Mr X has much pleasure in accepting.

The time of a function is specified on the invitation; for lunch or dinner it is considered a politeness to arrive at the time stated, or preferably five minutes later. For most receptions and cocktail parties the time of arrival is more flexible, as it must be if two or more have to be attended on the same night. In these circumstances it is not unknown for husband and wife to fulfil an engagement separately, usually meeting at the final function; and in the case of representation at national day celebrations, members of a mission will often take it in turn to be present. If however, the reception is given for an occasion when a speech is likely to be made, for example the award of a decoration or a farewell, then it is important to arrive within 15–20 minutes of the time stated on the invitation.

The time of departure from a function varies, but it is better to be brief than to overstay one's welcome.

## SAYING 'THANK YOU'

The counterpart to generous hospitality by the host or hostess is appreciation on the part of the guest, and ways of showing this will depend both on the occasion and the custom of the country. After a mixed dinner, a mark of appreciation would normally be appropriate, and this might take the form of flowers to the hostess either before or after the occasion, or for those of less exuberant temperament the humble 'thank-you' letter. This follows the simple rule that it should contain only sentiments of appreciation, and might be on the following lines:

Dear Mrs ..........................

I am writing to say how very much my husband and I appreciated your kind hospitality last night.
The dinner was a most enjoyable occasion, and we are very grateful for your kind invitation.

Yours sincerely,

## INTRODUCING PEOPLE

A gentleman is normally presented or introduced to a lady; and a junior is always presented to a senior, e.g.

'Mrs Smith, may I introduce Mr Jones.'

Similarly:

'Your Excellency (Ambassador), may I present Mr Robbins, Counsellor in the Ruritanian Embassy.'

When introducing two people, the simple presentation of the one to the other by name is rarely adequate. If, as at a reception, they may be expected to embark on a conversation it is essential to give a brief description of their respective functions, e.g. 'Mrs

Smith, may I introduce Mr Silva? Mr Silva is Cultural Attaché at the Brazilian Embassy and knows Scandinavia well. Mrs Smith's husband is a director of Wotherspoons, and they have just arrived from Oslo.'

## VISITING CARDS

The visiting card is a useful device in that it performs functions on behalf of its owner. It may be delivered personally, delivered by chauffeur or sent by post, according to local custom and the degree of intimacy that it is designed to convey. For example, if the Ruritanian Counsellor, who is married, arrives at a post he may (if it is the local practice) send or take to Counsellors of other missions (who are married) two of his own cards and one of his wife's; and the two parties would consider themselves as being formally introduced to each other and free to act accordingly. The reason for the Ruritanian Counsellor presenting two of his own cards and one of his wife's is that he may present his compliments to another Counsellor and to that Counsellor's wife; but a lady in these circumstances will only present her compliments to another lady: it would not be correct for her to present them to a man unless she were herself a diplomat. To those who are unmarried he would send or take one card of his own.

Visiting cards may also convey specific messages, which take the form of initials pencilled at the bottom. The most common ones are:

p.p. *pour présentation:* to introduce or present somebody

p.p.c. *pour prendre congé:* to take one's leave, or say farewell

p.r. *pour remercier:* to thank, e.g. for a dinner

p.c. *pour condoléances:* to express condolences

p.m. *pour mémoire:* to remind.

Visiting cards may be 'cornered' (i.e. the top lefthand corner is folded down, then back nearly to its original place) to indicate that they have been presented personally.

It is usual for a married diplomat to have at least two sets of cards: one with his name, rank and embassy; and one bearing only his name and that of his wife.

Perhaps the most important function of a visiting card is to serve as a reminder of new acquaintances made at receptions and other functions – their name, initials, address and rank. Diplomats on all such occasions should go well equipped with a supply of their own cards for distribution, and in their turn can build up a valuable collection of other people's as a source of reference.

# WINES AND LIQUEURS

## WINES

Wines are part of the tradition of diplomatic entertainment in many countries, and although the past decade has witnessed the transformation of wine-production from the age-old skill of viticulture to its modern status as a branch of the agro-chemical industry, a basic knowledge of the subject is not entirely irrelevant.

*(a) Table wines*, i.e. those drunk with a meal, may be categorised in various ways, e.g. by colour – red, rosé (pink) or white; by taste – sweet, medium or dry; by effervescence – sparkling or still; by 'body' – full-bodied or light, and, of course, by country. The 'vintage' of a wine is the year in which the grapes were harvested.

*(b) Fortified wines* are wines to which alcohol (usually brandy) has been added. They may be drunk before a meal as aperitifs, or at the end of a meal as dessert wines.

At the end of a meal port wine is a traditional drink in many countries. Vintage port is matured mainly in the bottle; tawny (and ruby) are matured in the wood and should not be kept long in the bottle.

Vintage ports and some red wines develop with age a deposit at the bottom of the bottle and need decanting; the clear wine is poured carefully into another vessel (usually a 'decanter') and the dregs or lees are left behind: the process also airs the wine.

*(c) Spiced and fortified wines* which include vermouths: red (sweet) and white (dry).

*Choosing wines*
The choice of wines with a meal is essentially a matter for individual taste, but as a general rule dry white wine goes with fish; red wine with meat, and sweet wine with sweets. Most red wines are best if served at room temperature; all white wines should be served chilled; sweet white wines may be served cold.

Many countries now produce excellent wines of appropriate type, and in such countries it is always a compliment to one's guests to serve their 'national' wine.

The transformation of wine production in recent years has had two major consequences: the emphasis on 'varietal' wines i.e. those made of one or two specific grape varieties (e.g. Cabernet Sauvignon, Merlot, Pinot Noir, Syrah among the reds and Chardonnay, Riesling, Sauvignon Blanc, Steen and Tokay among the white) in place of 'regional' wines usually containing traditional grape varieties; and the increase in the number of wine-producing areas. Apart from the traditional European producers, wines eminently suitable for diplomatic entertainment are available from other parts of the world, particularly Australia, California, Chile and New Zealand; whilst South Africa is making a welcome return, with its 300-year-old tradition of wine-making being reflected in the excellence of its products.

France and Germany nevertheless remain in the forefront of producers of 'fine wines', and whilst the wording on the label cannot in all cases be taken as a precise indication of the contents of the bottle, the following information is a useful guide.

## FRENCH WINES

There are three categories of French table wines: *'Appellation d'Origine Controlée'* (A.C.), *'Vin Délimité de Qualité Supérieur'* (V.D.Q.S.) and *'Vin de Table'* (Vin de Pays); the two latter being mainly for local consumption.

*Bordeaux* is the most prominent producer of fine *red A.C. wines* (claret) which bear the year of the vintage and the name of one of its regions, e.g. Haut Médoc, or alternatively one of its communes, e.g. St-Estèphe. *The white A.C. wines* which are famous are sweet: from Sauternes, which includes Barsac, and Château Yquem. Certain wines from Bordeaux in the Appellation Controlée category are entitled to be described as *'classed growths'* on the basis of classification awards, and may add to their label 'premier cru', 'deuxième cru', etc., to 'cinquième cru' depending on their rating in 1855 when the awards were made. Some of lesser standing may be styled 'Cru Bourgeois'.

 *Burgundy* may come under varous general headings such as 'Bourgogne', 'Côte de Beaune Villages', etc., but the fine wines are from the *Côte de Nuits* (preferably red), and from the *Côte de Beaune* (preferably white). Further south in the Burgundy region come *Macon* (red and white); and *Beaujolais* which is almost entirely red. Beaujolais *primeur* is drunk within a few months of the vintage.

 The *Côtes du Rhône* produces full-bodied red wine especially from Châteauneuf-du-Pape; the *Loire Valley* produces a wide variety of red, rosé and white wines, bearing famous names such as Sancerre and Muscadet, and wines from *Alsace* are mainly light, clean and dry; and *Champagne* is a wine mainly for celebration.

## GERMAN WINES

Production of German wine falls into three categories: (1) Table wine, (2) Quality wine and (3) specially graded Quality wines.

1. *Tafelwein:* consumed mainly in Germany.
2. *Qualitätswein:* quality wine made from approved grape varieties. Within this category falls *Liebfraumilch*, which is a Qualitätswein from Rheinpfalz, Rheinhessen, Nahe or Rheingau.
3. *Qualitätswein mit prädikat:* the highest category of German wine; must also be from approved grape varieties.
   *Kabinett:* lightest of these wines, usually dry.
   *Spätlese:* literally means late harvest; wines have more body, and a degree of sweetness.

*Auslese:* rich wines made from the ripest bunches of grapes, picked individually.
*Beerenauslese:* wines of exceptional quality, from individually selected grapes; sweet and full-bodied.
*Trockenbeerenauslese:* highest category of German viticulture; a wine rarely made; from individually selected grapes, shrivelled almost to raisins.
*Eiswein:* rare wine made from grapes harvested and crushed while still frozen.
*Sekt:* sparkling wine, whose effervescence reflects characteristics of the Rhine and Mosel.

The label will normally also include the name of the vineyard/property (e.g. the Weingut) and the region (the Bereich); the official growers' number (the Amtliche Prüfungsnummer); the type of grape (e.g. Riesling, Müller-Thurgau, Sylvaner); and the word Erzeuger-Abfüllung if the wine is estate bottled.

LIQUEURS

Liqueurs are potent, concentrated drinks and are taken after a meal. Mostly they have a brandy base to which herbs, fruit and/or syrup are added.

# NON-ALCOHOLIC DRINKS

It should always be borne in mind that many people, for a variety of reasons, drink non-alcoholic beverages, and that as much care should be taken in providing for their taste as is taken for those preferring alcohol. Orange juice (unless freshly pressed) is often the last resort of the unimaginative.

# INTERNATIONAL ABBREVIATIONS

The letters 'q.v.' indicate that the subject is referred to elsewhere in the text.

| | |
|---|---|
| ACP | African, Caribbean and Pacific Countries, European Union/Lomé Convention (q.v.) |
| AFTA | ASEAN Free Trade Area |
| AID | Agency for International Development (US Government Agency) |
| ALADI | Latin American Integration Association |
| APEC | Asia-Pacific Economic Cooperation |
| ARF | ASEAN Regional Forum |
| ASEAN | Association of South-East Asian Nations (q.v.) |
| ASEM | Asia-Europe Meeting |
| | |
| BCEAO | Banque centrale des Etats de l'Afrique de l'Ouest |
| BIS | Bank for International Settlements (q.v.) |
| BSEC | Black Sea Economic Cooperation |
| | |
| CABEI | Central American Bank for Economic Integration |
| CARICOM | The Caribbean Community (q.v.) |
| CBM | Confidence-building measures |
| CCCN | Customs Cooperation Council Nomenclature |
| CCD | Conference of the Committee on Disarmament |
| CD | Committee on Disarmament |
| CEEAC | Economic Community of Central African States |
| CEI | Central European Initiative |
| CERN | European Council for Nuclear Research |
| CFCs | Chlorofluorocarbons |
| CGCED | Caribbean Group for Cooperation in Economic Development |
| CIPEC | Intergovernmental Committee of Copper-Exporting Countries |
| CIS | Commonwealth of Independent States |
| CITES | Convention on International Trade in Endangered Species |
| COMESA | Common Market for Eastern and Southern Africa |
| COREPER | Council of Permanent Representatives (EU) |
| CPISA | Convention on the privileges and immunities of Specialised Agencies |
| CPIUN | Convention on the privileges and immunities of the UN |
| CPLP | Lusophone Community |
| CRSIO | Convention on the representation of states in their relations with international organisations |
| CSM | Convention on Special Missions |

| | |
|---|---|
| DAC | Development Assistance Committee (OECD) |
| DCM | Deputy Chief of Mission |
| | |
| EACC | Euro-Atlantic Cooperation Council |
| EBRD | European Bank for Reconstruction and Development |
| ECA | Economic Commission for Africa (UN) |
| ECE | Economic Commission for Europe (UN) |
| ECLAC | Economic Commission for Latin America and the Caribbean (UN) |
| ECOMOG | ECOWAS Monitoring Group |
| ECOSOC | Economic and Social Council (UN) |
| ECOWAS | Economic Community of West African States |
| EDF | European Development Fund (EC) |
| EEA | European Economic Area |
| EEZ | Exclusive Economic Zone |
| EFTA | European Free Trade Association |
| EIB | European Investment Bank (EU) |
| ELDO | European Launcher Development Organisation |
| EMU | Economic and monetary union (EU) |
| ENEA | European Nuclear Energy Agency (OECD) |
| ESCAP | Economic and Social Commission for Asia and the Pacific (UN) |
| ESCWA | Economic and Social Commission for Western Asia (UN) |
| ESRO | European Space Research Organisation |
| EURASEC | Eurasian Economic Community |
| | |
| FAO | Food and Agriculture Organization |
| FCO | Foreign and Commonwealth Office (UK) |
| | |
| GAB | General Arrangements to borrow (IBRD) |
| GATT | General Agreement on Tariffs and Trade |
| GDP | Gross Domestic Product |
| GEF | Global environment facility (IBRD) |
| | |
| HABITAT | United Nations Centre for Human Settlements (Nairobi) |
| | |
| IADB | Inter-American Development Bank |
| IAEA | International Atomic Energy Agency |
| IATA | International Air Transport Association |
| IBRD | International Bank for Reconstruction and Development |
| ICAO | International Civil Aviation Organization |
| ICBM | Inter-Continental Ballistic Missile |
| ICFTU | International Confederation of Free Trade Unions (Brussels) |
| ICJ | International Court of Justice |
| ICRC | International Committee of the Red Cross |

| | |
|---|---|
| ICSID | The International Centre for the Settlement of Investment Disputes |
| IDA | International Development Association (IBRD) |
| IDB | Inter-American Development Bank |
| IEA | International Energy Agency |
| IFAD | International Fund for Agricultural Development |
| IFC | International Finance Corporation (IBRD) |
| ILC | International Law Commission |
| ILO | International Labour Organization |
| IMF | International Monetary Fund |
| IMO | International Maritime Organization |
| INF | Intermediate Nuclear Forces |
| INIS | International Nuclear Information System |
| INSTRAW | International Research and Training Institute for the Advancement of Women |
| INTERPOL | International Criminal Police Organisation |
| ITU | International Telecommunications Union |
| | |
| LAFTA | Latin American Free Trade Area |
| LAIA | Latin American Integration Association |
| LDC | Less-developed country |
| LLDC | Least-developed country |
| | |
| MBFR | Mutual and Balanced Force Reductions |
| MCCA | Central American Common Market |
| MERCOSUR | Southern common market |
| MFA | Multi-fibre arrangement |
| MFN | Most-favoured nation |
| MIGA | Multilateral Investment Guarantee Agency (IBRD) |
| | |
| NAB | New Arrangements to Borrow |
| NACC | North Atlantic Cooperation Council |
| NAFTA | North American Free Trade Agreement |
| NATO | North Atlantic Treaty Organisation |
| NBC | Nuclear, Biological, Chemical |
| NEA | Nuclear Energy Agency |
| NGO | Non-governmental Organisation |
| NIC | Newly industrialising country |
| NORDEK | Nordic Union |
| NPT | Treaty on the Non-Proliferation of Nuclear Weapons |
| | |
| OAPEC | Organisation of Arab Petroleum Exporting Countries |
| OAS | Organisation of American States |
| OCAS | Organization of Central American States |
| ODA | Official Development Assistance (UNCTAD) |

| | |
|---|---|
| ODECA | Organisation of Central American States |
| ODIHR | Office for Democratic Institutions and Human Rights (OSCE) |
| OECD | Organisation for Economic Cooperation and Development |
| OECS | Organisation of Eastern Caribbean States |
| OIC | Organisation of the Islamic Conference |
| OPEC | Organization of the Petroleum Exporting Countries |
| OSCE | Organisation for Security and Cooperation in Europe |
| | |
| p.a. | per annum: yearly |
| PALOP | Organisation of Lusophone African States |
| p.c. | per capita: per person |
| PECC | Pacific Economic Cooperation Council |
| PfP | Partnership for Peace (NATO) |
| PLO | Palestine Liberation Organisation |
| PPP | Purchasing power parity |
| PTA | Preferential Trade Area |
| | |
| q.v. | Quod vide: the immediately preceding word or phrase appears elsewhere in the text |
| | |
| R and D | Research and Development |
| RDF | Rapid Deployment Force |
| | |
| SAARC | South Asian Association for Regional Cooperation |
| SACLANT | Supreme Allied Commander Atlantic |
| SACEUR | Supreme Allied Commander Europe |
| SACU | Southern Africa Customs Union |
| SADC | Southern African Development Community |
| SALT | Strategic Arms Limitation Talks |
| SAM | Surface-to-air missile |
| SATCOM | Satellite Communication |
| SDR | Special drawing rights (IMF) |
| SEANWFZ | South-East Asia Nuclear Weapon-Free Zone |
| SELA | Latin American Economic System |
| SPC | South Pacific Commission |
| SPF | South Pacific Forum |
| SPOCC | South Pacific Organisations Coordinating Committee |
| STABEX | System of Stabilisation of Export Earnings (Lomé Convention) |
| START | Strategic Arms Reduction Talks |
| SYSMIN | System of Stabilisation of Mining Exports (Lomé Convention) |
| | |
| TAC | Treaty of Amity and Cooperation |
| TNC | Transnational Corporation |

| | |
|---|---|
| UAM | Union Africaine et Malagache |
| UN | United Nations |
| UNAMIR | UN Assistance Mission to Rwanda |
| UNCDF | United Nations Capital Development Fund |
| UNCITRAL | UN Commission on International Trade Law |
| UNCTAD | United Nations Conference on Trade and Development |
| UNDC | UN Disarmanent Commission |
| UNDOF | UN Disengagement Observer Force |
| UNDP | United Nations Development Programme |
| UNEP | United Nations Environment Programme |
| UNESCO | United Nations Educational Scientific and Cultural Organisation |
| UNFPA | United Nations Fund for Population Activities |
| UNHCR | United Nations High Commission for Refugees |
| UNICEF | United Nations Children's Fund |
| UNIDO | United Nations Industrial Development Organisation |
| UNIFIL | United Nations Interim Force in Lebanon |
| UNITAR | United Nations Institute for Training and Research |
| UNMOT | UN Mission of Observers in Tajikistan |
| UNRISD | United Nations Research Institute for Social Development |
| UNRWA | United Nations Relief and Works Agency for Palestine Refugees and the Near East |
| UNSSD | UN Special Session on Disarmament |
| UNTSO | United Nations Truce Supervision Organisation |
| UNU | United Nations University |
| UPU | Universal Postal Union |
| | |
| VNR | Video News Release |
| | |
| WFC | World Food Council |
| WFP | World Food Programme (UN/FAO) |
| WHO | World Health Organization |
| WIPO | World Intellectual Property Organization |
| WMO | World Meteorological Organization |
| WTO | World Trade Organization |
| | |
| ZOPFAN | Zone of Peace, Freedom and Neutrality (ASEAN) |

# ISLAMIC FESTIVALS

The two major festivals in the Islamic calendar, apart from the Prophet's birthday, the Ascension of the Prophet and the Islamic and Christian New Years, are: (a) the *īd al fitr* or Little Festival which marks the end of the month *Ramadān* and is held during the first days of the following month, *Shawwāl*; and (b) the *īd al adha al mubārak* or Great Festival which lasts for four days and is associated with the sacrifice at Minv made by the pilgrims who are undertaking the *Hajj* to Mecca.

During the entire month of *Ramadān* fasting takes place from dawn to sunset, and a special festival is the Day of Decrees on the twenty-seventh of the month.

The Islamic calendar takes as its starting point the Prophet's move from Mecca to Medina (the *Hijra*) on 16 July AD 622 (or 'CE' for Christian era) which became the first day of the Islamic era ('AH' for *Anno Hegirae*). The calendar is based on the lunar month of $29^{1}/2$ days with twelve months in the year (the months consisting of twenty-nine and thirty days alternately) which results in a year of 354 days. The Islamic year is consequently shorter by approximately eleven days than the solar year, and *Ramadān* and other festivals are therefore eleven days earlier each year according to the non-Islamic (or Gregorian) calendar. It should be noted that, traditionally, a 'day' starts at sunset. Friday is the Day of Prayer when all offices are closed; and in some countries the Thursday is included in this 'week-end'.

In addition, Shī'ite Muslims celebrate the death at Kerbela of Husain, grandson of the Prophet and son of Ali the fourth Caliph. This festival begins on the first day of Muharram (the first month of the Islamic year) and comes to a climax on the tenth day, the anniversary of Husain's death in the year 61 AH (10 October AD 680). The occasion is one of deep mourning.

# THE ENVIRONMENT

The protection of the local environment (as exemplified by the U.K. Clean Air Act of 1956) has long been a matter for national politicians, whilst the protection of the regional environment has been dealt with by diplomats, negotiating such treaties as the Rhine River Treaty and the 1991 Protocol for the Protection of the Environment in the Antarctic.

Now, as a result of man's ability to influence the world's climate through rapid advances in technology and a dramatic increase in population, it is accepted that the global environment is under threat, and it has become a matter of major international concern, of urgency and priority for the international community as a whole. Population pressures, industrialisation, deforestation, new technologies, a build-up of carbon dioxide ($CO_2$) and other 'greenhouse' gases in the atmosphere, new pollutants, man's enhanced material expectations, changes in methods of farming the land and sea – all have combined to threaten the stability of the world's climatic system, and with it the world's existing ecosystem. It is difficult to gauge the extent of this threat to the world's climate, since change is the essence of climate as a consequence of global and universal factors outside man's knowledge and influence – such as the change in the earth's angle on its axis or the phases of sunspots, and little is known of the interrelationships between these factors. Accurate measurements have been available only for decades, whereas climatic changes are to be reckoned in millennia. The destructive effect of present practices on the ecosystem – such as desertification, soil erosion and loss of bio-diversity as well as acid rain, toxic waste and marine pollution are being actively tackled, but there are four major areas of global concern, which can only be resolved by positive diplomacy on a comprehensive international basis:

## 1. THE OZONE LAYER

A major factor in maintaining the world's existing ecohabitat is a concentrated layer of ozone gas approximately fifteen miles above the earth's surface. This acts as a shield preventing a harmful quantity of the sun's ultra-violet rays from reaching the earth. It is only in recent years that appropriate technology has enabled the ozone layer to be measured, but during this time it has become evident that it is decreasing steadily and substantially. It is also known that chlorofluorocarbon gases (CFCs) destroy ozone molecules. These are being produced and used especially as refrigerants, in the production of foam plastics, and in aerosols. If the depletion of the ozone layer and the creation of 'ozone holes' were to continue, the increased impact of ultra-violet rays could affect not only the animal food chain, but also human health; and whereas cause and effect cannot be conclusively proved there is sufficient reason to justify a total and worldwide ban on CFCs which also have an effect on global warming.

As a result of initiatives in this direction, the Vienna Convention for the protection of the Ozone Layer was signed in 1985, followed by the 1987 Montreal Protocol on Substances that Deplete the Ozone Layer, as amended in June 1990. Incremental costs relating to the phasing out of CFCs can be funded in developing country signatories from the Montreal Fund which was established by the Montreal Protocol. The European Union and other major industrialised countries have agreed to forbid the manufacture and use of CFCs.

## 2. GLOBAL WARMING AND THE GREENHOUSE EFFECT

Whereas change is the essence of the earth's climate, whether in cycles of decades, centuries or millennia, it remains a fact that the rapidly increasing use of fossil fuels by a rapidly increasing world population could result in unexpected and dangerous consequences; resulting products such as carbon dioxide, methane and nitrous oxide are known to trap heat and create a 'greenhouse' effect. There is always the possibility that global warming might trigger off unexpected and potentially disastrous changes, but its main impact would be to alter the regional emphasis of the world's climate and consequently the agriculture – with unknown social and political consequences – and gradually raise the level of the seas and influence ocean currents and marine life.

Apart from natural causes such as volcanic activity on land and in the oceans, as well as the inevitable consequences of the glacial cycle, the major cause of global warming is judged to be the use of fossil fuels – oil, lignite, coal, and wood – mainly in industry, transport and the generation of electricity, but also for domestic purposes; but reservations in respect of the use of nuclear fuels prevent serious reduction of the output of carbon dioxide. This potentially threatening situation was addressed at the meeting of the Earth Summit in Rio de Janeiro in 1997 and subsequently in New York, Tokyo and Bonn, where agreement was reached on the text of the Kyoto Protocol to the United Nations Framework Convention on Climate Change. The most significant element of this agreement was that approximately 40 industrialised countries undertook to cut their emissions of greenhouse gases by the year 2010 to 5.2% below their 1990 levels, and to purchase 'emission credits' from countries not listed in Annexe 1 to the treaty if they failed to meet their target.

## 3.  BIODIVERSITY

The relatively recent discovery of DNA has opened up the field of genetic engineering, with its prospects of worldwide benefits especially in medicine. Bio-technology, however, is dependent upon the preservation of biodiversity – the vast number of different forms of life existing on the planet – and the ability to have access to such sources. These two matters – preservation and access – more particularly the financial basis on which access is permitted, were the subject of the Convention on Bio-Diversity signed at the 1992 Earth Summit in Rio de Janeiro.

## 4.  THE PRESERVATION OF FORESTS

The preservation of forests – particularly the rainforests – is seen as the major element in the maintenance of biodiversity, and their diminution or destruction would, in addition, undoubtedly result in a change of influence of the world's climate and accentuate the problem of soil erosion.

The origins of the 1992 United Nations Conference on Environment and Development, the 'Earth Summit', are to be found in an instruction from the Secretary General to create a World Commission on

'how the human species could make economic progress within nature's strict laws'.

It would be hard to find words that more precisely sum up the essence of the problem that diplomats have to face. The 1992 Earth Summit produced a non-binding Earth Charter and Agenda 21 with excellent intentions, but supreme diplomatic skills will be necessary if the imperative of economic progress is to be reconciled with the inflexibility of nature's strict laws. In the meantime it may be noted that, according to the UNFPA, within twenty years more than half of the world's ever-increasing population will be urban dwellers, thus increasing pressure on water resources, waste disposal and other potential hazards to the environment.

# GLOSSARY OF DIPLOMATIC, CONSULAR, LEGAL AND ECONOMIC TERMS

*above the line payments and receipts*, payments and receipts contained in that part of the government's budget dealing with expenditure to be met out of revenue raised mainly from taxation

*abrogate*, to annul, revoke (e.g. a treaty)

*ad hominem*, on an individual basis

*ad interim*, temporary; during the intervening period of time

*ad referendum*, subject to confirmation

*ad valorem tax*, a duty imposed on goods in proportion to their value, i.e. a duty expressed as a percentage, and not a specific amount

*amortisation*, the gradual repayment of a debt by means of a sinking fund

*annexation*, the acquisition by a state of additional territory

*appellation d'origine*, the name given to a commodity indicating its place of origin

*arbitration*, the judgment of a dispute by an agreed third party, the matter to be resolved on the basis of international law, and the decision to be binding on the parties concerned

*autarky*, self-sufficiency (e.g. national economic self-sufficiency)

*autocracy*, government or control by a single person

*balance of payments*, the relation between the payments of all kinds made from one country to the rest of the world and its receipts from all other countries

*balance of trade*, the relationship between a country's merchandise imports ('visible imports') and its merchandise exports ('visible exports'). It excludes current payments and receipts for services and capital account items

*bank rate*, the minimum rate at which a central bank will discount first-class bills

*basket*, a jargon term, first popularised at the meetings of the Conference on Security and Cooperation in Europe, to refer to a grouping of items or subjects. In financial circles it refers to a collection of different currencies

*becquerel*, unit of measurement of radioactivity

*belligerency*, a term of legal significance to describe a particular state of aggression

*below the line payments and receipts*, payments and receipts contained in that part of the government's budget dealing with capital items

*bill of exchange*, an order for the making of payment, mainly used in international trade. A term bill may not be payable until, say, ninety days after acceptance; a sight bill is payable upon acceptance

*bill of lading*, a document of title to goods received for shipment

*bonded warehouse*, warehouse in which dutiable articles may be stored without payment of duty until they are withdrawn

*Bourse*, the Paris Stock Exchange and money market; term widely used for similar institutions in other countries

*boycott*, the refusal to do business with a state (or person)

*broker*, an intermediary between two or more persons engaged in a business transaction

*budget*, an estimate of national revenue and expenditure for the ensuing fiscal year

*buffer state*, one situated between more powerful neighbours which relies for its security largely on the fact that no one neighbouring state is prepared to let it be occupied by a third state

*bullion*, gold and silver in bulk

*buyers' market*, a market in which producers, suppliers and dealers experience difficulty in selling the goods which are available

*capital expenditure*, expenditure of a non-recurrent nature resulting in the acquisition of assets

*capital intensive*, forms of production in which there is a considerable use of capital equipment per person employed relative to the labour employed

*capital market*, a market comprising institutions which deal in the purchase and sale of securities

*cartel*, a central selling organisation which assigns to each of its members a specific share in the total output of a commodity

*casus belli*, an action justifying a declaration of war

*caveat*, a request for action to be deferred, a proviso

*Central Bank*, a bank which in any country is (a) banker to the government, (b) banker to the commercial banks and (c) implements the currency and credit policy of the country

*certificate of origin*, a declaration by an exporter or by a chamber of commerce stating the country of origin of goods shipped

*chargé d'affaires ad interim*, the member of the diplomatic staff of a mission (save in exceptional cases) who acts as head of mission during the latter's absence or indisposition, or in the interval between appointments

*chargé d'affaires en titre*, the head of a diplomatic mission accredited to a Minister for Foreign Affairs

*cheap money*, a description applied to money when the bank rate is low

*c.i.f.*, cost, insurance and freight, i.e. a quoted price for goods shipped c.i.f. includes all charges up to the point where the goods are deposited on board ship (f.o.b.) and also the cost of their insurance and freight

*cold war*, a term used to denote the *degree* of hostility between states when their foreign policy interests clash one with another: the final stage in the spectrum of aggression conducted by non-military means

*commission (consular)*, a commission of appointment

*concordat*, an agreement concluded between a state and the Holy See *confrontation*, a situation (usually between two states) which threatens to develop into a physical conflict in which neither party shows a willingness to give way

*consular invoice*, an invoice certified by the consul of an overseas country relating to goods shipped to that country

*consumer goods*, products in the actual form in which they will reach domestic consumers

*Contadora Group*, consisting of Colombia, Mexico, Panama and Venezuela, and joined in 1985 by a Support Group consisting of Argentina, Brazil, Paraguay and Peru. Their objective is to seek peace, respect for frontiers, democracy, human rights and arms reduction in Central America through negotiation

*contract*, an agreement, either oral or in writing, whereby two or more parties mutually undertake specific commitments

*convertibility*, the freedom to exchange any currency for another currency at the ruling rate of exchange

*conveyance*, legal description for the transfer of property from a seller to a buyer

*countervailing duty*, a tax levied on imports to counteract an unfair advantage, especially government subsidies and dumping, and to protect a domestic industry

*coup d'état*, unlawful seizure of control of a government by persons (often military) occupying positions of authority

*currency dumping*, derogatory term for competitive devaluation

*current expenditure*, expenditure recurrent in nature and not resulting in the acquisition of assets

*customs cooperation council nomenclature*, the internationally accepted standardised system of describing goods for customs purposes (successor to the Brussels Tariff Nomenclature)

*customs duties*, duties levied on goods entering one state or region from another

*customs union*, a grouping of states or regions which form a single customs territory: tariffs and other trade restrictions between the member states or countries are abolished, and the union maintains a common external tariff against other countries

*debt–service ratio*, the relationship between a country's foreign debt repayments (interest and capital) and its export earnings, expressed in percentage terms

*de facto* (recognition) as a matter of fact

*deficit financing*, the financing of a budget deficit by a government by means of borrowing in the market or from the central bank

*deflation*, a situation in which prices and money incomes are falling, accompanied by an increase in the value of the monetary unit

*de jure* (recognition) in accordance with international law

*delegate*, a person to whom responsibility to act (usually to a specified extent) has been delegated (e.g. by a government)

*démarche*, an initiative or approach by a government, often based on a fresh policy following an unsatisfactory situation

*demurrage*, delay caused to shipping, goods, etc., and the payment of fees or compensation as a result

*de rigeur*, obligatory

*derogation*, the temporary suspension of the enforcement of a provision

*détente*, relaxation of tension

*devaluation*, the determination of a new and lower (i.e. fewer units of foreign currency per unit of home currency) fixed exchange rate for a currency

*diplomatic asylum*, political asylum granted in the premises of a diplomatic mission or other such premises entitled to inviolability

*diplomatic conference*, as for plenipotentiary conference (q.v.)

*disinflation*, the removal of inflationary pressure from the economy in order to maintain the value of the monetary unit

*dobson*, unit of measurement of ozone level

*domino theory*, the theory that in a certain set of circumstances the fall of a government or state will bring about the downfall of a neighbouring government or state which, in falling, will set in train a succession of similar downfalls (a similar concept is 'to fall like a house of cards')

*double taxation agreement*, an agreement to prevent the same income being taxed twice

*drawback*, the repayment of the import duty an exporter has had to pay on foreign materials or components contained in the goods he exports

*dumping*, the sale of goods in foreign markets at less than their net cost in the domestic market. The term 'non-commercial competition' is similarly applied to services, e.g. shipping

*economic growth*, the growth per head of the population in the production of goods and services of all kinds available to meet demand

*en clair*, in clear (as opposed to being in code or in cipher)

*en marge*, incidentally: used in the sense of discussions held during the course of a meeting but not necessarily related to the topic of the meeting

*en poste*, having assumed duties at the authorised (diplomatic or consular) post

*en principe* (English), as a matter of principle

*en principe* (French), generally speaking, as a rule

*entrepôt*, a place where merchandise is collected and stored for subsequent distribution

*entrepreneur*, a person who undertakes trading transactions on his own account

*escalate*, to accelerate and increase in intensity or magnitude

*euro*, the unit of currency of the European Union

*euro-dollar(s)*, private dollar balances held in European commercial banks

*exchange rate parity*, the fixed rate of exchange between one currency and another

*excise duties*, duties or taxes imposed on goods produced and distributed within a country

*ex officio*, by virtue of a specific post or office. Appointments to committees may be *ex officio*, i.e. the holder of a particular post is appointed for so long as he holds the post: the appointment does not relate to him personally

*explanations of vote*, verbal statement explaining why a vote has been cast in a particular way

*export duties*, duties or taxes imposed on goods exported from a country *exposé*, revelation in public of a matter hitherto secret

*extra-territorial*, outside the jurisdiction of a territory

*fait accompli*, an act that has been committed and is therefore no longer open to discussion

*f.a.s.*, free alongside (see f.o.b.): a quoted price for goods shipped which includes all payments and charges up to the point of the goods being deposited on the quay alongside the ship

*fast track*, a procedure adopted by the American Congress whereby they agree to accept or reject (but not amend) an agreement within ninety working days

*faux pas*, a blunder (literally a false step)

*feasibility study*, the study of a proposed project in its technical and economic aspects to ascertain the possibility of commercial exploitation

*fiduciary issue*, that portion of the bank note issue which is not backed by gold

*fiscal policy*, the policy adopted by a government for raising revenue to meet expenditure and for influencing the level of business activity

*flag of convenience*, the flag of a state whose laws relating to shipping are less onerous on shipowners than other states: vessels registered in such a state fly its flag, and their crews are subject to its laws

*floating debt*, that part of the national debt which involves short-term borrowing

*floating exchange rate*, the exchange rate of any currency free to float to any level which supply and demand may determine

*f.o.b.*, free on board (see f.a.s. for elucidation)

*force majeure*, unavoidable and usually unforeseen circumstances

*free port*, an enclosed and policed area in an airport, seaport or other locality into which goods may be imported and processed or manufactured without payment of customs duty of the country in which it is situated provided that they are re-exported subsequently to a third country

*free trade*, trade which is unimpeded by tariffs, import and export quotas and other devices which obstruct the free movement of goods and services between countries

*Free Trade Area*, a grouping of states or regions within which customs duties and other barriers to trade are removed, but which has no common external tariff

*funding*, the conversion of short-term debts into long-term debts

*futures market*, a market in which goods are sold for delivery at some future date

*generalised system of preferences*, arrangement whereby the exports of developing countries are admitted to the industrialised countries duty-free up to a certain level, or at reduced rates, on a non-reciprocal basis

*giro system*, a mechanism for the transfer of payments

*gold standard*, a monetary system in which each unit of currency is worth a fixed amount of gold. The rules of a gold standard are:

(a) all paper currency must be convertible at its face value into gold;

(b) there must be no restrictions on the import or export of gold;

(c) a gold reserve must be maintained, fully sufficient to meet all demands made upon it.

*gross domestic product*, the value of goods and services produced within the state

*gross national product*, gross domestic product plus net income from interest, profit and dividends derived from assets abroad

*Group of Three* (G3) is a forum for political discussion on the promotion of economic integration with a view to the creation of a Free Trade Area. Members are Colombia, Mexico and Venezuela, and the Secretariat is in Bogatá.

*Group of Eight* (G8), major industrialised countries: Canada, France, Germany, Italy, Japan, Russia United Kingdom, and the United States of America together with the President of the European Commision and the header of the country holding the Presidency of the European Council. Regular meeting are held primarily to discuss the world economic situation

*Group of Ten* (G10), the countries with a controlling majority in the IMF (currently eleven in number)

*Group of Fifteen* (G15), association of 17 developing countries with mutual economic interests

*Group of twenty* (G20), committee of the ten controlling members of the IMF and ten members of developing countries

*Group of 77*, group of developing countries (originally formed at UNCTAD I)

*Holy See*, the legal and symbolic personification of the Roman Catholic Church of which the Pope is Supreme Pontiff. He is also Sovereign Pontiff of the State of Vatican City

*hot money*, money which is transferred between countries in order to benefit from advantageous rates of interest or in anticipation of a change in the parity of a currency

*hot pursuit*, a legal doctrine originally of nautical application permitting the apprehension of vessels which are believed to have committed an offence within a state's territorial waters, and then have escaped to the high seas. The term is also used to attempt to justify similar actions in respect of persons escaping from one state to another by land

*impasse*, a situation of immobility or stalemate, in which no party involved can make a move

*incognito*, without revealing one's identity

*inflation*, a condition in which the volume of purchasing power is constantly running ahead of the output of goods and services, with the result that as incomes and prices rise the value of money falls

*infrastructure*, services regarded as essential for the creation of a modern economy, e.g. power, transport, housing, education and health services

*innocent passage*, the right of any sea-going vessel of any state to pass through the territorial waters of another state provided that this is done innocently, and to stop and anchor but only in accordance with navigational requirements, *force majeure* or distress. Certain states demand prior notification or approval for warships. Submarines must travel on the surface and show their flag

*inter alia*, among other things

*invisible earnings*, in national accounting, receipts for services rendered (e.g. shipping, banking, insurance, tourism)

*junta*, a committee or a group of people working together; usually used to refer to a
  revolutionary government consisting of members of a group (e.g. the army)
*jus sanguinis* (nationality), based on blood relationship
*jus soli* (nationality), based on the place of birth
*labour-intensive*, form of production in which there is a considerable use of labour in
  relation to the amount of capital equipment per unit of output
*laissez-faire*, a policy of non-interference by the state in economic affairs
*laissez-passer*, a permit to travel or to enter a particular area
*lapsus linguae* (Latin), a slip of the tongue – a spoken error
*legal tender*, money which a person is obliged by law to accept in payment of a debt
*liquid assets*, assets either in the form of money, or which can be quickly converted
  into money
*Lombard rate*, the rate at which a Central Bank makes loans to commercial banks
  against eligible securities (e.g. government bonds)
*memorandum of association*, a document specifying the aims and objects of a commercial company
*merchant banks*, banks whose business consists mainly of the accepting of commercial bills and the financing of trade
*mixed economy*, an economy in which resources are allocated partly through the decisions of private individuals and privately-owned business enterprises, and partly
  through the decisions of the government and state-owned enterprises: the two sectors are respectively known as the private and public sectors
*modus vivendi*, an arrangement which enables all concerned to carry on their activities in spite of disagreements, or while a disagreement is being resolved
*most-favoured-nation clause*, a clause which may be included in a commercial treaty
  between two countries that they will mutually grant to each other any favourable
  treatment which either may accord to a third country in respect of customs duties
*motions for division*, provision for separate voting on separate sections of a resolution
*multi-fibre arrangement*, an agreement between developed and developing countries
  to protect the textile industries of the former by limiting imports from the latter
*national debt*, the debts of a government, both internal and external
*national income*, a measure of the money value of the goods and services becoming
  available to a country from economic activity during a prescribed period, usually
  a year
*nautical mile*, a distance of 2,025 yards or 1,852 metres, equal to one minute of the
  earth's measurement
*non-aligned movement*, group of 177 states originally uncommitted in the Cold War;
  now concerned with a new world order and economic development
*notarial acts*, the acts of an official (e.g. a consular officer) who attests and certifies
  documents
*oligarchy*, rule by a very small section of a state or community
*oligopoly*, a market structure in which only a few firms compete
*ordre du jour*, agenda
*package deal*, an agreement incorporating a variety of diverse elements

*pacta sunt servanda*, the legal doctrine that a treaty constitutes a contract between the parties, and that its conditions are binding and must be observed

*pari passu*, in step; by equal stages

*Paris club*, association of major creditor states concerned with renegotiating and, where appropriate, rescheduling official foreign debts

*plenipotentiary conference*, a conference meeting for the purpose of drawing up or revising an international instrument at which delegates have full powers

*post mortem*, an analysis or enquiry into an event, primarily to see what lessons for the future can be learnt from it (Latin: 'after the death')

*Pressler amendment*, policy of limiting US aid to non-nuclear states

*prima facie*, on the basis of the evidence immediately available

*private sector*, the private sector of the economy is the combination of elements in the economy which are not organs or agencies of central or local government and therefore includes the company sector and the personal sector

*procedural motion*, relates to the conduct of a meeting and must immediately be put to the vote by the presiding officer

*procès-verbale*, the minutes of a meeting

*producer goods*, goods made for the purpose of producing consumer goods, e.g. machinery of all kinds

*productivity*, the efficiency with which productive resources, i.e. labour, capital and land, are used, usually expressed as output per unit of input

*pronunciamiento*, a proclamation or manifesto, usually associated with the revolutionary takeover of a government

*protocol*, (i) formal diplomatic behaviour; (ii) an international agreement, usually supplementary to a major treaty

*protocol of signature*, an addendum to a treaty usually recording clarifications or reservations

*proviso*, an exception

*public sector*, the public sector of the economy usually denotes the combination of the central government, the local authorities, the nationalised industries and other public corporations.

*purchasing power parity*, the exchange rate between two currencies that would result in equal purchasing power in the currency areas concerned

*quid pro quo*, something given in return for something else; a consideration

*quiproquo* (French), a misunderstanding; at cross-purposes

*rapporteur*, the person who makes a summary of e.g. the proceedings of a conference

*rapprochement*, a renewal of improved relations between states

*real terms*, sums of money expressed in 'real terms' take account of the changing value of money; the change is usually related to a particular 'base year'

*rebus sic stantibus*, the legal doctrine which asserts that if the conditions under which a treaty was concluded have fundamentally altered, then the treaty may be said to be no longer binding

*shipping conference*, an association of shipowners, the main purpose of which is to fix rates to be charged and to allocate ports of call

*sine qua non*, an essential, something without which something else would not be possible

*sinking fund*, a fund built up by periodic instalments in order to accumulate a certain sum at a given date for some specific purpose

*social dumping*, in a free trade or low-tariff area, the transfer of industry or other sources of employment from a member country where the levels of social costs and labour legislation are high to a member country where they are low

*special drawing rights*, a system of international reserve assets created by the International Monetary Fund

*specific tariff*, a tariff reckoned in terms of a specific amount of money for each unit of the commodity concerned (e.g. 30 cents per kg)

*spot market*, a market in which goods are sold for immediate delivery

*status quo*, the existing situation

*suaviter in modo, fortiter in re*, firm in purpose, courteous in manner

*super-301*, US legislation relating to unfair trade

*tariff*, a duty or tax charged by a country on its imports from other countries; a customs duty

*territorial asylum*, political asylum granted by a state to an alien in its territory

*trade creation*, in a Common Market or Free Trade Area the replacement of high-cost imported goods by low-cost articles produced within the area (e.g. benefiting from the economies of scale)

*trade deflection*, in a Free Trade Area the importation of goods into a member country with a low external tariff for consumption in another with a high external tariff in an attempt to pay the minimum duty

*trade diversion*, in a Common Market or Free Trade Area the substitution of cheap imported goods by more costly articles produced within the area

*trade gap*, the difference between the value of imports c.i.f., and exports (and re-exports) f.o.b.

*trademark*, the brand name or other device used to relate a commodity to the particular firm owning, producing or distributing it

*tranche*, literally a slice or segment: term used by the IMF referring to a credit granted to a member state. This is allocated in four tranches, each being dependent upon the acceptance by the member country of increasing degrees of financial stringency

*ultimatum*, final demand

*ultra vires*, not within the law

*unit of account*, in the European Union, the monetary unit used for fixing the price of agricultural produce, etc.

*veto*, a negative vote

*volte face*, an abrupt and complete reversal of previous policy

*visible exports*, exports which consist of tangible goods such as plant and machinery, consumer goods, etc.

# NUCLEAR NON-PROLIFERATION

A concomitant of the Cold War was the development and proliferation of nuclear armaments, both on the part of the major antagonists and of various non-aligned states. The end of the Cold War has presented the world community of states with the opportunity to reduce and eventually eliminate nuclear armaments: failing which they will inevitably continue the process of proliferation as every regional 'superpower' seeks either to extend its hegemony or to match the nuclear capability of a potential rival or aggressor.

The Treaty on the Non-Proliferation of Nuclear Weapons (NPT) came into force in March 1970, and its basic aims are to prevent the further spread of nuclear weapons; to foster peaceful nuclear cooperation under safeguards, and to encourage negotiations to end competitive development of nuclear weapons with a view to their eventual elimination.

Under the terms of the treaty, nuclear-weapon states agree not to assist non-nuclear-weapon states to acquire nuclear explosive devices; and the latter agree not to manufacture or otherwise acquire such devices. Provision is made for the International Atomic Energy Agency to apply safeguards, including inspection in respect of nuclear material used in the peaceful programmes of non-nuclear weapon states which are parties to the treaty. The dangers of nuclear proliferation, not least of nuclear technology and know-how, have increased considerably since the break-up of the Soviet Union, and the member states of the European Union have made recognition of those members of the Commonwealth of Independent States on whose territory nuclear weapons were stationed, conditional on their adherence to the treaty as non-nuclear-weapon states.

Parties to the treaty include the existing nuclear powers (with the exception of North Korea) who have also agreed to the Missile Technology Control Regime.

Review Conferences have been held every five years in accordance with the treaty, and in 1995 when the treaty came to the end of its twenty-five-year duration, the contracting parties agreed by consensus to an indefinite extension of the treaty. They also accepted three non-binding Declarations of Principle:

1.  A restatement of previous commitments, particularly in respect of nuclear disarmament and an undertaking to end all nuclear tests.
2.  A strengthening of the verification procedures in relation to disarmament.
3.  The establishment of a nuclear-free zone in the Middle East and the adherence of all states, without exception, to the Non-Proliferation Treaty.

# INDEX

*See also* glossary of diplomatic, consular, legal and economic terms, pages 172–180